Power, Knowledge and Anti-Racism Education

Power, Knowledge and Anti-Racism Education

A Critical Reader

edited by George J. Sefa Dei and Agnes Calliste
with the assistance of Margarida Aguiar

Fernwood Publishing • Halifax

Editing: Donna Davis
Design and production: Beverley Rach
Printed and bound in Canada by: Hignell Printing Limited

A publication of:
Fernwood Publishing
Box 9409, Station A
Halifax, Nova Scotia
B3K 5S3

Fernwood Publishing Company Limited gratefully acknowledges the financial support of the Department of Canadian Heritage and the Canada Council for the Arts for our publishing program.

Canadian Cataloguing in Publication Data

Main entry under title:

Power, knowledge and anti-racism education

Includes bibliographical references.
ISBN 1-55266-030-3

1. Racism -- Study and teaching -- Canada. 2. Canada -- Race Relations -- Study and teaching. 3. Discrimination in education -- Canada.
I. Dei, George J. Sefa (George Jerry Sefa), 1954- II. Calliste, Agnes M. (Agnes Miranda)

LC1099.5.C3P68 2000 306.43 C00-950046-4

Contents

Contributors

Gabriele Bedard is a master's graduate of the Ontario Institute for Studies in Education at the University of Toronto. He was a co-ordinator for the Multicultural Centre at Portland State University, facilitating alliance-building among students of diverse ethnic/racial/linguistic and sexual groups. He has also done extensive community development and education work with regards to HIV/AIDS in underrepresented groups in Portland, Oregon. He is now living in Toronto, and is furthering his commitment to anti-racism policies and pedagogy.

Agnes Calliste is an associate professor in the Department of Sociology and Anthropology at St. Francis Xavier University. Her academic research has focused on anti-racism and feminism in employment, immigration and education. She has several scholarly publications in refereed journals; most notable is her work on nurses in the health care system.

George J. Sefa Dei is a professor in and associate chair of the Department of Sociology and Equity Studies in Education at the Ontario Institute for Studies in Education, University of Toronto (OISE/UT). He is also director of the Centre for Integrative Anti-Racism Studies, Indigenous Knowledges, and International Development. He has written several books and has had numerous articles published in refereed journals.

Annette Henry is an associate professor at the College of Education, University of Illinois at Chicago. She has numerous publications and is the reviews editor for the journal *Race Ethnicity and Education*. Among her recent publications is *Taking Back Control: African Canadian Women Teachers' Lives and Practice* (SUNY, 1998).

Awad El K.M. Ibrahim is a visiting professor in the Faculty of Education at the University of Ottawa. He teaches in the areas of anti-racism and critical multiculturalism, applied socio-linguistics, cultural studies, critical pedagogy and educational foundation. He is interested both in exploring the connections between race, language and culture and the politics of identity, and in film and popular music studies, especially hip hop and rap.

Carl E. James is an associate professor in the Faculty of Education at York University, Toronto, where he teaches courses in foundations of education, urban education, and the teacher as researcher. He has also taught at community colleges and, before that, was a youth worker in Toronto. He holds a doctorate in sociology and works in the areas of anti-racism and multicultural education, urban education, youth and sports.

Joy Mannette is an associate professor in the Faculty of Education at York University. She is an activist engaged in union work, Aboriginal treaty rights and the development of applied research with communities working for social change. She holds a doctorate in sociology from Carleton University. Her academic writing has focused on anti-racism, feminism, poverty and indigenous ways of knowing.

Evangelia Tastsoglou is an associate professor of sociology at Saint Mary's University in Halifax. She earned a doctorate at Boston University and has published in the areas of ethnicity, migration and gender, cultural studies, families and community development. She is an affiliated researcher to the Prairie Centre of Excellence for Research on Immigration, an elected member of the Canadian Sociology and Anthropology Association (CSAA) Status of Women Committee and a former member on the CSAA executive.

Handel Kashope Wright is an associate professor of cultural studies and co-ordinator of the Urban/Multicultural Teacher Education Program at the College of Education, University of Tennessee, Knoxville. He is a doctoral graduate of the University of Toronto. He works and is published in the areas of cultural studies, anti-racist and multicultural education, literature studies and critical pedagogy.

Acknowledgments

Any academic work on anti-racism borrows and builds on a long history of intellectual scholarship and community politics in the field. Therefore we dedicate this book to the long years of collective struggles and battles waged, particularly by Canadian parents, students and educators of racial and ethnic minority backgrounds, to ensure that our schools respond to the concerns of a diverse body politic. We owe a tremendous intellectual debt for this book to many unheralded community workers who have challenged our academic discourses to speak to the material and lived realities of the disadvantaged in our communities. Special thanks go to students and colleagues who have shared their knowledge with us over the years, thus sharpening our thoughts and insights into anti-racism discourse and practice. To students of the Ontario Institute for Studies in Education at the University of Toronto and to those at St. Francis Xavier University we say a big thank-you for sharing and creating a community. We also thank the contributors to this book for their patience as we negotiated towards publication of this anthology and for their unwavering dedication to the cause of anti-racism. We give special thanks to Margarida Aguiar of the Department of Adult Education, Community Development and Counselling Psychology of the Ontario Institute for Studies in Education/ University of Toronto; christine connelly, Marcia James and Leeno Karumanchery of the Department of Sociology and Equity Studies, Ontario Institute for Studies in Education/University of Toronto; and Debbie Murphy of the Department of Sociology and Anthropology at St. Francis Xavier University for their invaluable comments on the text and their committed work/labour. Thanks also to the anonymous reviewers who commented on earlier drafts of the manuscripts. Finally, we send heartfelt regards to the folks at Fernwood Publishing for their continued commitment to publishing works that speak to the fundamental issues of social justice, equity and human freedom.

Toronto
January 2000

Introduction

Mapping the Terrain:

Power, Knowledge and Anti-Racism Education

George J. Sefa Dei and Agnes Calliste

This book looks specifically at the rhetorics of anti-racism and the implications of discourse and political practice for educational change in Euro-American contexts. In collaborating on this work we recognize the necessity for extending the discussion of anti-racism beyond schools to other institutional settings, a challenge that we have taken up in Calliste and Dei (2000). In this collection before you, however, our strategy focuses on the academy—schools, colleges and universities. Our academic objective is simple. We believe it is important to target educational institutions as one of the foremost places for producing societal change and transformation. Questions about how we construct social identities and seek representation still plague our academy. Our schools, colleges and universities continue to be powerful discursive sites through which race knowledge is produced, organized and regulated. Marginalized bodies are continually silenced and rendered invisible not simply through the failure to take issues of race and social oppression seriously but through the constant negation of multiple lived experiences and alternative knowledges. Colonial and imperial discourses and practices heavily influence how learners come to know race today. Racialized tropes deployed in the social construction of racialized identities and the representation of marginalized bodies as racial "others" are heavily encoded in prevailing ideologies that maintain the validity of conventional academic knowledge. The academic ideologies have become powerful mechanisms of control as conventional ideas produce material consequences. Fortunately, amid dominance and resistance the production of oppositional knowledges is flourishing. Counter and oppositional knowledges such as anti-racism are questioning the privilege to claim neutrality. A new and contemporary theorizing of anti-racism and social difference is speaking to the power of human agency. The historical specificity of understanding the myriad oppressions is espoused in critical anti-racism. We are learning that race, gender, class and sexuality have neither fixed nor essentialized meanings; that producing academic theory is simply not enough to challenge the workings of multiple oppressions; that there is a danger in presenting race [and social difference] discourse in the academy "as though the biological basis for racial distinctions has been banished by the intervention of social theory" (Grandy 1998: 37). In other words our understandings of race have not shifted far beyond the ills of biological determinism simply through the social theorizing of race (see John 1999).

Recognizing that educational institutions such as schools and universities play a critical role in reproducing or analyzing, critiquing and transforming our understandings of how we have come to view and construct our world, the contributors to this anthology examine practices at these formal educational sites. All of the authors have lived, worked and/or studied in Canada and, therefore, address the Canadian context. Some are currently working in the US, however, and all, if not most, have lived and worked elsewhere in the world (in particular the Caribbean and Africa); therefore their insights and perceptions—their subject positions—have been influenced by those experiences also. From these locations, we believe the book has theoretical and practical implications for understanding anti-racism and difference in the broader Euro-American schooling contexts. The unprecedented pace of global change has significant implications for understanding contemporary social practices. An important academic and political goal of anti-racism is to understand current practices, social barriers and new approaches to collective existence. We need to search for new, alternative and multiple knowledge forms in diverse social sites to provide meaning and understanding to individual and collective experience and action.

This book addresses important questions of anti-racism and its connection with difference in a variety of educational contexts and schooling practices. It focuses on the Canadian context but draws on broad global implications. It offers critical readings of multiple oppressions revealed in different sites and sources. Individual chapters take up the challenge of anti-racism and the dynamics/relational aspects of difference (race, gender, class, language, culture and sexuality) through a critical examination of daily social practice in educational settings. Positioned within a critical examination of the historical, political and economic roots of racism and other social oppressions, the book highlights the unassailable connection between anti-racism and difference. The focus is on systems, structures and relations of domination, particularly the racist, classist and sexist constructions of reality that serve as dominant paradigms for viewing and interpreting lived and historical realities. The anti-racist concern with difference matters only if it contributes to an understanding of difference within contexts of social domination, which is a critical reading of difference structured along the power-asymmetrical relation of class, race, gender and sexuality. Disturbingly contemporary forms of racist expressions and actions celebrate culture, difference and identity within oppressive contexts. And within such oppressive contexts, the rhetorical manipulation of difference fails to address the fundamental question of power and privilege.

In this collection, we propose anti-racism as a counter-hegemonic strategy for dealing with oppression based on race, class, gender and sexuality. We examine how contemporary representations of race, class, gender and sexual differences connect to a broader power politics of authority, morality, knowledge and speech that denies people (particularly minoritized groups) their agency as resisting and creating subjects. We ask, for example, why it is that in the politics of representation certain forms of identity, agency and subjectivity are privileged in order to sustain dominant causes, meanings and ideologies. Why do certain textual and discursive representations help stabilize social relations in the service of capital? How are the views of the dominant group in society accepted, naturalized or taken for granted at the level of common-sense knowledge? We also enthuse that critical anti-racist workers develop effective pedagogic and communicative practices that not only interrogate how questions of power, politics and ethics are framed and mediated in textual, material and other discursive representations of society but that also seek to transform society.

Three pertinent issues at the heart of the collection provide readers with a knowledge base on the general field of anti-racism: first, the retheorizing of anti-racism to acknowledge the intersections of difference as well as the situational and contextual variations in intensities of oppressions; second, the implications of anti-racism for rethinking schooling in Euro-American contexts; and third, the strategies, meanings and implications of pursuing anti-racism in a variety of educational settings. Respective writers, in engaging diverse subject areas, inform readers about academic and political debates in the ever-expanding field of anti-racism studies and about the different positions of anti-racist scholars and workers.

We define anti-racism as an action-oriented, educational and political strategy for institutional and systemic change that addresses the issues of racism and the interlocking systems of social oppression (sexism, classism, heterosexism, ableism) (see Dei 1996a expanding on formulations of Thomas 1984 and Lee 1985). We understand education as referring broadly to the options, strategies, processes and structures through which individuals and communities/groups come to know and understand the world and act within it (Freire 1993). Existing scholarly critical works on race and anti-racism use schools as a focus of discussion. This edited collection marks a refreshing departure. It includes the school as a significant site but broadens the theoretical discussion on critical anti-racism to the emerging challenges of inclusive education into Canada. We build on existing scholarship and contribute to the knowledge of the integration of race, class, gender and other aspects of social difference. We present anti-racism as a pedagogical discourse and academic and political practice. Furthermore, we utilize a critical anti-racism discursive framework to understand the issues of race, class and gender identity and representation beyond the classroom to the schoolyard, through the various educational institutions and points of entry and exit and into professional practice.

Our fundamental quest is to define the place of race in critical studies of social difference. There are two academic observations of interest to us: first, the idea that race is theoretically and empirically a meaningless term, that it lacks scientific and analytical status and must accordingly be discarded (Miles 1980;

Miles and Torres 1996); and second, the problematic of according primacy to race in a supposedly integrative approach to social oppressions that works within an anti-racist discursive framework (Lee 1985; Dei 1996a). Quite a bit of scholarship has been devoted to explaining the different positions on these issues. Rather than rehash these debates, we move on and urge the readers to join us. On the first matter, it may be useful for us to reiterate that there is a social, political, cultural and intellectual meaning to race despite its lack of "scientific" status. No amount of intellectual gymnastics and skirting around issues can evade or deny the powerful social and political currency of race and its intellectual and emotional meaning in our society. The tyranny of theory emerges in the academic commatization of race. In other words, the theoretical position that race is meaningless because it lacks scientific validity/clarity and the public discourse of a colour-blind society is as insidious as the practice of racism itself. Our society is colour-coded. The acknowledgment of racial differences per se is not the problem. It is the power behind the construction of these differences and the interpretation put on the perceived differences that are at issue. Rather than deny race because it is not scientifically valid, we must critique science for its inability to account for race (see Miles 1997 and Dei 1999).

In the discourse of anti-racism change, an important clarification needs to be made regarding the evocation of race, and this is crucial in focusing anti-racist political work. Working with the race concept means acknowledging the power of constructing racial differences. But the anti-racist politics requires that we disassociate negative meanings from race. We argue that, rather than deny race as meaningless, anti-racist workers must problematize and disassociate the injurious and negative meanings from race. The fight against racial inequality cannot be predicated on the abolition or minimization of race. Race has profound social, material and political consequences. In fact Benedict (1999: 43), in speaking of racial persecution, has pointed out that "race is not in itself the source of the conflict." Conflict stems from the institutional and social practices that create and sustain injustice and inequality among groups and individuals defined in racial terms. Race, as a concept or an idea, does not signify inferiority or superiority. As a term, race need not imply any supremacist assertions. Thus race is not connected to racism except through deliberative human action and response. Nevertheless, we recognize that the affective, cognitive and material meanings embedded in the race concept have created the invidious distinction or hierarchy of superiority and inferiority. John Rex argued that

> sociology ... has ideological and political competitors whose speeches and writings are so influential that it is difficult for sociologists to ignore them and to insist upon pure academic discourse. If their work is to have any influence on public debate they are bound to take up the

> terminology of the ideologies and politicians, even if in so doing they seek to use it with greater precision. (1999: 149-50)

In fact Rex (1999: 148) has cautiously stressed that we

> might, for example, eliminate the use of the term "Jew" or "black" in its current meaning and see that its implications have to do with universally shared rights of [hu]man[kind]. What we cannot do is to eliminate culture and meaning altogether.

On the second issue, there is a historical and ongoing critique of the conventional and simplistic reductionist analysis that diminishes race, class, gender and gender interrelations (see Miles 1980, 1989; Miles and Torres 1996; Gabriel and Ben-Tovim 1978, 1979; Stasiulis 1990; Solomos 1986). However, George Dei argues in Chapter One of this book that a political practice that recognizes the primacy/saliency of one form of oppression in the lives of a people at a particular historical moment should not, by and in itself, deny other trajectories of social difference. It should not negate the lived reality of "simultaneity of social oppressions" (Brewer 1993). Highlighting race in a discussion of critical anti-racism studies is political. That is, the politics of anti-racism demands that race be central, that its salience is primary even when other dimensions of oppression co-exist with racial ones. It is important to reiterate this position because of the academic temptation of an easy slippage to, for example, an orthodox, Eurocentric, Marxian position, which subsumes race and difference under class (see Solomos 1986 and Solomos and Back 1995 for excellent critiques).

A genuine anti-racism "project" demands space for race to be analyzed outside of class and gender, so that race is reduced to neither class nor gender. Distinguishing race, class and gender as separate analytical (albeit interconnected) categories is an important step in unravelling the ideological effects of specific racialized material processes and structures. In terms of race and class relations, this position in no way negates the fact that, historically, specific racisms have arisen from the matrix of socio-economic political relations and structures. We believe that an important conceptual and analytical distinction needs to be made between the production of racism and the reproduction of racisms. The function of a social attribute may not necessarily explain its origins. Additionally, we must be careful not to allow structure to become overdeterminant in ways that deny individual agency and collective action.

The historical specificities of racist practices challenge a general theory of race. At the same time, the permanence of skin-colour racism suggests a degree of autonomy for the race concept. Discourses of social change and class struggle are intertwined in ways that constrain an understanding of the internal character (emotionality) of racism, which exceeds the struggle against capitalism. In the context of global capitalist development we must ask why it is that, unlike race, "class struggle and gender inequality are more comfortable places from which to launch a critique of global inequality" (Fischer 1996: 4).

Race is a central but not exclusive theme of this book. Each chapter maintains the focus on race to ensure that a racial analysis is not subsumed under the other axes of multiplex identifications and relations of difference as we continue to draw the trajectories of difference. Striving for inclusivity does not necessarily entail giving equal treatment to all dimensions of difference and experience. In conventional discourses articulating a multiplex of oppressions, race is the category that often gets lost. We refer to how dominant discourses erase or deny race and yet accentuate class and perhaps gender in part because of the discomfort of speaking about race and racism. This erasure usually begins with talk about race not being the only oppression and then the discussion shifts quickly to other forms of oppression. Of course, it is through critical writings that race is recognized in the evocation of multiple subjectivities, plurality of oppressions and ways of seeing and acting in the world. Often times race gets lost in the zeal to connect equity issues and social oppressions. For example, this is the problem in creating a single undifferentiated category of "other" when devising specific policy measures to address educational inequities and social oppression. We need an anti-racist project to highlight race so as to pinpoint the specific needs of various communities just as discursively we draw the connections between oppressions and social equity issues. Our political and academic strategy, therefore, is to talk about inclusion in a way that highlights race. Nevertheless, the entire book weaves through the nuances of oppressions by showing how systems of oppression (race, class, gender, sexuality) intersect.

The strength of an integrative analysis to race, gender, class and sexuality lies in the fact that such a discursive approach captures the subtleties and complexities of social oppressions. Race, class, gender and sexuality are interrelated concepts. And, as this book demonstrates, racisms work differently for groups, depending on history, culture and identity. An integrative analysis to understanding the structural practices and effects of racisms and other forms of oppression captures the nuances and complexities.

The ideology of racism recognizes the multiplex oppressions and the roles in sustaining institutionalized power. The ideology of racism is not defined as false consciousness. Rather, it is an ideology rooted in commonsensical thought and the material and non-material human condition. There is the power of ideology in the Gramscian sense of a reproduction of hegemonic interests, which is beyond capital/material interests. No doubt racism as an ideology has powerful material consequences when combined with class, gender and sexual identities. The consciousness of race and difference (class, gender, sexuality) is related to existing conditions of privilege and lack of privilege, that is, the structures of material production, distribution, exchange and representation. However, the struggle against racism (like other forms of oppression—sexism, classism and homophobia) cannot simply be equated with the struggle against capitalism. For example, the function of state interests is not solely linked to capital and capital accumulation. The state reproduces its interests beyond the mere concerns of capital. Yet the intersections of race, class, gender and economic issues cannot be downplayed in contemporary society. Today many communities face disturbing moves by fiscally conservative governments to renege on their responsibilities to a larger citizenry. To fight budget deficits, economic recession and other monetary woes national governments are reneging on equity commitments. The practice of "reforming" government has sidelined equity and social justice concerns. Race and equity issues remain peripheral to social policy despite the fact that profound inequities continually affect certain groups in society.

This book also presents multiple readings of anti-racism discourse and praxis by focusing on the structural issues that play important roles in race, gender, class conflict and social policy. Authors situate discussions in broad socio-historical contexts and events that make anti-racism and difference a critical and necessary area of academic inquiry and political practice today.

No doubt, geographic inclusiveness is important. The book does not claim to address the particularities of racisms in various regions of Canada. We agree that issues involving Asians in Western Canada or Aboriginal peoples in the North and the West deserve treatment. However, at the level of discourse, this book speaks to a myriad of racisms in a theoretical and practical sense. We hope the book stands on its theoretical significance in the face of gaps relating to geographical representation. The idea of multiplicity of voice must leave room for other historically marginalized voices to be heard loud and clear.

Individual authors explore the sites and spaces of individual and collective resistance to the culture of dominance in society. They discuss diverse but connected issues ranging from the nuanced politics of representation, race and cultural work in a post-modern age to the radical politics of contemporary educational engagement and the role of power and ideology in understanding the structuralization of differences in society.

The book touches on many aspects of anti-racism education, but generally deals with the implications of anti-racism and critical race, gender and class studies for critical pedagogy. As mentioned earlier, education is broadly defined to include the varied options, strategies and ways in which people come to know their world and act within it. The chapters examine anti-racist challenges and interventions in education. George Dei moves our theoretical understandings to the development of an outline for a discursive anti-racist theoretical framework. He argues that confronting the dynamics and relational aspects of social difference (race, class, ethnicity and gender) is a key to inclusivity and power-sharing in Euro-Canadian contexts. He asserts that a critical anti-racism discursive framework deals foremost with equity: the qualitative value of justice. The anti-racist approach also addresses representation: a multiplicity of knowledge and the pursuit of a diverse body politic with academic discourse and texts and the public terrain. Further, anti-racism responds to the social construction of race, class, gender and sexual difference within society.

Bedard presents a succinct discussion of how the discourse of multiculturalism has been utilized within Canadian schools. Multiculturalism has recently come under scrutiny by critical educators for not meeting the needs of non-White students. This author explores the identity development of White bodies through histories of colonialism, imperialism and capitalism and the ways in which this development continues today through multicultural discourses. Hidden within the multicultural paradigm are the historical legacies and racial imageries of a past that perpetuates systems of power and domination within educational institutions. Anti-racism has emerged as a response to these discontentions and directly addresses issues of power and privilege. The author notes, however, that for anti-racism to be effective in promoting educational change, educators must first interrogate their identities and histories of privilege. Bedard discusses the need for a decolonizing process for White teachers in order to implement an anti-racist praxis into the existing educational system. Without this process the author feels that White teachers cannot teach in an anti-racist framework. Racism and institutional racism are so embedded in what it means to be White that there is a need to decolonize White people and create a White identity based on equity and social responsibility.

Awad Ibrahim's chapter on popular culture is relevant to the debate about connecting anti-racism and cultural politics in the school setting. He answers two questions: first, where do students form the identities that they bring with them to the classroom (if not in and within the discourse of popular culture, which is negated most often by the "official" education system); and, second, what are the implications of these negations in developing an anti-racism curriculum. The author, based on an ethnographic study, contends that a group of continental African students do develop aspects of a null curriculum and that, in the case of Black popular culture, such a null curriculum can contribute to bringing in Black students' previously unwarranted and non-validated forms of knowledge. The null curriculum, it is argued, can address the feeling of alienation that Black students have in their relation to Eurocentric curricula and can also contribute to a more relevant, engaging and integrative anti-racism curriculum.

James and Mannette explore the concept of post-secondary access programs in Canada, arguing that access programs within the existing inequitable structures of universities have merely added "colour" to the student body. Utilizing the comments of African Canadian students who are enrolled in a university with an access initiative, they demonstrate that to survive academe these students must constantly negotiate the hegemonic structures and official discourses of universities that have operated, and in some cases continue to operate, to exclude them. The authors suggest that access fulfills the aspirations and expectations of neither its architects nor its historically disadvantaged target populations. What access has become, for institutions and access students who enter universities through access programs, is an episode in living with difficult knowledge.

Annette Henry raises significant questions about the meanings of anti-racist policy from the standpoint of Black women. She uses three vignettes from the lives of Black women in teaching and teacher education as her point of departure. Henry frames the discussion in feminist/womanist literature and concludes that, for an anti-racist movement to take place, Black women must take transformative positions rather than remaining complacent, silent and invisible.

Evangelia Tastsoglou interrogates the subject of cultural, political and pedagogical border crossings. Starting from a critical overview of the sociological literature on boundaries and border crossings and a sociological and political vision of a society that although seeking to be equitable includes classifications and group boundaries, the author examines myriad social, cultural, epistemological and political boundaries in classrooms. Critical feminist and anti-racist pedagogy is treated as an attempt at egalitarian border crossings in the school and in the process of learning for citizenship. Tastsoglou also highlights challenges to such crossings.

Handel Wright addresses questions of academic exclusion of the "other" from discourses of empowerment. The author steps inside/outside the discourses of empowerment that inform and sustain his praxis as an educator to examine them critically. He argues that, paradoxically, discourses of empowerment are complicit in the very problem of exclusion that they attempt to address in mainstream academic discourses. To illustrate this, he holds up the politics of one discourse against another in what he calls critical skepticism. He points to the exclusion of minorities (Blacks, more specifically) from the discourses of feminism and post-modernism and to the exclusion of non-African American women from the discourse of Afrocentrism. Arguing that the operation of power within and between discourses ensures that we are all both victims and perpetrators of exclusion, Wright calls for the evolution of a politics of identification (as opposed to a politics of identity) and the forging of alliances (a search for solidarity rather than consensus) as a means of working with difference and avoiding the immobilizing dualism of *j'accuse* on the one hand and *mea culpa* on the other.

Agnes Calliste provides a critical analysis of the structures and practices within universities that overtly and subtly discriminate against minority faculty and students. The chapter is grounded in research on anti-racist organizing and resistance in two Nova Scotia universities. The author examines the conditions under which these anti-racist struggles materialized, the constraints placed upon them and their effects.

Authors have focused on the structural issues that play important roles in race and anti-racism conflict with implications for social policy. Discussions have been situated in the broad socio-historical contexts and events that make anti-racism and difference a critical and necessary area of today's academic inquiry and political practice. As mentioned earlier, one of our major learning objectives is to reframe anti-racism debates and not merely to revisit the old, tired discussions. We have urged our readers to move on. Particular sites have been taken up for discussion in this text, but we do not claim to address all that needs to be addressed in anti-racism discourse. This book contributes to a dialogue on lived experiences at specific sites and times, which leaves room for further critical dialogue voicing different experiences and experiencing difference at multiple points of intersection and gaps. We urge others to join in the debate on what anti-racism means and how we can work with the intersections of varied forms of difference.

Anti-racism practice cannot afford to be caught up in high theoretical debates. There are several paths to equity in education. For example, it is clear to most anti-racist educators that racialized minorities experiencing a deracialized approach to schooling feel the material consequences of race profoundly. A modernist approach to improving schools focuses on academic excellence without simultaneously addressing the unequal educational effects of race, gender and social class. Common-sense knowledge allows a Conservative government in Ontario to view education through the metaphor and lens of market capital. The stakes are very high for the racially disadvantaged.

Anti-Racism or Multiculturalism

We cannot end this introduction without clarifying a question continually asked by some educators, students and parents, namely the distinction between anti-racism and multiculturalism. It is easy for the distinction between multiculturalism and anti-racism to be blurred as community workers and theorists resist a placement in neat theoretical boxes. Some writers appear to conflate both terms as if they mean the same thing (see Lyons 1994). In other cases scholars may refer to multiculturalism even when working with some of the basic tenets of anti-racism.

In US discourse, McLaren (1997) speaks of "critical/revolutionary multiculturalism" in a way that is akin to anti-racism as understood in Canadian contexts. Other authors such as Kailin (1994) and Lawrence and Tatum (1997) describe their work as "anti-racist." In the British literature the understanding of anti-racism has been clearly articulated (Brandt 1986; see also Mullard 1980, 1985; Carby 1982; Jeffcoate 1984; Troyna and Williams 1986; Cohen 1989). In the Canadian context it is significant that we draw the distinction between anti-racism and multiculturalism (see Thomas 1984 and Lee 1985, 1994). Our attempt here will not be comprehensive as we recast the points of divergence and convergence. The subject has been covered at length (see Kehoe n.d. and Tator and Henry 1991) and is critiqued from a schooling perspective in Gabriel

Bedard's chapter. Our aim is to highlight the key areas of distinction that are significant to understanding the anti-racism approach adopted in this book.

The question for us is not whether multiculturalism shares certain ideas in common with anti-racism. Rather, we seek to explain where to draw the boundary and operationalize the distinction between these two terms. Multiculturalism has become an ideology in Canada that, with the passage of Bill C-93 ("An Act for the preservation and enhancement of multiculturalism in Canada") on July 12, 1988, was enshrined into law (see Lynch 1992 and Price 1993). It is a political doctrine officially promoting cultural diversity as an intrinsic component of the social, political and moral order (Fleras and Elliot 1992). The Liberal claim for multiculturalism sees it as a cornerstone in nation-building. It is an ideal of a democratic pluralistic society that recognizes a community and advocates empathy for minorities on the basis of a common humanity. It also envisions a future assured by goodwill, tolerance and understanding of diversity among all (Price 1993). In other words, multiculturalism works with the notion of our basic humanness and downplays inequities of difference by accentuating shared commonalities. Anti-racism, on the other hand, views as suspect the whole nation-building enterprise as pursued by the dominant, together with the underlying assumptions of empathy, commonality and goodwill. Anti-racism shifts the talk away from tolerance of diversity to the pointed notion of difference and power. It sees race and racism as central to how we claim, occupy and defend spaces. The task of anti-racism is to identify, challenge and change the values, structures and behaviours that perpetuate systemic racism and other forms of societal oppressions.

We are well aware of creating binaries of thought but nevertheless posit the following as fundamental differences between multiculturalism and anti-racism. As a discourse and discursive practice, multiculturalism heralds the mosaic, cherishes diversity and plurality and promotes an image of multiple, thriving, mutually respectful and appreciative ethno-cultural communities. The anti-racism discourse highlights persistent inequities among communities, focusing on relations of domination and subordination (Thomas 1984; Lee 1985; Walcott 1990; Dei 1996a). To a multiculturalist the issue is one of a lack of recognition of the positive contributions of minorities, which stems from misunderstanding and miscommunication. An anti-racist sees the issue starkly as entrenched inequities and power imbalance. Multiculturalism views the problem as manifested in intolerance and lack of goodwill. Anti-racism troubles the manifestation of the problem as bias, discrimination, hatred, exclusion and violence (Price 1993). Multiculturalism perceives prejudice as a violation of democratic rights. Anti-racism perceives prejudice as an integral part of the social order. Consequently, multiculturalism presents the mechanism of redress through education-sharing and exchange of ideas while anti-racism views the mechanism of redress through fundamental structural/societal change. The assumption underlying empathy, commonality and goodwill promoted by multiculturalism is that we start from a relatively level playing field, that we have access to similar resources and that we have comparable values, aspirations and concerns. Nothing can be further from the reality of the racially minoritized in our communities. How we name our discursive practice is equally as important as that in which we are engaged politically. For those whose discursive, political and community work is located in the basic tenets of anti-racism, it is important to call our work anti-racist.

Chapter One

Towards an Anti-Racism Discursive Framework

George J. Sefa Dei

From the outset, let me emphasize that this chapter is largely a theoretical discussion and not is strictly concerned with the "how" of policy, although this is crucial. My goal is to present anti-racism as a useful analytical framework for understanding society. I examine the theoretical tools for popularizing a critical integrative anti-racism framework for understanding and resisting social oppressions. I critique the practice of racializing human subjects for differential (negative) treatment in schools, workplaces, communities and other institutional settings in society. The discussion is anchored in the politics of race and representation of social difference. It goes without saying that, if left standing, the wave of ultra-conservativism currently sweeping across North America will constitute a mortal danger to anti-racism work for educational and social change. I am not speaking only of what Ku (1996: 8) calls the "distancing of racism." The fact is that race and equity issues are no longer "officially" supported in some political circles; they are openly challenged. The dominant discourse of individual rights and concerns about censorship are privileged over racism.

Anti-racism praxis (Freire 1993) has become an untenable political engagement in the fears and anxieties of critics and right-wing ideologues. Some law-makers in North America have discovered that unashamedly attacking anti-racism and equity issues as "special interests" wins strong public approval. One need only witness the wide public appeal of the right-wing conservatives in Canada and the United States who openly attack employment equity and affirmative action policies. In both public discourses, political and social capital can be gained by encoding racial meanings into terms like "immigrant" and "welfare." The subtext of the mission to "reform" welfare is to get the pathological culprits—Blacks and racial minorities (constituted as "immigrants")—off the welfare rolls. As an African Canadian male living in Toronto, I vividly recall the Toronto media's late 1980's and early 1990's portrayal of Somalian refugees as welfare cheats. In fact, when the Progressive Conservative government later ran an election campaign promising to reform the welfare system, what was left unsaid, but clearly understood, was that they would put an end to practices that allowed immigrants to abuse the system and drain the patience of White, middle-class, Canadian taxpayers. It is by understanding the nature of anti-racism resistance that the pain of collective identification through negative racialization can be countered.

There is a need to develop a more critical anti-racism discursive praxis. The urgency for developing an anti-racism discursive framework can be found in current local, national and global struggles for equity and justice. Theory must undoubtedly inform such practices, just as these practices themselves shape theoretical discourses about society. Recent developments offer some impetus for an anti-racist discursive framework: the denial of the significance of race in academic discourse and practice; the open renunciation of racial differences in social practices; the trend towards the use of strictly class-based criteria in formulating social policy for equity; the call for a transracial coalition praxis devoid of any symptoms of the politics of identity; the majority's embracing of the argument that race-specific practices should receive less attention in progressive political agendas; and the backlash against racial and ethnic minorities clamouring for change (see Winant 1997). Elsewhere I have categorized these concerns as "the politics of denying race and difference" (Dei 1999). The consequences and implications of the denial and negation of race and racial differences are significant; anti-racist workers need to sharpen their theoretical and discursive practices to legitimize the social struggles for race justice and equity. As has been noted, there is a distinction between associating (negative) meanings to race and the insidious politics of denying racial differences in formulating social policy for justice. The recognition of difference in itself is no problem, unlike the interpretations of the differences. Therefore a popular reframing of anti-racist discourses will enable progressive anti-racist politics to work more effectively for change. It will ensure that anti-racism is evoked not simply at the theoretical/discursive level but also at the level of informed political practice.

Far from diminishing the significance of race, these developments have added to the unsettling of race in public consciousness. Winant (1997: 49) further reminds us that we in North American society daily "articulate our anxieties in racial terms: wealth and poverty, crime and punishment, gender and sexuality, nationality and citizenship, culture and power ... primarily though race." Our society is racially stratified. As Fine, Powell, Weis and Wong (1997: x) point out, raced and colonial hierarchies are embedded in institutions, and everyday racism "travels like a virus through institutional structures, policies, practices, relationships, fights and identities."

By clearly articulating an anti-racist discursive framework, we[1] are able to offer both theoretical and practical responses to challenging questions about the nature and practice of race and racism and the intersections with power and difference. We can answer questions such as: What do we know about diversity in social settings? What is the relationship between race and social practice? How do teachers and educators teach about race and racism in schools? What do we understand by power and privilege? What are the challenges of being a "minority" in Canadian society? What does it mean to be "different"? What are the strengths of having "difference"? What do you see as your personal and collective responsibilities in fighting racism and social oppression? What is and who can do anti-racist work? What are the risks and consequences involved in doing anti-racist work?

Historically, academic knowledge[2] has had an influence in framing public discourse and policy, and race issues have been no exception (see van Dijk 1993). Given the continuing hostility towards anti-racism work, new knowledge must be produced to refocus attention and efforts on addressing social justice and equity issues. New knowledge should critically examine the socially constructed ways of making meaning in a racialized, gendered and classed world. Reading the world is a political act in which we, the readers, must account for how we come to appreciate and interrogate established hegemonic ways of knowing. It is in this context that questions of subject positionality arise in anti-racism praxis.

In this chapter I will develop the anti-racism discursive framework by first spelling out how the subject(ive) defines the academic and political project on anti-racism. I will then discuss the importance of acknowledging situational and contextual variations in intensities of oppression by highlighting the saliency of race in anti-racism discourse. Since racisms work differently depending on group history, culture, class and gender, we cannot underestimate the relevance of an integrative analysis to understanding the structural processes, practices and social effects of racisms and other forms of oppression. Race, class, gender and sexuality are not absolute conceptions of difference. These concepts/categories are not mutually exclusive. They are not deterministic of character, behaviour and identity. However, by working with these categories in an integrative manner, we can help promote community cohesion. We may also help advance the cause of destabilizing/disrupting the real interest-group politics promoted by those who defend the current status quo.

The Subject and the Academic/Political Project

Referencing one's subject position can be an entry point from which to pursue political praxis. Anti-racism work begins when the individual practitioner takes stock of his or her relative positions of power, privilege and disadvantage. Anti-racism entails a recognition of the individual and collective responsibility to use multiple positions and differential locations of power, privilege and social disadvantage to work for change. As an African Canadian educator privileged to be teaching in a Canadian institution of higher learning, I have a responsibility to use my position, power and space to speak against what I consider to be the social injustices structured around the negative evaluation of difference. While I am privileged by my class and gender, I also experience the racial subordination that is very much a part of Euro-American society and therefore work with others to remove all forms of oppression and injustice.

Such collaboration is possible only if I recognize that while I may experience racial oppression, I also "enjoy [the] hetero sexist and ablest privilege that society offers" (I.M. James 1996: 36). I must also be aware of the limits and possibilities of my anti-racism pedagogical praxis in challenging the structures of knowledge production in academia. In the face of the pressing concerns of African Canadian parents, community activists, students and educators about educational inequalities in school systems, I cannot distance myself and naively ask, "Aren't our schools working?" I have to ask the poignant political question, "What can be done to transform schools into working communities?" The questions that I ask, emerging as they do from a particular subject position, must be more practical and more urgent than if they were asked by someone for whom the consequences of educational inequity may be less crucial or pressing. Our individual and collective histories shape how we come to read and interpret the world around us. I would not claim to have the truth or the authentic voice on racial oppressions. I do feel, however, that while we may not agree on what constitutes justice, we can recognize injustice when it is done.

The rush to move beyond race is couched in a denial of racialized positionality of power and privilege. Many believe that we live in a phase of race neutrality. There is the supposed disappearance of race evident in current processes of deracializing human subjects. This is commonly witnessed among White teachers who state, "I don't look at the race; I see only the child." This colour-blindness and/or racelessness is not a social equalizer; it is a "racial act" (Morrison 1992a: 46) and an "enactment of White normativity and dominance" (Chater 1996: 24).[3] Indeed, it masks and denies the existence of racism and provides an excuse for complacency or the outright dismantling of anti-racism programs and initiatives.

Within Euro-Canadian/American contexts, the normativity of Whiteness is powerfully entrenched in schools. In an ongoing study of "best practices" of inclusive schooling in which I have been involved (Dei et al. 1996), two White teachers stated in interviews with researchers that they did not see why they had to teach diverse histories and multiple ways of knowing. One teacher said "We don't have a Muslim week, we don't have a White week" (11/16/95). The other teacher argued that she saw "no reason to teach, you know, that particular history [Black/African history]": "I really get tired of people labelling [and distinguishing] 'Black' history.... Do I teach 'White' history?" (12/5/95). This is an example of "racelessness" as an enactment of White normativity and dominance. Some educators do not even recognize that what they see as a "normal" curriculum suited to all students is actually a White, Eurocentric curriculum (see also Castagna 1995: 8). As observed by Joyce (1995), only White people can afford to be raceless.

The politics of negation and erasure of race is pervasive in contemporary North American schools, government, media and popular culture. As hooks (1992b) argues, issues of race and racism are continually replaced with "evocations of pluralism and diversity." "Anti-racism" is replaced with "managing diversity" in many institutional settings. This erasure "allows for assimilation and forgetfulness" (hooks 1992b: 345). But this is no innocent strategy. In Canadian contexts, it perpetuates the association of Whiteness with innocence, thus bestowing upon neo-conservative Whites the "right" to dismantle anti-racism initiatives such as mandatory employment equity policies.[4]

I define anti-racism as an action-oriented educational strategy for institutional, systemic change to address racism and interlocking systems of social oppression. It is a critical discourse of race and racism in society that challenges the continuance of racializing social groups for differential and unequal treatment. Anti-racism explicitly names the issues of race and social difference as issues of power and equity, rather than as matters of cultural and ethnic variety (see Brandt 1986; Lee 1985). The anti-racism discourse draws on broad definitions of race and racism, extending beyond skin colour as the only signifier of difference (see Gillborn 1995). While recognizing the saliency of skin-colour racism, critical anti-racism asserts that a discussion about racism should not be restricted to "White racism" but must explore the myriad manifestations of racism in society. Racialization of society and its subjects distinguishes and subjects social groups to differential and unequal treatment on the basis of supposedly biological, phenotypical and cultural characteristics (Miles 1989; Li 1990; Goldberg 1993). The new social markers or indicators of difference are evident in the discourse of language, politics, culture, religion and social difference (see Macchiusi 1993). These racist discourses still stem and emanate from White racism, from the discourse of the dominant White society, which has prescribed what is and is not normal and acceptable. In other words, racism is fully entrenched in dominant White Christian ideology regardless of who is perpetuating it.

Furthermore, critical anti-racism asserts that racial minorities cannot simply be presented as victims, powerless and subordinated in the study of race relations and conflict. Their histories of resistance against social domination (e.g., race, class, gender and sexual oppressions) contain important lessons for anti-racism praxis for social change. A critical anti-racism approach must also deal with differences in a way that moves beyond multiculturalism's celebratory approach to diversity and towards a discourse and praxis of fundamental power-sharing in communities. One cannot simply earn the "badge of diversity" (I.M. James 1996: 33) without dealing with key questions of equity and power-sharing within a social context that sees Whiteness as the norm. The next section addresses the need to question the "normality" of Whiteness.

Anti-Racism's Interrogation of "Whiteness"

As many have argued, an important dimension of any critical discussion of anti-racism and difference is challenging the normality of Whiteness and the pervasive effects of White privilege. White privilege allows the dominant to define and articulate difference. It is a relational phenomenon that has emerged from the counterplay of complex social, cultural, political and historical forces and contexts (see Frankenberg 1993; Dyer 1997; Roediger 1994). Today White privilege is continuously asserted by the dominant; and, in assessing this privilege, anti-racism targets claims to innocence. As others have shown, it is important that our articulation of Whiteness be seen as more than the sum of White privilege, power and identity (see Giroux 1997; McLaren 1997). The creation of an open and equal opportunity school system with effective social outcomes for all groups means disrupting the dominance of Whiteness. Frankly, the mere superficial claim of diversity does not allow for a critical reading of Whiteness (see Nanacoo 2000). Frankenberg (1993) has called for the unmasking of Whiteness as an unracialized category. In our anti-racist praxis we must centre the interrogation of Whiteness in a way that does not shift attention away from the plight and concerns of society's disadvantaged. A rupturing of Whiteness is crucial to further subversion of Eurocentrism because Whiteness promotes a cultural practice of race-based hierarchies (Fine et al. 1997; see also McLaren 1997; Giroux 1997). It is a power base defining normalcy. Notions of meritocracy, excellence, ethical neutrality and rugged individualism are rationalized in the understandings of Whiteness. Whiteness is also a privileged signifier of difference; identity; and power for domination, resistance and change (Post and Rogin 1998; Wray and Newitz 1997). An analysis of the discourse on White racial hierarchies not only suggests that there are different complicities in the maintenance of racism but also that hierarchies end up benefiting the dominant.

A critical approach to difference asks what it means to claim Whiteness in a racialized context. Whiteness must be examined as an active component in the maintenance of domination. Whiteness exists within a system of economic, political, cultural, psychological, emotional and social advantages for dominant groups at the expense of racialized others. Whiteness is a racial category, a social marker of power and privilege; but rather than posit "who exactly is Whiteness," we must adhere to Giroux's (1997) caution against conflating a warranted critique and careful interrogation of Whiteness with criticisms of White people. We must reframe the question "who" is Whiteness to ask "how and why is Whiteness produced, maintained and elaborated upon in the social order." Whiteness is a social construction with political, cultural and economic capital. It is produced by and productive of the social contexts of power that constructs difference, normality and privilege. It is also an ideology in the way it conjures images, conceptions and promises that provide the frameworks through which dominant and other groups represent, interpret, understand and make sense of social existence. Whiteness is a form of self identity and a marker of material, political, symbolic and psychological worth.

Roediger (1994) and Dyer (1997) have written extensively on Whiteness as a marker of identity that is nothing but oppressive and false, "an empty category" that is fragile and fluid, an "identity based on what one isn't and on whom one can hold back" (Roediger 1994: 13). But Whiteness has become a point of cultural attachment. For anti-racist educational change, then, a key question is: how can we think through "Whiteness" and its complexities without avoiding or evading racial injustice and deep systemic inequities. Whiteness is institutionalized privilege. Therefore progressive politics for change must focus on Whiteness as a system of dominance. The ontological reality is that Whiteness is a powerful conception of identity that cannot be destroyed (see McLaren 1997); but we can hope for its critical deconstruction, beginning with an acknowledgment of the normalcy of Whiteness. Educators must challenge "merit based on individuality," which erases privilege, and they must teach that Whiteness reproduces itself regardless of intention, power differences and goodwill (Dyer 1997). Whiteness as property is privilege, which excludes and appropriates.

Chater (1994: 102) long ago noted that "privilege and power have historically sedimented along lines mediated by class, caste, nation, race, gender, sexuality and so on. Many, if not most people, have a complex and contradictory relationship to power and powerlessness, to privilege and oppression." She further enthused that the experiences of White working classes, women, disabled people, gays and lesbians indicate that we must interrogate seriously any generalizations of White privilege (see Wray and Newitz 1997). In conceding to this assertion I also concur with Harris (1993: 1759) that the benefits of Whiteness are available to all dominant groups, regardless of class, gender and sexual positions. While those who benefit from Whiteness may be disadvantaged in society, it is "not because of their race, but in spite of it" (Harris 1993: 1786). Admittedly, Whiteness is not the universal experience of all Whites. Therefore the anti-racist discursive practice must explore how gender, class and sexuality make the experience of being White different for different people, because there is no "fictive homogenous community of Whites" (Roman 1997: 274).

We require a historical approach to contextualize and situate Whiteness and the complicities of dominant groups in myriad forms of racisms. We also require a renegotiation of Whiteness as a productive and critical force within the politics of claiming, knowing and naming difference. To articulate Whiteness as an oppositional category, anti-racism must work with racial identity as a form of agency and resistance. The political, economic and educational advantage of Whiteness (McIntosh 1990) must be used to create a resisting space that challenges dominance/hegemony (Giroux 1997). When Whiteness is destabilized, both the claim to own, possess and be privileged and the claim to normalcy are challenged and resisted, and the right to have a larger share of societal resources is made suspect. Our vision should be one in which no group has an automatic right to privilege, supremacy and a disproportionate share of the valued goods and services of society (see Dei 2000).

On the Saliency and Centrality of Race in Anti-Racism Praxis

A call to move beyond race and racism, however well-intentioned, can be a luxury. To the critical anti-racism worker, such a call can be shallow and hypocritical. We cannot deny our subjectivities and positionalities. The call to move beyond race is particularly unacceptable when issued by members of the dominant group. The intention usually is to evade or cover up their own positioning in locations of race privilege and power (Frankenberg 1993; Fiske 1996: 48). Rather than move beyond race, what we ought to move beyond is a "denial of race as a social issue, in a society with a profoundly racist history and where institutional racism still exists" (Lutz and Collins 1993: 165).

I share Yuval-Davis' (1994: 408) contention that "all identity dimensions can, in specific contexts, have higher or lower salience, but often the primordial components of one's identity ... provoke the most powerful emotions for the individual, through processes of identification which ... can blur individual and collective boundaries." Bishop (1994) is also correct in pointing out that all oppressions do not necessarily operate in the same way or at the same time (see also Barrett 1996). What then is the politics of affirming the centrality of race in anti-racism praxis? Anti-racism advocates for social change whereby race is acknowledged as a central axis of power and racist inequities are ameliorated. The politics of anti-racism demands that race come first, that its salience is central even when other dimensions of oppression co-exist with racial ones. For the anti-racism worker, the decision to speak of the saliency of race is a political one.

Race is a salient aspect of human identity. To ignore race difference and the social practices and actions engendered by race categorization is to deny the individual–social subject connection and to "neutralize a person's experiences" (Varma 1996: 19) as situated in broader socio-political contexts. The recognition of the centrality and saliency of race in anti-racism praxis is not tantamount to a hierarchical positioning of difference. It is informed by the realization that, historically, other oppressions have been privileged and allowed to replace racism in the public discourse on social injustice. It is a recognition that academic discussions on race are often avoided, negated or erased in schools. All of this is compounded by disturbing evidence that racial knowledge, meanings and organization permeate school life in ways that have the most negative impact on minority youth in White-dominated societies (see Alladin 1995; Dei et al. 1995; Brathwaite and James 1996). In countering the omission, erasures and negations of race, the anti-racism project intends to bring racial difference to the centre of schooling and education in Euro-American contexts. The centring of race in anti-racism, then, stems the continued official denial and marginalization of race.

But anti-racism cannot reify race. The centrality of race in anti-racism discourse and praxis recognizes the need to de-essentialize the race concept and to see race and racisms in their multifarious complexities (Gillborn 1995; Dei

1996a). This means shifting from a competitive and dichotomous thinking of a simplistic Black/White duality to the inclusive "and/with" position (that is, different/multiple racisms). It also means refocusing on the relational aspects of race and difference rather than using the lens of race to produce a unidimensional picture of social reality.

As already remarked, we occupy multiple subject positions of privilege and disadvantage, power and subordination. Matthews (1996: 2) argues that often the location "on which we fail to cast our gaze is that location from which we dominate." White anti-racist workers may recognize and discuss systemic racism and yet fail to see themselves as implicated in the structures that perpetuate and reproduce racism. Similarly, a racial minority male anti-racism worker may focus on race while failing to explore how gender and class issues complicate racial concerns.

Multiplex Oppressions: Race, Gender, Class and Sexuality

Race, class, gender and sexuality are primary social categories that inform the complexity of human experience. The individual does not possess a one-dimensional identity. Individuals have constructed and defined race, gender, class and sexual identities. Individuals are also socialized into identities that correspond to the categories of race, gender and class. One's identity is a complex mesh of race, gender, class and sexual orientation. These identities are also sites of shifting power relations that inform, constrain and determine the human experience and condition. Identity, as Hall (1991) cautions, is history in the making. Identities are constantly reconstituted and reformulated, particularly in the representational politics of social difference.

A critical understanding of racism must not be premised on a narrow individualistic frame of reference in which both the complexity of the human subject and the connection to larger socio-political forces are denied. For example, cases brought before human rights tribunals in Canada reveal how the courts' inability or refusal to see the interconnectedness of race, ability, gender and class oppressions can impede the delivery of justice. This narrow frame of reference, as Duclos (1992) indicates, means that a First Nations woman with a motor disability who has been refused service in a liquor store is unable to win her case of discrimination on the basis of race, colour or ancestry. In this particular case, the tribunal accepted the allegations of discrimination based on disability but rejected allegations based on race (see Duclos 1992).

There are further manifestations of this inability to see the interconnectedness of social differences. For example, race and gender oppressions are implicated in ways that view foreign domestic workers as suitable for household labour and, more importantly, child and elder care. In addition to race and gender, social class is also a significant factor in the understanding of Canadian immigration policy. Desirable live-in caregivers are now being advertised by agencies as nurses, teachers and midwives, sufficiently middle-class to provide the necessary environment for White middle-class children. Evidence abounds concerning the social stratification that determines which domestics receive immigrant status sooner. And this hierarchy of privilege tends to be based on race and class, with European "nannies" (often from France and England) being most desirable, followed by Filipino nurses, many of whom are part of an export industry in which they train in high-technology, Western medical techniques and then go abroad to earn foreign currency. African Caribbean women are below European and Filipino women in the hierarchy of preference. Many questions can be asked of this social stratification of women workers in a global context. Why does the Philippines so value North American knowledge and experience that it will send its already highly qualified women to Canada to gain additional training as a nanny in a middle-class home? What are the consequences of inadequate working and childcare programs for poor women and children both in this country and abroad? Makeda Silvera (1993) speaks of the racism, classism and sexism that domestic workers from the Caribbean have experienced throughout history. Silvera also notes that the concerns expressed by racial minority domestics were never addressed under the previous immigration policy (The Domestic Scheme of 1955); rather their situation worsened when the practice of automatically granting landed immigrant status after a period of a year was replaced by the practice of issuing temporary employment visas. Without this automatic granting, individual applicants must hope to gain landed immigrant status on the recommendations of employers and immigration officers. They are now more vulnerable to continued exploitation, systemic racism (which may be why this policy was brought in) and increased individual racism. The Canadian state and employment agencies, as gatekeepers, have determined that African Caribbean women are not "most desirable" as live-in caregivers (see Bakan and Stasiulis 1995). Consequently, race, class and gender conspires to determine which people are allowed into Canada, where they are permitted to work once admitted and the conditions under which they work.

The expression or articulation of individual particularities/specificities and the recognition of (fundamental) diversity in human experience must acknowledge how individuals are inserted asymmetrically into broader political economic structures. A major consequence of individualizing experience is that identity is depoliticized. Politics constitutes identity (Hall 1992a). Individual identities emerge at the intersections of political, social and historical realities. Mary John (1989: 50) spoke about the need to question "'what one is' through a more extensive questioning of the intrications of one's history within History." The lodging of meaning strictly in individual subjectivity can preclude "the possibility of political criticism or action because meaning becomes simply a matter of individual opinion, lacking political power" (O'Neil 1993: 20).

Our understanding of racism can be enriched only by an understanding of the intricate web of intersecting and interlocking oppressions (Dei 1998). In the interrogation of racist and racialized practices of society, the complexity and dynamics of social categories of race, class, gender and sexuality could constitute the point of reference. Chater (1996: 30) adds that the individual as a social subject cannot exist outside of a social group context of power relations, which determine or constrain agency. Anti-racism praxis cannot valorize the individual through a denial of the collectivity of peoples. It is also crucial that critical anti-racism work does not essentialize difference by romanticizing or overdramatizing it. The articulation and/or enforcement of individualism can lead to an erasure of collectivities and collective group differences.

Specifying the Anti-Racism Discursive Framework

Collins (1990: 234) aptly reminds us that "subjugation is not grounds for an epistemology." The anti-racism framework does not emerge simply from a knowledge of the racial atrocities in human history. Narratives of victimhood—victimologies—help us to understand social reality. Victims of racism resist in order to survive and tell their stories. Similarly, while theory can be created from a critical interrogation of individual and collective social experiences, the individual and collective identity of subjects cannot be reduced merely to a resistance to racism (see Gilroy 1990). What this implies, then, is a theorization of anti-racism that transcends a reification of the victimhood and the resistance status to fully comprehend the complexities of social reality.

The diverse and complex ways in which minority youth, parents and community workers negotiate their identities with the school and broader society speak to these complexities. When a parent who is dealing with a hostile/inflexible school administrator, for example, chooses words such as "bias" rather than "prejudice," "culture" rather than "race," he or she is fully aware that choice of language will affect whether or not he or she will gain a hearing (Fine 1993). At the same time, understanding the complexities of social reality necessitates a deconstruction of what is seen as normative by the dominant society, deconstructing, for example, White acts of empathy (Roger 1996). The anti-racism discursive framework can develop from a critical understanding of the history and context of race, racist and racialized practices and knowledge production around difference and sameness. Anti-racism discourse emerges out of the recognition of the importance of race identity, social difference and representation in educational practice.

Following up on the pioneering works by Brandt (1986), Mullard (1980, 1985), Carby (1982), Jeffcoate (1984), Nixon (1984), Gilroy (1982), Cohen (1989), Bains and Cohen (1988), Abella (1984), Thomas (1984), Lee (1985), Troyna and Williams (1986) and Reed (1994), I would specify what constitutes an anti-racism discursive framework and praxis. I prefer the term "discursive" to "theoretical" because I find it problematic to focus on a grand theoretical bedrock when trying to explain social phenomena. It is important to work with a guiding framework that takes into account the fact that academic and political questions are continually changing to reflect social realities as well as the narration of different histories and experiences.

Anti-racism is about social change. The anti-racism discursive framework is an interrogation of both structural barriers to and social practices for systemic change. As already argued, anti-racism not only acknowledges the reality of racism in society and the potential for changing that reality, it also moves beyond acknowledgment to question White power and privilege and its accompanying rationale for dominance. Anti-racism questions the marginalization of certain voices in society and the delegitimation/devaluation of the knowledge and experience of subordinate/minority groups. It challenges definitions of "valid" knowledge and interrogates how knowledge is produced and distributed, both nationally and globally.

Anti-racism education questions pathological explanations of the family or home environment as the source of the problems that youths face in the schools. It is argued that such explanations divert attention from a critical analysis of the institutional structures of schooling, which treat youth inequitably and which justify the (educational) status quo by attributing causal priority to the victims themselves. Anti-racism also questions public discourse that criminalizes Black youths and presents educational problems in isolation from the material, ideological and structural conditions in which students find themselves. The cause of youth academic failure is attributed to inadequate parental responsibility and a deviant home and family. The individual youth is subjected to blame without any appreciation of how larger socio-economic and political forces and conditions structure individual family lives. Pathologizing family and home reinforces/produces/depends on gendered racial stereotypes such as welfare mothers and absentee fathers.

The anti-racism discursive framework questions the roles that societal institutions (school, home/family, museum, workplace, arts, justice and media) play in reproducing inequalities of race, gender, sex and class. It acknowledges the pedagogic need to confront the challenge of diversity and difference in society and the urgency for a more inclusive social system that is capable of responding to minority concerns and aspirations. Anti-racism praxis opposes established hegemonic social, economic and political interests and forces underpinning domination. The institutional structures of society historically have served the material, political and ideological interests of the state and the capitalist social formation. Anti-racism deals foremost with *equity*; that is, the qualitative value of justice. It deals with *representation;* that is, the need to have multiple voices and perspectives involved in the production of mainstream social knowledge. Anti-racism also examines institutional practices to see how institutions respond to the challenge of *diversity and difference*; understood as the intersections of race, gender, class, sexuality, language, culture and religion.

The concept of race is an entry point to anti-racism praxis. Anti-racism recognizes the social effects of race despite its lack of "scientific basis." The concept of race is a fundamental tool for community and academic political organizing for social change. *But racism is the problem, not a definition of what race is or is not.* Racism cannot be dealt with by simply rejecting the idea and concept of race. In fact, as Ku (1995: 2) aptly expressed it, "the debunking of scientific justification for race has not resulted in the obsolescence of the concept of race." Racial classification has become an important criterion for social and political interactions. Race is as much a reality as class and gender (see W. Ng 1995). Race is a socio-political construct, but it is also real in terms of material consequences. Race is central to all structures, institutions and social discourses in Euro-American society. Race is used to include, exclude, superiorize and inferiorize peoples. Race defines who has access to public resources, social goods and social benefits, and the means by which they gain that access (see Omi and Winant 1994; Henry et al. 1995). The knowledge that race is an ideological, social/material construct does not take away the consequences when one is faced with actual racist incidents or practices. However, one cannot understand the full social effects of race without understanding the intersections of all other forms of social oppression (race, class, gender and sexuality). Therefore, a key understanding is that all systems of oppression intersect and interlock and a study of one such system—racism—necessarily entails a study of classism, sexism and homophobia. For this reason a critical anti-racism praxis must incorporate gender, class and sexuality as fundamental and relational aspects of the human experience, which intersect both the historical and contemporary reality of peoples (Leah 1995:2; Ng 1991; Belkhir and Ball 1993; Collins 1993). To undertake effective anti-racism praxis is to question White power and privilege and the rationality for dominance in the global community.

In the anti-racism discursive framework, race is not the focus of academic discussion and political action. Rather centrality is accorded to the examination of particular social practices made possible or politically engendered by racial identifications. Anti-racism knowledge is necessarily political and situated knowledge. Anti-racism education is transformative learning in the sense of promoting an educational agenda for social change. Anti-racism seeks to comprehend racist events and racialized practices by asking critical and destabilizing questions from the standpoint of both the marginalized and the privileged. Furthermore, in constructing anti-racism knowledge, the focus is more on the interactions between racist structures and racialized practices than on individual intent and motivations. As Anthias and Yuval-Davis (1992: 13) have argued,

> the question of racist practices need not rely on a notion of racism as explicitly underlying the structures and practices involved. Racist practices do not require the racist intentionality of structures which underpins so much of the work on institutional racism. Practices may

> be racist in terms of their effects. These practices may exacerbate or even produce exclusions and subordinations which are coterminous with supposed "racially" different populations.

Racism is more than an ideology and structure. It is a process. For example, anti-racism acknowledges how the entrenched norms and values (as ideology) of dominant groups can and do constrain the individual agency and collective resistance of subordinate groups. The ideology supports a structure of inequality in society. Systemic racial inequity is also reproduced though a process of daily interactions and routine practices. As Essed (1991: 39) shows with her concept of "everyday racism," macro-structures of society are not independent of the practices of everyday life. Institutions and structures shape and are influenced by everyday practices and experiences. Macro-structural and cultural properties of racism create the micro-inequities very much evident among individuals and groups. Both micro- and macro-structures impact on each other, and they maintain and reproduce systems of domination and subordination in society (see Nazim 1996; Essed 1990).

The implication for developing a critical anti-racism framework, therefore, is to understand the interplay between macro- and micro-dimensions of racism. Racism, as both a historical process and a system of structural inequities, is created and recreated through routine everyday practices. Similarly, individuals practise and understand racism from the existing knowledge of macro-structures of racial inequality in the system. In other words, while the structures of racism are created by agents, specific racialized practices are racist by definition when they activate existing structural inequities in the social system (Essed 1991: 39; Nazim 1996: 12).

Consequently, the anti-racism discursive framework draws on the notions of identity, practice and experience. Identity is linked with knowledge production in terms of how we can make sense of our world through individual and collective histories and experiences. The standpoint of marginalized people has special validity, and we need to incorporate the critiques and experiences of marginalized people into the process of knowledge production about race and racialized practices. An epistemic privilege of the marginalized and oppressed voices enriches and strengthens critical race studies because the voices add experiential accounts to race knowledge production. Production of critical race and anti-racism knowledge requires the examination of the historical and daily lived experiences of subordinate groups in White-dominated society. It also requires an interrogation of the system supporting White privilege and dominance.

Understanding the complexities of fighting racisms calls for a knowledge of individual and collective experiences of racism as well as the general knowledge of racism that connects individuals to a structure (see Essed 1991: 6). As argued elsewhere (Dei 1996a), a key consideration in the pursuit of anti-racism political organizing for social change is theorizing the personal and the political. A theoretical understanding of the personal is, in fact, a prerequisite for effective political action. Understanding the trajectories of individual and group experiences may point to significant lessons about alternative forms of social and political resistance to a myriad of oppressive human conditions. It is necessary for anti-racism workers to critically theorize both individual and collective historical and contemporary experiences to provide a methodology of social change (see Butler and Scott 1992; Scott 1991; Pierson 1991 in other contexts). Theorizing the personal and the collective starts with a critical interrogation of voice and experience. The voice that claims authority based on experience must be problematized without necessarily denying individual agency. Self-criticism is crucial to anti-racism politics. As Butler and Scott (1992) argue, experience should not be a source of truth or the "origin of knowledge." Experience cannot be taken for granted. While we may seek to understand experience and practice as a contextual basis of knowledge and political action, it must be noted that experience itself requires an explanation.

hooks (1994b) elaborates on how important personal experience is and how the telling of such experience can help "transgress" the boundaries of intellectual exploitation, appropriation and misrepresentation in education. Personal experience by itself is not enough to provide a complete account of social oppression. There are problems in claiming an "authority of experience" without recognizing how power relations shape the process of knowledge construction. Personal experiences are lived through social relations of power.

Anti-Racism in Schools: Putting Theory into Practice

A contemporary challenge is moving from rhetoric to political action, which ensures that change is accomplished in meaningful ways. In the context of capitalist and racist schooling in North America, there is a relation between developing a genuinely anti-racist perspective and the attainment of academic and social competence for the educator. While a case can be made for teaching anti-racism, given the diversity and differences exhibited in North American schools a rationale for anti-racism rests on the importance of teaching critically about difference. Social justice is not a per capita issue (Varma 1996: 21). All students need to be exposed to a complete and full account of human history and development.

Anti-racism education, as Varma (1996) enthuses, is not about creating a new hegemonic structure in the schools. It is about allowing every student to share in the centre. An inclusive anti-racist educational practice is the pursuit of interactive and co-operative learning strategies that teach all learners critical thinking skills to question the status quo. To accomplish the task of centring all students, the school system's hegemony and dominance of Whiteness must be ruptured.

Notions of visibility and credibility are always racialized and gendered.

Throughout human history, Whites have been racialized for privilege and credibility. Non-Whites, on the other hand, have been racialized for visibility (see Philip 1995 for a discussion on the criminalization of Blacks in Euro-American contexts). Students enter the school system as racialized, gendered and classed subjects. As I have argued elsewhere (Dei 1997), to deal with racism in the schools is, in effect, to decentre and destabilize Whiteness. Critical anti-racist work acknowledges that, through articulations of difference, Whiteness can be constructed as an "invisible border" to keep minority groups on the margins (Harris 1996: 1).

Every learner has the knowledge to produce situated understandings of the ways in which race and social difference work to accord/determine privilege and punishment. Unfortunately, not all learners can critically reflect on such knowledge. Schools contribute to the lack of self-criticality by privileging received academic knowledge over personal, cultural and social knowledge (see Hesch 1996).

Critical scholars can incorporate the study of the impact and consequences of racism on the perpetrator of racism in the development of a body of anti-racism scholarship (Morrison 1992a: 11; Chater 1996: 10). We may do this by allowing anti-racism scholars to work from multiple subject positions of privilege, power, domination and subordination. Thus, members from the dominant group can engage their anti-racism practice by first unpacking Whiteness in a racialized, gendered and classed society. This entails the examination of power and privilege and the rationality for White dominance in society. But Whiteness cannot be understood in static or frozen terms. Critical anti-racism must seek to understand the shifting positions and meanings of Whiteness as a "flexible positionality from which power operates" in society (Fiske 1996: 49).

In the populist, contemporary call to move beyond race, critical race studies should be able to draw an important distinction between "disassociating race from meaning" (Sleeter 1994a: 16) and hypocritically denying or negating race privilege. A refusal to talk about race would not necessarily end racism. The problem lies not in the articulation of racial differences but in the act of fastening negative meanings to them.

Conclusion

I conclude this essay with the question: What does our discussion here mean for actual political practice? One implication of the discussion thus far is that we cannot take a strictly theoretical view of race, racism and difference. Such an approach separates theory and practice. Theorizing about race does not certify anti-racist behaviour/work. In truly progressive anti-racism work, practicality must acknowledge the limits of theory. It also implies developing a clear strategy to put theory into practice. Given the existence of oppressive social structures it may be daunting, but it is nonetheless a surmountable task. This is why resistance must be broadly conceived. Our interpretations of resistance must include multiple actions directed towards change, either through a critique of dominant ideologies or through concrete action that systemically ruptures institutions. We should continually explore "all those micro forms of power and resistance which are organized around the discipline and control of racialized [as well as gendered, classed and sexualized] bodies" (Lattas 1993: 241). Also as Moore (1997: 90) argues, we must look for alternative conceptions of resistance, and "[r]ather than measuring resistance against a yardstick of widespread social and political economic transformations, the micro-politics of tactical manoeuvres [must take] centre stage." In other words, we must view resistance as collective actions and strategies for processual and incremental change. Resistance starts by using received knowledges to ask critical questions about the nature of the social order. Resistance also means seeing small acts as cumulative and significant for social change. Resistance must also eschew pragmatism and recognize the limits of agency.

How then do we put these ideas into practice? There are many spaces from which to address social inequities through anti-racist resistant work. Anti-racism practice begins with the inner self and a commitment to removing every bit of oppression in one's life. In schools for instance, anti-racism work can start by asking critical, theoretically informed questions and then proceeding to demand that schools address the absence of minority teachers and staff, the lack of curricular sophistication and the failure to link identity to schooling and knowledge production. Of course, there must be political commitment on the part of those who have power and privilege, but the acknowledgment of personal and collective complicity, responsibility and agency (and the limits of human agency) on the part of all is critical.

Notes

1. In the context of this paper, "we" refers to all who read this piece and share in the ideals of the anti-racism project.
2. Within the context of Canadian public policy and discourse, we recognize academic knowledge as an important alternative to "think tanks" such as the C.D. Howe Institute and the Fraser Institute. There is no doubt as to the interests of such institutes and their role in seeking to influence public policy and attitudes. Progressive academics and other professional cultural workers must not shrink from naming their positions in the quest for a more equitable and just society, from critiquing oppressions and injustices and from collectively working towards transforming them. Shrinking from that responsibility allows these positions to be usurped by those espousing a more inequitable market-driven society. Gramsci would suggest that our goal is to counter this by encouraging and supporting the development of organic intellectuals who are committed to the creation of just communities.
3. Chater (1996: 24) goes on to make an excellent point that the idea that an African Canadian "does not want to be recognized as such, or should not be, carries the underlying assumption that there is something wrong with that social/cultural/

racial location ... [rather than an acknowledgment that] the only thing wrong with it is the imposition of racism."

4. In the Province of Ontario, this negation of race and denial of racism has allowed the current Conservative government to problematically dismiss the employment equity commissioner from office (see *Share*, July 20, 1995: 1, 26). It also has allowed provincial government officials, on the International Day for the Elimination of Racial Discrimination, to insult and humiliate an opposition member who questioned the government's commitment to anti-racism after it gutted anti-racism programs (see *Globe and Mail*, March 25, 1996: A7).

Chapter Two

Deconstructing Whiteness:

Pedagogical Implications for Anti-Racism Education

Gabriel Bedard

> Racial imagery is central to the organization of the modern world. At what cost regions and countries export their goods, whose voices are listened to at international gatherings, who bombs and who is bombed, who gets what job, housing, access to health care and education, what cultural activities are subsidized and sold, in what terms they are validated—these are all largely inextricable from racial imagery. (Dyer 1997: 1)

Multiculturalism has become a site of great contention for many educators. It has become a site in which Whiteness continues to remain the centre and difference is relegated to the margins of social experience. Anti-racism education has emerged as a response to this discontention; it is a discourse that directly challenges White domination and power while at the same time allowing a space for White people to produce a new anti-racist identity. Since a large proportion of Canadian schools have a disproportionate amount of White teachers, I have a fear that anti-racism will not reach its full potential without serious work and commitment from White pedagogues. In this chapter, I take on the political project of exploring the identity development of White bodies through histories of colonialism, imperialism and capitalism and the ways in which this process continues today through multicultural discourses. It is throughout these histories that Whiteness became invested in an identity based on power and domination. As a White male educator who has been dissatisfied with the lack of critical engagement with race and difference in our schools, and especially with how Whiteness invests itself in racialized systems, I feel this is an important exploratory project. It allows space for White pedagogues to deconstruct their identities and decolonize their minds, creating an identity that does not rely on the bodies of non-White peoples but creates an oppositional space to fight for equality and social justice. It is only when Whiteness de-invests itself from an identity of power and domination that White pedagogues can begin teaching in an anti-racism framework.

At the core of White identity are racial imageries that exist at an unconscious level and comprise both the human psyche and our cultural systems and images. Racial imageries are cognitive structures that assist White people in categorizing the vast majority of information about their world and themselves.

How we explore, define and contextualize the world around us is controlled by racialized images; in this way we create knowledge and social institutions that reflect the assumptions that these images convey. How we know about ourselves and others cannot be disconnected from how we represent and imagine ourselves; we know ourselves through others and how we define the other affects how we define ourselves (Giroux 1998). Through the histories of colonialism and imperialism, we as White people have defined and known other peoples and ourselves through racialized imageries, and our assumptions about others and ourselves reflect the knowledge that has been created through these systems. This is a process that continues presently—even in our multicultural educational system—and it needs to be disrupted.

Understanding racism and other oppressions that intersect and interconnect to create systems of domination requires a contrapuntal exploration of White bodies throughout the histories of colonialism, imperialism and capitalism. These histories have shaped language, art, popular culture and knowledges through racialized cognitive structures, making particular bodies—bodies that are defined, judged and accorded privileges and disadvantages based on racial markers. Without a contrapuntal exploration, the White identity will continue to be based on domination, relying on the control and subjugation of other bodies to define itself. Racialized imagery and knowledge have become vital to the sustenance of White identities, and they have created social relations and institutions that rely on created differences. There is "[a]n epistemology so basically driven by difference it will 'naturally' find racialized thinking comfortable; it will uncritically [come to] assume racial knowledge as given" (Goldberg 1993: 150). The formulation of these differences are evident in Western concepts of knowledge, which are based on binary distinction—good/evil, Black/White, superior/inferior, light/dark. Thus racial knowledge and imagery use theories such as binary differentiations to support notions of White as superior. "Primitive societies were theorized in binary differentiation from a civilized order: nomadic rather than settled; sexually promiscuous, polygamous, and communal in family and property; illogical in mentality and practicing magic rather than rational and scientific" (Goldberg 1993: 156).

Before exploring the making of Whiteness, particularly Canadian Whiteness, through the development of racial imagery and knowledge, a working concept of race must be conceived. Michael Omi and Howard Winant (1993) have envisioned a racial formation approach to race that takes into account the complex dynamics of race as a discourse. Their definition consists of three main elements.

First, race must apply to contemporary political relationships. "New [race] relationships emerge chiefly at the point where some counter-hegemonic or post-colonial power is attained" (Omi and Winant 1993: 7). Race is used as a political tool, and depending on the social milieu and the historical context of the body politic, race will be used differently. This phenomenon is articulated in Henry Giroux's concept of a "new racism," where race is coded in discourses of "welfare reform," "neighbourhood schools," "toughness on crime" and "illegitimate births" (1997: 287). If this political climate were not analyzed, racial imagery would continue to control the minds and bodies of White and non-White peoples, and race would continue to be invisible within those political discourses. I theorize that, in Canada, race is used in differing ways; multicultural discourses are utilized to mask discomforting racist practices and policies, allowing most Canadians the illusion that we live in a relatively non-racist country.

Second, race must apply in an increasingly global context. "The geography of race is becoming more complex ... the breakdown of borders in both Europe and North America all seem to be internationalizing and racializing previously national polities, cultures, and identities" (Omi and Winant 1993: 7). With the increase of migration and immigration, race has taken on a much more complex meaning, one that is intertwined with national identities and the globalization of markets that expand to third worlds. First worlds utilize racial discourses to rationalize the control of world markets and resources. "Westerners may have physically left their old colonies in Africa and Asia, but they retained them not only as markets but as locales on the ideological map over which they continued to rule morally and intellectually" (Said 1993: 25).

Third, race must also apply across historical time. Race is a slow inscription of innate characteristics to phenotypical body types that arose out of the knowledge creation and accumulation of White peoples throughout the histories of colonialism, imperialism, slavery and capitalism. This language of race was usually anchored in the signification of certain forms of somatic difference (skin colour, facial characteristics, body shape and size, eye colour, skull shape), which were interpreted as the physical marks that accompanied and that in some unexplained way determined the nature of those so marked (Miles and Torres 1996: 27).

Analyzing race across historical time allows one to map the changing meanings and rationales for using racial markers to justify certain behaviours and practices. It helps the deconstructing process by revealing how the identities of White bodies have become so intertwined with our racist perceptions of others and the subjugation of those non-White bodies. It also exposes the ever changing and increasingly complex meanings of race in contemporary times.

We began George Dei's class The Sociology of Race and Ethnicity (Fall 1998) by creating a working definition of race based on our own personal experiences and learnings. The following definition emphasizes some of the above and contributes a few more important components to the understanding of race as a socially constructed yet real category.

- Race is socially constructed in a historical and contextual environment.

- Race has everything to do with skin colour but isn't just skin colour, it can include markers such as language, culture and religion. Any of these can create racialized bodies, even if physical markers are not apparent.

- Race is phenotype + social construction + social reality.

- Race is a social/relational (power and dominance) category determined by socially selected, physical characteristics. Race was created and is used to justify power over other bodies.

- Race is the construction of difference which is the construction of power.

- Race is historically specific and has constantly changing meanings.

Race has been defined as a socially constructed but real category, which should be analyzed as a political, global and historical discourse. Analyzing race using these tools can uncover how White peoples have created and relied on racial imageries and knowledges to maintain their own sense of self, while at the same time perpetuating White domination and racism. Stemming from the historical and social creation of race are the physical acts and institutional structures of racism. One must be aware that racism is not a problem of prejudice, but prejudice is certainly a result of racism. Racism is characterized by slowly learned ways of knowing, which are believed to be universal truths. They appear so natural that most White people are unaware of their existence.

Paul Kivel (1996: 2) distinguishes "racism" from "White racism." He defines racism as "the institutionalization of social injustice based on skin colour, other physical characteristics, and cultural and religious difference." He defines White racism as "the uneven and unfair distribution of power, privilege, and material goods favouring White people." These definitions are very similar: the institutionalization of social injustices is the unfair distribution of power and privilege. Because of the power and privilege of Whiteness, we as White people have created and continue to create institutional systems that remain racist. In making this distinction, Kevil is separating himself and White people from the truth that White racism is the perpetration of social injustices based on phenotypical differences. In separating White people from racism he then can theorize White racism as being grounded in existing systems of privilege and not in physical moves of Whiteness, which are created and recreated every day by White people. Utilizing the term "White racism" instead of racism is dangerous because it allows White people the space to negate their own racist practices and attribute racism to pre-existing systems of privilege and not to themselves. I theorize that Canadian identity discourses are about Whiteness and that images of Whiteness are evoked when discussing Canadian identity. It is problematic to distinguish between racism and White racism because, in the Canadian context, racism and White racism are synonymous. In Canada, Whiteness holds political, economical and moral power, and racism is based on both phenotypical differences and unfair power distribution. Creating the term "White racism" diverts attention from the important issues, which are dismantling racism and its effects.

Many theoretical ideas and pedagogical tools may be used to dismantle racism, although many also incorporate colonial and imperialist mentalities. Goldberg (1993: 92) suggests two distinct approaches to racism education and tradition, both of which produce entirely different outcomes. One perceives racism as an issue of personal prejudice; the other as a social structural problem. The personal prejudice approach posits that changing personal beliefs and discarding stereotypes will eliminate racism and that exposure to other cultures will make people more sensitive and, thus, less racist. Multiculturalism is one such paradigm. Advocates of this approach employ pedagogical methods that perpetuate racist ideals that stem from our colonial and imperial past. This approach fails to incorporate issues of power and privilege and to interrogate the making of White bodies in the development of racist systems. The social structural approach slides to the other end of the spectrum. Rather than analyze the psychology of racism, it targets socially created structures that maintain racism. This approach has its strengths since it explores how racism is created and maintained at an institutional level, and this can include an investigation of issues of power and privilege. Like the other approach, however, it fails to explore the connections between power and White identity and the ways in which Whiteness is invested in maintaining racialized systems of domination.

The Making of White Bodies

I will begin my analysis of multiculturalism and how its employed today by first exploring the historical making of White bodies and so reveal how White domination becomes implicit in multiculturalism. Mary Louise Pratt (1992) explores White subject identity through discourses of natural science. "In 1735 The System of Nature was written and attempted to classify all plant forms on the planet" (Pratt 1992: 15), and it was through this investment in exploration and naming that Whiteness came into contact with other peoples. Explorers who travelled to ever further lands and oceans in their quest to classify and interpret the world around them returned with "tales and texts which produced other parts of the world for Europeans" at home (Pratt 1992: 18), contributing to the formation of racialized imagery of distant lands and peoples. These explorers interpreted the cultures of these new people, creating a White identity that defined itself as that of a civilized people making contact with the uncivilized and dark other. Since Darwinism also influenced the making of White bodies,

> The theory of types in its purest form stated that underlying the superficial variations in human constitutions there was a limited number of permanent types of distinct origins,... [that] there had been pure races in the past and that interbreeding was leading to degeneration. Social Darwinism also saw relations between peoples of different races as biologically determined,... operations of natural selection would create pure races out of the prevailing diversity. (Banton 1977: 89)

Darwinism produced knowledges that contributed to racial imageries, it naturalized human differences as biologically determined and innate. White bodies were constructed through these discourses as racially superior; science was utilized to prove White superiority over other bodies and other lands.

The emergence of natural science and Darwinism was contemporaneous with the expanding search for commercially exploitable resources and markets and for lands to colonize. These ventures created systems of domination that necessitated Whiteness superiority and other inferiority to rationalize broken treaties, genocide, mass displacements and enslavement (Pratt 1992). The production of subjugated bodies is discussed at length by Ann Laura Stoler, who utilizes Foucault's concept of "bio-power" to explore the making of White bourgeois bodies:

> A political technology ... brought life and its mechanisms into the realm of explicit calculations and made knowledge/power an agent of transformation of human life.... Within this schema, technologies of sex played a critical role; sex occupied the discursive interface, linking the life of the individual to the life of the species as a whole. (1995: 3-4)

Sexuality became a "dense transfer point" of power, and it was through bio-power that bourgeois sexuality was "shaped on the imperial landscape where the politics and language of race were utilized" (Stoler 1995: 3). In Western dichotomous thinking Whiteness needed an opposite against which to define itself; thus other bodies were racialized and defined as contrary to the White bourgeois vision. Non-White bodies, defined as highly sexualized and degenerate, were foils for White bourgeois sexual virtue. Bio-power was used to identify and control the degenerate not only outside the European state, but within it as well. Bio-power secured a relationship among racism, sexuality and class that defined the White bourgeois as racially pure and sexual virtuous (Stoler 1995: 10). Those within the state who failed to meet the stringent requirements of bourgeois identity were also racialized and sexualized. When the English colonized Ireland and incorporated it into the European state, they defined the Irish in terms similar to those used to describe the dark inhabitants of their other colonial acquisitions. It was not uncommon to hear the Irish described as "Black" Irish: The Irish were described as lazy, "naturally" given to "idleness" ... and dominated by "innate sloth" and "loose, barbarous and most wicked" behaviour—"like beasts" (Takaki 1993: 27).

Discourses around cleanliness, hygiene, morality and family were also used to control and define populations, and these in turn created the dichotomous identities needed to uplift bourgeois Whiteness. White men embarked on their exploratory and colonial expeditions and identified themselves in opposition to the ways in which they defined those dark others. Representing themselves as virtuous and racially pure necessitated great psychic energy. They projected their own degenerate desires and fantasies onto other bodies. McClintock argues that "the European imagination" perceived these conquered lands as the "porno-tropics," "a fantastic magic lantern of the mind onto which Europe projected its forbidden sexual desires and fears" (1995: 22). Whiteness has been "occupied with creating its own sexuality and forming a specific body based on it, a class body with its health, hygiene, descent, and race" (Stoler 1995: 53). It is through these mechanisms that Whiteness began to define itself as the centre and non-White bodies as marginalized. White bourgeois bodies became dependent on the bodies of non-White peoples to maintain their created image of themselves. A climate was created in which "racisms provided truth claims about how the social world once was, why social inequalities do or should persist, and the social distribution on which the future should rest" (Stoler 1995: 91).

What Is a Canadian?

Canadian identity has many complex components. To deconstruct what it means to be White, we need to examine the discourses that create our identity as Canadian. I refer to dominant notions of Canadian identity, although I am aware of the many competing claims to Canadian identity—such as those of First Nations—that are struggling to gain political recognition. I am concerned with analyzing and dismantling dominant forms of Canadian identity because it is this identity that is coupled with Whiteness to create a particular citizen. Much of our identity is based in opposition to our American neighbours. Shields (1991: 163) argues that Canadian nationalist narratives identify Canada as natural/nature, struggling "against American mass culture, entirely originating, or so we are asked to believe, south of the border." Canada's geography positions it in the shadow of the politically and economically powerful United States, which means that we as Canadians continually struggle for an identity that is separate from that of the United States. These national narratives try to distinguish us, to identify Canadians as non-American, to create cohesion among peoples in a particular geographical space. But these same narratives can also be used to exclude segments of the population who are not desirable in the making of a national identity. Edward Said sees national narratives as powerful tools to subjugate populations and their narratives:

> Nations themselves are narrations. The power to narrate, or to block other narratives from forming and emerging, is very important to culture and imperialism, and constitutes one of the main connections between them. Most important, the grand narratives of emancipation and enlightenment mobilized people in the colonial world to rise up and throw off imperial subjection. (1993: xiii)

Multiculturalism has become a discourse within the Canadian national identity, but it has silenced the voices of those less desirable people or sanitized them to suit the political climate of the time. Those competing claims to Canadian identity that continue to struggle for recognition are the ones that push for political change.

Multiculturalism is a narrative that defines Canadians as different from the United States. This is observable in the language used to narrate our countries. The United States uses the analogy of the "melting pot"; Canada is analogous to the "tossed salad" or "mosaic." But imbedded in the multicultural narrative is the belief that we as Canadians are not as racist as the citizens of the United States; we are sometimes referred to as non-racist. White Canadians visualize our country as multicultural, a country with a diverse population and a history pleasingly devoid of slavery and segregation; we even visualize ourselves as a benevolent country because of our kindness in the Underground Railroad. I have heard these narratives most of my life, and I continue to hear them. While friends and I were having a heated debate about multiculturalism and Canadian identity one evening, I posed the question "What is a Canadian?" and their responses reflected those multicultural national narratives: there is no single "true" Canadian, they said, because we are a multicultural and diverse country. I suggested that many would argue that Canadian identity is White, male and heterosexual, but they stuck to their comfortable notion that Canada is multicultural. Some in the room began to understand my position when I asked my non-White friends if they have ever been asked, "Where are you from?" This argument helped them realize that the Canadian multicultural narrative included them superficially but still rendered them invisible. Multiculturalism is a trope to satiate non-White peoples while relieving White anxiety and guilt about their colonial and imperial past.

Today, Canadian White identity is continually being created and contested but still constitutes the same histories of colonialism and imperialism. The discourse of multiculturalism has recently become important to the making of White subjects, and it is of critical importance that the contrapuntal mapping of Whiteness be undertaken both historically and in contemporary times. Deconstructing White subject identity, and in particular the Canadian White subject identity of teachers, becomes even more crucial when looking at the shifting population of Canada due to mass migration and immigration. Our educational system has a disproportionately high number of White teachers, and those White teachers are utilizing racialized knowledge and imagery in their classrooms, which has devastating results for all students. Deconstructing the histories of Whiteness can create a space for White teachers to explore their investment in racist imagery and allow them to challenge the racist knowledge systems embedded within multiculturalism.

The discourse of multiculturalism was created by White men with particular political projects, and since multiculturalism has been created by those in power there are certain knowledges that are given authority. Multiculturalism has been sanitized and/or censored so as not to offend, and it allows White people to utilize it in ways that legitimate or delegitimate certain knowledges. Those knowledges, which are "easy to swallow," will be permitted to enter the classroom, but those that challenge notions of Whiteness or White authority will not be legitimated. The danger is that all of this is achieved while still allowing White people to appear as Liberal proponents of multiculturalism. Looking at the historical beginnings of multiculturalism and how multicultural discourses have evolved to constitute the same colonial practices of our past will open a space in our classrooms for White Canadian teachers and students to uncover the colonial, imperial and racialized practices that stem from the histories of their White identities. They then can begin to challenge multicultural discourses and move towards an identity based on an anti-racist praxis.

Ideologies of Canadian Multiculturalism

The 1960s were a socially and politically turbulent time for both the United States and Canada. The US experienced many civil rights movements, the most widely known fulfilled by a history of slavery and Jim Crow laws directed towards Black populations (Raines 1977: 135). Canada faced the French–English national language debate and this unease became extremely volatile. Also, increasingly vocal and militant minorities, such as First Nations, youth and immigrant groups, made the government look seriously at its policies regarding equity (R. Ng 1995). This forced then Prime Minister Pierre Trudeau to re-evaluate government policies and consider the future of a Canada with increasing multiracial populations; he established multiculturalism as a cultural policy on October 8, 1971. Roxana Ng (1995) describes multiculturalism as an ideological frame put in place to govern a new reality. An ideological frame, she writes, is produced and constructed through human activities/process. But once the ideological frame is in place, the ideologies and processes that produced it are rendered invisible and the ideals become "common sense" (Ng 1995). Any remaining pressures can now be ignored because multiculturalism is believed to rectify these issues. Multiculturalism becomes common sense and the language surrounding the discourse becomes commonly used by White people who wish to appear liberal and progressive to the pressure groups without having to relinquish power. This notion of "common sense" is similar to what Michel Foucault calls the "power of truth," where the most effective and non-obtrusive power is exercised through discourses, not physical force.

> There can be no possible exercise of power without a certain economy of discourses of truth which operates through and on the basis of this association. We are subjected to the production of truth through power and we cannot exercise power except through the production of truth.... We are forced to produce the truth of power that our society demands, of which it has need, in order to function: we must speak the truth. (Foucault 1980: 93)

This power of truth is present within the multicultural discourse. Its creation and enforcement works through a liberal White male hegemonic discourse created by the same government whose ultimate goal is to remain in power. The government constructed a truth discourse in the name of multiculturalism and based it on similar racist discourses of the past. Once multiculturalism as an ideological frame was implemented, liberal White teachers began to employ multicultural pedagogies, in turn perpetuating racisms and failing to initiate changes to eliminate institutional racist practices. Multiculturalism has not only allowed Whites to feel non-racist because they "celebrate diversity," but it has satiated some of the non-White populations also. As Foucault (1980: 119) says:

> What makes power hold good, what makes it accepted, is simply the fact that it doesn't only weigh on us as a force that says no, but that it traverses and produces things, it induces pleasure, forms knowledge, produces discourse. It needs to be considered as a productive network which runs through the whole social body, much more than as a negative instance whose function is repression.

Multiculturalism has been used as a "power of truth," and it is the making of a Canadian White identity that perceives itself as liberal and non-racist. Power and domination continue to work through discourses of multiculturalism, and I will demonstrate how this is happening in the educational system.

Many pedagogical approaches to multicultural education are utilized in Canada. Goli Rezai-Rashti (1995: 4) separates them into five main approaches. The following is not an exhaustive list but a short breakdown of the main approaches used in Canada.

- Education of culturally different groups. This is designed to sensitize and prepare teachers to meet the needs of minority or culturally atypical students. Here we find programs such as English as a Second Language and Transitional Programs.

• Education promoting the understanding of cultural difference. Programs of this sort emphasize the responsibilities of educational institutions to understand the positive contributions made by culturally diverse groups.

• Education stressing cultural pluralism. These programs recognize ethnic and cultural diversity and accept the rights of citizens to retain their cultural identity.

• Bicultural education. These programs recognize two cultures and are designed to teach and prepare students to function in those two cultures.

• Cultural/intercultural education. This approach highlights every aspect of multicultural education, namely the concerns for cultural and linguistic continuity, issues related to ethnic and race relations, Aboriginal peoples' rights, integration of immigrants, bilingualism and human rights.

Each of these multicultural approaches was created through good intentions and some serious concerns about education for all students. When critically exploring its implications for students and teachers, however, one can see the inability of multiculturalism to eradicate racism and create a Canadian White subject that does not base its identity on the bodies of non-White peoples. The first approach, education of culturally different groups, is implemented in programs that help students to learn about and adapt to their new country. Most commonly students, usually immigrant students, learn English and the cultural ethics and practices of Canada. These programs are designed to prepare "minority students for their social and cultural negotiations with dominant White mainstream society. At the same time, it is expected that White students will also acquire knowledge and familiarity with the language and culture of minority groups" (McCarthy 1995: 31). Attempting to prepare students for social and cultural crossover, however, sends them on a trajectory towards assimilation into the dominant White culture. Assimilationist theory does not tackle issues of racism but attempts to strip students of cultural traits that are not similar to or desirable in the dominant White culture of Canada. Unfortunately, most of these students are non-White and their bodies have already been racialized, which carries with it many consequences and makes full integration into Canadian society impossible since the dominating definition of a Canadian is defined as White, male, heterosexual and able-bodied. As for White students, the opportunity to acquire knowledge of the language and customs of differing groups is deemed unimportant in a country that values and rewards White languages and cultures. As well, it is impossible for these White students to learn the language and customs of minority groups who are being forced to shed those cultural traits.

The second approach, education promoting the understanding of cultural difference, although seemingly practical, is problematic. "By fostering understanding and acceptance of cultural differences in the classroom and in the school curriculum, educational programs based on the cultural understanding approach, it is expected, will contribute towards the elimination of prejudice" (McCarthy 1995: 27). There are three reasons why this approach is destined to fail.

First, lack of integration of multicultural pedagogies into the curriculum creates an "us and them" dichotomy, with Whiteness at the centre of valued knowledge and other cultures relegated to the margins. This approach usually encompasses thematic cultural studies, such as Black history month, which present multicultural education as marginalized knowledge too primitive to be included in the White canon.

Second, the fact that cultural fears present only static and outdated images of non-White cultures also dooms the cultural understanding approach to failure. Displays featuring cultural dancing, food, clothing, art and customs exhibit only essentialist representations of culture based on nostalgic notions of the past. This negates the dynamism and present-day existence of these cultures. For example, Aboriginal cultures are often represented by images from their past; museums and books attempt to preserve a dying culture and fail to recognize that Aboriginal peoples and their culture have changed with time. Anne McClintock (1995: 30) writes that "[c]olonized people do not inhabit history proper, but exist in a permanently anterior time within the geographic space of the modern empire as anachronistic humans; the living embodiment of the archaic primitive." We witness their cultural celebrations only, negating their struggles against domination. Cultural fairs also "overemphasize the differences among ethnic groups, neglecting the differences within any one group ... which results in multicultural approaches that treat ethnic groups as monolithic entities possessing uniform, discernible traits" (McCarthy 1995: 28). Once a group of people is believed to have discernible traits, innate characteristics are allocated to them, allowing a climate for racist beliefs to flourish.

Theorizing racism as stemming from prejudices and stereotypes is the third reason that multicultural education will fail to achieve its objective. Attempting to solve racism by correcting prejudiced attitudes, stereotypes and lack of information about non-White peoples falsifies White racial knowledge and imagery. Moreover it fails to explore how this knowledge came to be known and how it is linked to positions of power and privilege. Christine Sleeter (1993) cites a study of twenty-three White pre-service students who undertook intensive course work on multicultural education and spent one hundred hours with low-income minority children. She notes "the remarkable phenomenon of students generally using these direct experiences to selectively perceive and reinforce their initial preconceptions" of non-White students (Sleeter 1993: 158). She also found that "while some studies find White students' attitudes to improve somewhat immediately after receiving instruction, studies do not report lasting changes in Whites' perspectives and/or behavior patterns" (Sleeter 1993: 158). So the very aim of this approach—to dismantle stereotypes by disseminating information re establishes or strengthens those stereotypes because this approach relies on White essentialist notions of the past as cultural information. Educators must disrupt racial knowledge by deconstructing Whiteness. Otherwise, when non-White peoples attempt to disrupt essentialized representations of themselves, they will be invalidated as inauthentic knowers.

> For the most part, [White scholars] seem to be very disappointed that modern Indians do not act like the Indians of their undergraduate textbooks or the movies they enjoyed as children and they seem determined to attack contemporary expressions of Indian-ness as fraudulent and invalid because modern Indians fall short of their expectations. (Deloria 1992: 399)

Even when presented with alternative representations, Whites do not dismantle their essentialized notions but de-authenticate the Aboriginal view because "Indians do not have the right to have a point of view when scholars know reality to be different" (Deloria 1992: 399). Multicultural education that attempts to eliminate racism by changing White prejudices creates a White subjectivity that continues to identify their canon or knowledges as superior to those of non-White peoples. Whiteness also essentializes culturally different groups to define, name, and thus control them. In the end, White identities become defined in opposition to those non-White bodies.

The third approach to multicultural education—education stressing cultural pluralism—is based on the premise that if the learning environment of non-White students fosters a "universal respect for the individual ethnic history, culture, and language of the plurality of students" (McCarthy 1995: 32), it will have a positive effect on individual self-concepts and boost their academic achievement. Improving self-concepts of non-White students is rooted in a cultural-deficiency perspective, which assumes that students of colour have poor self-concepts. Embedded in this approach are the colonial mentalities that consider White people as saviors to non-White people. Many people believe that the "main causes of their difficulties [are] located in their homes and communities such as parental attitudes, gang influences, and 'deficient' language skills" (Sleeter 1993: 160). Also, since modernist discourses are prevalent within Western thought and since we use universal and essentialist notions of culture, deficiencies can be attributed to innate characteristics of the students themselves. This is dangerous because it shifts the blame for the poor retention and low success rate of non-White students away from the educational system and onto the student and his or her community environment. Although improving self-concept through a better learning environment can help, we are climbing a slippery slope by pathologizing the egos of non-White students instead of examining the institutional structure of the educational system.

To live in a society that holds merit as a key component of national identity is to encounter the belief that proper education will improve academic achievement and that hard work will help non-White youth break the cycle of unemployment by entering a labour market that will absorb large numbers of qualified non-White youths. I want to stress here that those who create these programs of multicultural education may have good intentions but that those intentions are couched within a White supremacist discourse that connotes pathology of non-White peoples. Joblessness among non-White youths often is attributed to their innate racial characteristics or to their culture. Instead of viewing the racist structure of the educational system as problematic they find fault in non-White youths' weak self-concept, which in itself is racist. Some in the educational system fail to see their own complicity in perpetuating the racist knowledge and imagery that fundamentally affect non-White youth. The notion that the labour market will absorb qualified minority youth ignores the racism practised every day in the workforce. In his investigation of the fortunes of educated Black and White youth in the job market, Troyna concludes that "racial and social connections, rather than educational qualifications per se, 'determined' the phenomenon of better job chances for White youth even when Black youth had higher qualifications than their White counterparts" (1984: 81). Thus, cultural pluralism in the curriculum may boost minority youth self-concept, but it does not address the more crucial problem of systemic institutional racism and the racist identities of White teachers.

The fourth approach to a multicultural curriculum, bicultural education, educates students to become competent in at least two cultures. According to Henry et al. in *The Colour of Democracy* (1995), to be competent in another culture the student would have to learn and put into practice knowledge that is unattainable for non-members of a particular culture. The student would have to learn the following:

> The totality of the ideas, beliefs, values, knowledge and way of life of a group of people who share a certain historical, religious, racial, linguistic, ethnic, or social background.... Culture is a complex and dynamic organization of meaning, knowledge, artifacts, and symbols that guide human behavior, account for shared patterns of thought and

> action, and contribute to human, social, and physical survival. (Henry et al. 1995: 326)

How is a student expected to acquire knowledge that anthropologists have been attempting to understand for decades? The liberal multicultural discourse plays at teaching students about other cultures but presents an appropriated and colonized version of those other. That is the only way in which Whiteness can see the other—through the lens of the superior to the inferior. One must remember that, throughout history, Whiteness has attempted to understand other cultures and in doing so has either destroyed, misinterpreted or appropriated them as their own through colonialism, imperialism and capitalism. bell hooks (1992a) describes "eating the other" as a phenomenon taking place within popular culture. This can also be seen within the educational institution.

> Currently, the commodification of difference promotes paradigms of consumption wherein whatever difference the Other inhabits is eradicated, via exchange, by a consumer cannibalism that not only displaces the Other but denies the significance of that Other's history through a process of decontextualization. (hooks 1992a: 31)

White students are expected to consume or "eat the other" in this bicultural education approach to multiculturalism. How can this be achieved without essentializing and erasing the other's history? More importantly, should competency in other cultures be an educational goal? White students should not become competent in other cultures until they begin learning about themselves by constructing a White identity through the decolonizing process. Understanding cultural difference is unattainable when Whiteness continues to view others through colonial lenses.

The fifth approach to multicultural curriculum, cultural/intercultural education, highlights many aspects of multicultural education; the concerns for cultural and linguistic continuity, issues related to ethnic and race relations, Aboriginal rights, integration of immigrants, bilingualism and human rights (Rezai-Rashti 1995: 4). Many of the components in this type of curriculum are based on important concepts, such as Aboriginal rights, human rights and race relations, and can be a beginning at resistance and institutional change. But, since the curriculum combines most of the approaches discussed earlier, similar problems arise and make it very difficult to create institutional change when Whiteness is not contrapuntally interrogated.

Within liberal multicultural discourses, racism is understood primarily as the product of ignorance, which in turn is perpetuated by individual prejudice and negative attitudes. Also, Whiteness historically has been constructed on the backs of non-White peoples, so multiculturalism becomes a discourse that continues to use non-White peoples to create Whiteness. "The contemporary crises of identity in the west, especially as experienced by White youth, are eased when the 'primitive' is recouped via a focus on diversity and pluralism which suggests the Other can provide life-sustaining alternatives" (hooks 1992a: 25).

Pedagogical approaches need to address these serious issues in multicultural education. Since White teachers continue to perpetuate power and privilege and still represent non-White bodies in racialized ways, there needs to be a move towards examining Whiteness and its implications in education. In summary, multiculturalism fails to do the following: examine the power relations within social institutions as the main proponent in upholding systemic racism; examine the interconnectedness of social oppressions, their reliance on, and support of one another; eliminate from the educational system all methods that uphold White racial domination through an "us and them" dichotomy; integrate other forms of knowledge, histories and cultures into the curriculum, although it still "otherizes" by placing these discourses outside of the dominant White canon; and use critical pedagogy as a tool to create an environment in which students are not passive recipients of knowledge but political subjects.

But how does a White teacher join the anti-racism struggle for change without perpetuating colonial, imperial, paternalist and liberal notions of race? This is an important question because it points to our identities as White people and reveals how they are implicated in the types of knowledges we produce. Knowledge is not produced in a vacuum. It is effected by the identity and agenda of the knowledge producer and the socio-political climate in which the knowledge is produced. We see a move towards an anti-racist educational praxis in a lot of the educational literature, but there needs to be a commitment from White pedagogues to begin the work of exploring our identities as White people. We need to deconstruct how our identities have been created through colonial histories and how the knowledges we have come to know as "truth" have been created through these same colonial histories. It is time for White teachers to challenge their understanding of knowledge production and its connection to their identities as White people. We need to begin creating new knowledges that reflect the political agenda of anti-racism education instead of remaining complacent behind the mask of multiculturalism.

Chapter Three

"Whassup Homeboy?" Black/Popular Culture and the Politics of "Curriculum Studies": Devising an Anti-Racism Perspective

Awad Ibrahim

> Popular culture represents a significant pedagogical site that raises important questions about the relevance of everyday life, student voice, and the investments of meaning and pleasure that structure and anchor the why and how of learning. —Henry Giroux and Roger Simon

Some have argued that we live in a post-modern, poststructuralist moment: a moment of subjectivity, of movement from "margin" to "centre" and vice versa, of desire to belong and to re-present—a moment of agency (hooks 1990; McLaren 1994; Giroux 1992b; Usher and Edwards 1994; Haraway 1991). In this moment, to concentrate exclusively on Dewey's (1916: 16) notion of formal education—"the deliberate educating of the young"—is to miss a wide range of aspects of learning that go on in sites other than classrooms. These may include homes, hospitals, factories, clubs, sport sites, concerts, museums (see Cremin 1976; Beer and Marsh 1988), as well as school sites such as hallways and gyms. The tension between what goes on in the hallways and gyms, where learning can and does take place and where students' identities are formed (Ibrahim 1997; Giroux and Simon 1989a, 1989b), and what goes on in classroom pedagogies and practice strategies is scarcely seriously engaged in the field of "curriculum studies." This paper will re-articulate that tension and show the potency of popular culture, specifically Black popular culture, as it relates to students' identity formation, cultural and linguistic practices and sense of alienation from or relation to everyday classroom activities.

If our students embody subjectivities that have histories, memories, experiences and agency (McLaren 1994; McCarthy and Crichlow 1993), to wittingly or unwittingly negate these memories in classroom practices is to choose to weary and bore them. This is another way of talking about what I call *the politics of embodiment*. Here, sexualized, gendered, classed, race and racialized[1] identities that students bring with them to the classroom and how these identities come to be are vital to the praxis of schooling, especially to the praxis of anti-racism. Hence this chapter navigates the fields of "curriculum studies," (Black) popular culture and anti-racism. It asks two questions: where do students form their identities if not in and within the realm of popular culture, which is set aside and negated within the formal school settings; and what are the implications of these negations as far as the "anti-racism curriculum" is concerned. With regard to the last question, I borrow from Eisner (1979) in my discussion of three typologies of curriculum: explicit, implicit and null. The null curriculum, however, is where I want to draw the attention. It accentuates the relationship between identity, politics, experience, pedagogy and dis/engagement and the process of learning. By and large, different configurations of knowledge, which are linked to students' identities and ways of knowing, are directly related to students' identities and identity formation, but they are not taught at the school. Black popular culture is one such identity. Building on this, I argue that students do develop aspects of this curriculum and that, in the case of Black popular culture, such a curriculum can be utilized in and as a form of anti-racist praxis. The curriculum can contribute to instituting Black students' previously unwarranted and non-validated forms of knowledge. It can address their everyday sense of alienation from Eurocentric curricula, and it can contribute to a more relevant, engaging and anti-racism curriculum (Dei 1996a).

The arguments advanced in this chapter are based on ethnographic research that took place in early 1996 in a high school in southwestern Ontario. First I will discuss some of the theories around "curriculum studies" so that my project can be located within the field. Second I will outline some features of what constitutes an anti-racism curriculum praxis. I will introduce my own research, which argues that educators should pay closer attention to (Black) popular culture and that spaces need to be opened up in classrooms to validate and centre different forms of knowledge otherwise dehumanized. Finally, I conclude with the need to rethink what constitutes the school curriculum and to broaden and link "formal" education with "null/informal" education, which is the everyday experience of our students.

Curriculum Studies

In their discussion of different definitions of curriculum, Beer and Marsh (1988) distinguish between what they call "school" versus "non-school" curriculum. They equate school curriculum with classroom activities and practices and non-school curriculum with what goes on in places outside the school, such as a museum. What Beer and Marsh ignore are the different curricula within the school site itself; this is where Eisner's (1979) notion of curriculum becomes insightful. Eisner distinguishes, convincingly, between three types of curriculum: the explicit, the implicit and the null. He contends that, "although much of what is taught is explicit and public, a great deal is not" (Eisner 1979: 74).

In the explicit curricula, students enter a discourse and culture that is commonly called schooling, which has publicly sanctioned goals; for example, teaching how to read and write, learning the history and geography of a particular country and also studying science. These goals are often presented as ideologically neutral and pedagogically necessary if one is ever to be a successful/good citizen. In the implicit curricula, which some have identified as the "hidden" curricula (Apple 1982, 1990), students are expected to conform and follow certain patterns of cultural practices of schooling that are not stated explicitly.

> Take, for example, the expectation that students must not speak unless called on, or the expectation that virtually all of the activities within a course [or a class] shall be determined by the teacher, or the fact that schools are organized hierarchically, with the student at the bottom rung of the ladder, or that communication proceeds largely from the top down. (Eisner 1979: 76)

What the school is doing, through these implicit but firmly expected cultural practices, is preparing "most people for positions and contexts that in many respects are quite similar to what they experienced in school," that is "hierarchical organization, one-way communication, routine; in short, compliance to purposes set by another" (Eisner 1979: 77).

The "null curriculum" is defined as "what schools do not teach" (Eisner 1979: 83). Eisner argues that most subject matters that are now taught in school systems are taught out of habit. That is, schools teach geography, math, chemistry, etc., for no reason other than that these were always taught (Eisner 1979: 88). School systems rarely ask, "Why are we teaching what we are teaching?" (Eisner 1979: 83). This reminds us that "we ought to examine school programs to locate those areas of thought and those perspectives that are now absent in order to reassure ourselves that these omissions were not a result of ignorance but a product of choice" (Eisner 1979: 83).

Eisner identifies anthropology as an area that is unjustifiably omitted from the curriculum; in the same respect I add African studies and African history. Another area that has been omitted is what he calls "vernacular arts"—popular images shown on television and film which "would, at least in principle, help develop a level of critical consciousness that is now generally absent" (Eisner 1979: 89). These "vernacular arts" are what S. Hall (1990, 1992b), Wallace (1992), Grossberg (1994), Dyson (1993) and Giroux (1992b, 1994a) have called "popular culture," which has or should have a central place within anti-racism curriculum praxis.

Laying the Ground for an Anti-Racism Curriculum

In his introduction to a special anti-racism issue of *Orbit*, Dei (1994: 1) defines anti-racism education as "more than a discourse."

> [It] is an action-oriented educational strategy for addressing issues of

> racism and other types of social oppression. It is a call to make the theoretical discourse of "empowerment" real, a call for a fundamental restructuring of power relations in the schools and in the wider society.

I also articulate an anti-racism curriculum as an action-oriented pedagogical framework whereby theory and practice, identity and schooling are not and should not be disjoined and decoupled. This dissolubility of theory and practice is what Freire (1993) calls praxis.

The praxis of anti-racism,[2] according to this framework, "names the issues of race and social difference as issues of power and equity rather than as matters of cultural and ethnic variety" (Dei 1996a: 25). Hence, an anti-racism curriculum praxis is one in which the relations of power are centred and addressed, the interlocking net-like system of social oppressions is challenged and questioned; and the assumed social privileges of Whiteness are revisited. A vital and organic concern of anti-racism curriculum and pedagogy therefore is the deconstruction of the complex ways in which certain knowledges are legitimized while others are excluded from the corridors of our schools (Dei 1996a; Weiler 1991; Banks 1993). Anti-racism pedagogy investigates the role of race, gender, class, sexuality and ability in the process of legitimizing a particular knowledge and who teaches what, how and why (Feagin et al. 1996).

But power relations, as some have argued (Foucault 1977), have different sites, manifestations and socio-historical structures. The question, when addressing issues of power relation, is not so much its relativity, as for example Dei (1996a: 29) has argued, but at what moment and under what socio-historical structures is power exerted, by whom, how and to whose benefit? If we agree, for example, that Blacks might have power and agency at one historical moment, this should not be decoupled from the question: Do they have the structural set-up, on the one hand, and the social identity, on the other, that enable the exertion of this power? As I see it, power cannot be equated with agency. Agency is the individual ability to exert power. Power, however, is relational and takes different forms depending on identity (McCarthy and Crichlow 1993). Sex, ability, gender, class and race identities, for instance, are constructed in different manifestations of power relations, which can and do occur at the same time (hooks 1994b). An anti-racism pedagogy and curriculum therefore must acknowledge and critically uncover how these identities engage some students in the process of schooling but simultaneously disengage others. One way of doing so is through raising issues of voice and knowledge.

When it comes to the schooling process, it is paramount that all voices and knowledge should be accentuated and valued and not uncritically engaged. Yet the historically marginalized voices and knowledges demand special attention. Within an anti-racism curriculum praxis, this means creating safer and secure spaces (Dei 1996a: 30) where the heavy gaze of being the "expert" is not cast up on minority students as soon as minority issues are brought to the classrooms.

Anti-racism curriculum pedagogy should, moreover, work against a celebratory frame of consuming the other's (minority) voice, knowledge and cultural way of being. Within multiculturalism, for example, students from the hegemonic dominant groups sometimes naively gaze at and consume minority students as "exotica of difference," as Hall (1991) calls it. Here, food, clothing, ways of walking and talking, etc. rather than structures and power relations, are accented as the primary difference. In this way, history is massacred and obscured and social difference is reified. In a context like this, an anti-racism curriculum should not only value and create safer spaces for minorities so that their knowledge, voices and identities can be expressed and valorized, but it also should help them to return the gaze as full subjects who have desires to belong to histories and memories, to a place, to a language, to identities and to a future just as all of us do. "Schools, therefore," Dei (1996a: 30) poignantly argues, "have to constantly reflect on their teaching methodologies (both in terms of pedagogy and curriculum strategies) to ensure that they capture the wide body of community and off-school knowledge and expertise that students bring to the school environment."

This last point of on- and off-school sites needs further exploration. If identities are constructed in and within discourses (Foucault 1977), we must respond to instances in which people do not see themselves mirrored in the dominant discourses. Elsewhere, I argue that minorities find their representations, if not in negative stereotypes, then certainly in the margin of the dominant memory and re-presentations (Ibrahim 1997). One need only look to the newspapers, television and radio talk shows to know who is criminalized and whose whole race is at stake when a single member commits a crime. Undoubtedly, this construction is directly implicated in how minorities, including African students in my research, build memory, knowledge and identity (West 1993b; Banks 1993; Ogbu 1990; Bhabha 1994; Dei 1996a; hooks 1990, 1994b).

If identities, as Hall (1991) argues, are built in that "dirty" intersection between the self and the other, if identities are ever shifting, negotiated and multiplying (Bhabha 1994), moreover, if the self does not recognize itself without the other (S. Hall 1990), then the negative representations of the self by the other have tenacious and incalculable consequences. Anti-racism curriculum praxis must deconstruct these negative representations and the identities of those who benefit from them. It must also critically engage identities and memories of students in classroom activities and pedagogies.

This engagement of students' memory and embodied knowledge is understood in the notion of inclusive anti-racism curriculum. It is a praxis that is meant to centralize the historically marginalized "and not simply [graft them] ... into the existing order" (Dei 1996a: 84). This centralization, significantly, calls into question the very structure and the knowledge that create and sustain the dichotomy between margin and centre. The centre is centre only because of historical memories and power relations (Bourdieu 1990a). These memories and power relations, if ever an anti-racism curriculum is to open them up for resistance, have to be decentred and rendered as one among many other centres. In executing this move, however, vigilance is necessary and not simply vigilance against "eating" the marginalized other which raises the question of how the move itself is executed and by whom. The marginalized other must be located and positioned as a social subject with shifting, negotiated and multiplied but full agency. This agency does not need patronization. It needs instead pedagogues who should find strategies that will critically engage it.

Through the anti-racism curriculum, I am calling for pedagogy and praxis that make central, first, the crucial understanding of how to address "the marginalization of certain voices in society and the delegitimation of the knowledge and experience of subordinate groups in the educational system"; and, second, a recognition "that students do not go to school as "disembodied" individuals, but that their background and their identities are implicated in the schooling and learning process" (Dei 1994: 1).

Making the Connection

In the following section, I discuss how identities of a group of continental francophone African youths are implicated in the process of schooling. In so doing, I want to show that embodied identities are vital to the process of learning and that students do form their own "curriculum," depending on with whom they identify and how. The research data clearly shows that African youths choose Black popular cultural forms as sites of identification. The act of choosing here is located at the borderline between the subconscious and the conscious. African youths take up these cultural forms as part of their identity formation and their search for what it means to be Black in North America. As well, depending on their age and gender, they variably perform the North American Black-stylized English and hip hop identity, the signification of which I will explain later. In this way, they commence the odyssey of becoming Black.

The research findings point to the fact that continental African youths are constructed and positioned and thus treated as "Blacks" by the North American hegemonic discourses, representations and dominant groups, respectively. This positionality offered to continental African students in exceedingly complex ways through net-like representational discourses does not and is unwilling to acknowledge students' (ethnic, language, national and cultural) identity difference. Blackness, interestingly, becomes the encompassing category and the umbrella under which African youths find themselves. I am addressing here the White mindset in which all Black peoples become one entity ("Oh, they all look Black to me!") and in which Blackness is projected further into negative historical memory and representation (West 1993b). Elsewhere I show that this perception and treatment, which works within a race and racism framework, influences students' sense of identity, which, in turn, influences what they linguistically and culturally learn and how (Ibrahim 1998). What they learn, I will show, is Black-stylized English, which they access in Black popular cultural forms, such as films, newspapers, magazines and, more importantly, rap, reggae, pop, R&B and other types of music.

Research Methods

The findings and arguments I am advancing in this chapter are based on ethnographic research that was guided by the following series of questions. How and in what way does race identity difference enter the process of learning? What is the role of race and racism in students' identity formation? How are continental African youths positioned and constructed in and out of school? What are the implications of this construction in youths' social identity formation? And how are these identities formed and performed?

The site of the research is a small, urban Franco-Ontarian high school, which I will call Marie-Victorin and which is located in southwestern Ontario. Although the official language is French, the spoken language in corridors and hallways is English. Besides English and French, Arabic, Somali and Farsi also can be heard in the cafeteria and the gymnasium. Marie-Victorin has a population of approximately 389 students from different ethnic, language and national backgrounds. One-third to one-half of the 389 are students of colour. Despite this disproportionate percentage, all teachers, administrators and staff are White.

Based on the displays of photographs of *les étudiants gradués* (the graduated students), the school had an almost all-White population before 1991. In 1992–1993, a little over half were male (Heller 1993). The school itself is vital to the life of the Franco-Ontarian population and its various communities. French-language schools outside Quebec, Heller (1993) argues, are part of the larger cultural and linguistic struggle that francophone communities have to face in relation to the hegemonic English-speaking institutions and communities. Given this unequal dialectic between the two communities, francophones fear the loss of their French language and culture since English is the dominant language nationally and internationally. Nevertheless, in the midst of this struggle, the working-class segment, women and so-called "visible minorities" are usually left out. Thus, Heller (1993: 2) argues, francophone schools serve the privileged middle-class and elite populations. Linguistic norm is one manifestation of class inequality and domination. The school, in its pedagogy, practice and praxis, chooses the Parisian and/or Franco-Ontarian middle-class linguistic norm as the standard to follow (Heller 1993: 3). This practice dehumanizes and negates the linguistic practices of the working class. Heller (1993: 2–3) summarizes these tensions in broader terms:

> Schools like this have a "mission," namely to preserve French language and culture in an English-speaking society. This mission derives from the schools' role in the political mobilization of Canada's

> francophone minority. Francophone mobilization is primarily in the interests of an emerging francophone middle-class and new élite who have managed to compete with anglophones in both the public and private sectors by getting anglophones to accept French-English bilingualism as an important criterion of selection.... However, despite being primarily in the interests of one segment of the francophone population, this movement is successful because it claims to erase any internal differences among francophones. It appeals to ethnic solidarity which crosses gender and class lines. Raising questions of internal differences, let alone internal inequalities, has been difficult, often painful and frequently impossible.... This places front and center a struggle over how to define the "Frenchness" of the school.

The "internal differences" within the francophone community, and thus francophone schools, are pushed into the shadows. These internal differences include race, class and gender. The need to avoid reproducing the same inequalities that francophone communities face in the dominant English-speaking institutions arouses extreme sensitivity which often calls for urgent solutions.

When continental African students arrived en masse at Marie-Victorin from their homelands starting in 1991, they constituted from one-third to one-half of the school population. The continental African students' group now comprises students from cultural and linguistic backgrounds as diverse as their countries of origin: Somalia, Djibouti, Zaire, South Africa and Gabon, to name a few. The Somali speakers make up the majority within this group. The continental African students vary in age, gender and class. Most come from a middle-class or affluent background; their ages range from twelve to twenty; and they are spread from grade seven to thirteen.

Being one of the only two Black adults at Marie-Victorin helped me to establish good relationships with continental as well as diasporic African students. (By diasporic I refer to a small but active group of Haitian students.) I was able to initiate relationships with students of different genders and ages by "hanging out" and playing basketball and soccer with the students, but I was also cordially consulted for guidance when troubles occurred. I was invited to coach the basketball team, which was dominated by continental and diasporic African students. I was asked to speak to the school principal on some sensitive issues that concerned students, and I was enlisted to lend academic instruction.

Prior to this research project I had spent two years at the school in another research project, so I knew the school and its population well and received permission from the administration to conduct a second study. I started "hanging out" at least once, and in most cases, two or three times a week with continental students from January to June of 1996. In the beginning, I interacted aimlessly and freely with students of both genders and various ages. I took the role of a participant-observer, keeping regular notes and diaries. Having determined what they could offer to my research, I chose for extensive observation sixteen students—ten boys and six girls—between the ages of fourteen and twenty. The girls were Somali-speakers from Somalia and Djibouti. Of the ten boys, six were Somali, two Senegalese, one Ethiopian and one Togolese. I observed them in and out of the classrooms as well as in and out of school. With the consent of the students and their parents, I interviewed them. I also interviewed both the only Black counsellor and the only Black teacher: the latter had been employed at the school but was discharged by the board at the time of the interview.

I attended soirées, plays, basketball games and graduations. I videotaped and audio-taped interactions and exchanges among students. On two occasions, I gave a tape recorder to students to capture their "natural" linguistic exchanges. I was delighted to be invited to their residences. I transcribed the interviews and some of the videotapes, and I analyzed the data by grouping them by theme, category and subject.[3]

What about Hip Hop at Marie-Victorin?

Continental African students at Marie-Victorin identified with hip hop culture. This identification with hip hop, which is "Black" (male) cultural practice, especially hip hop dress, seemed to cut across all ages for the boys. However, it was a bit different for the girls. Girls in grade twelve and thirteen tended to be more post-modernly eclectic in their dress: oscillating between Parisian, chic North American middle-class, hip hop and traditional national dress. Some of them, for example, dressed in traditional Somali dress for the multicultural celebration day. In contrast, the younger girls in grades seven, eight and nine often dressed in hip hop and spoke in Black-stylized English. On one afternoon these younger girls, while behind the scenes preparing for an African dance performance scheduled as part of the Black History Month celebration and also while wearing the Islamic hijab (veil), were rapping to a recording of the African American rapper Cool J.

Hip hop cultural expressions, as performed by continental male and female African students at Marie-Victorin, have three distinctive but interlocking features (Butler 1990). Hip hop can be described as a way of dressing, walking and talking. Hip hop dress is eloquently described by Rose (1991: 277) in talking about a New York summer party: "Thousands of young Black folks milled around waiting to get into the large arena. The big rap summer tour was in town, and it was a prime night for one to show one's stuff." She then describes what I see as hip hop dress genres at Marie-Victorin: "Folks were dressed in the latest 'fly gear': bicycle shorts, high-top sneakers, chunk jewelry, baggy pants, and polka-dotted tops. The hair styles were a fashion show in themselves: high fade designs, dread, corkscrews, and braids" (Rose 1991: 277). Hip hop walk usually involves moving the hands simultaneously with the head and the rest of the body as one is walking or talking. The talk is what is generally referred to as "Black

English" or "Black talk" (Smitherman 1994), which I refer to as Black-stylized English.

Since continental African youths have no everyday interaction with African Americans, they access these "Black" (read African American) linguistic and cultural practices from Black popular culture, specifically rap music. Thus continental African students tend to "pick up" expressions and ways of talking and rapping that encompass stylistic and lexical features rather than grammatical ones.

Studies of what is known as Black English focus on linguistic features such as "negative attraction" and "negative concord" (Labov 1972: 65–130) or the use of "do" in place of "does" (Goldstein 1987). The work of these researchers certainly have historical and academic implications, but they almost never address issues of race and style; this is especially true of Goldstein. Had she endeavored to ask what it means for a Hispanic population in New York City to learn Black-stylized English, her opus would have been different.

Language, Bourdieu (1990a) argues, never was just an instrument of communication. Language is also an instrument and performance of power based on race, gender and class identity differences. My work, situated within these discourses, moves away from Goldstein's grammatically-based analysis towards a more cultural, political and stylistic analysis. The question of style is vital in dealing with continental African students' identity performance. Because continental African students have no day-to-day interaction with African Americans, when they use expressions like "yo yo," "whassup," "whadap," "wardap," "homeboy" and "homie," they are stylistically and lexically allying themselves with and translating what they conceive as "Black linguistic practice." This translation/imitation/citation, is expressed in and through students' speech, is a performance of the Black-stylized English.

Black-stylized English refers to a mannerism through which the linguistic performance is executed. For example, how continental African students dress goes hand-in-hand with how they speak. How they speak, however, given their desire to linguistically and culturally fit somewhere, and given more importantly their limited daily interactions with African Americans, is heavily dependent on certain stylistic codes: "yo yo," "whassup boss" (as one male student called me), "whadap," "wardap," and so on.

For continental youths, especially boys, these lexical expressions, which I discuss as performances of hip hop identity, are new cultural forms that they take up or "enter." Adopting hip hop influences not only their identity formation but also how they position themselves and are positioned by others (Foucault 1977). This is because when continental African students chose African American cultural and linguistic practices, they in fact chose an identification with a language and historical memory as well as a political and social stance.

Performativity, Language and Identities

These socio-political choices that African youths make, I argue, are performed in the language. The choices themselves, however, are different expressions, articulations of certain identity configurations. Identities are then performed in the language; that is, how one speaks, which lexical, phonological and syntactic choices one makes, articulates, at least in part, an identity that one would want to re-present to the rest of world. Hence, language is an expression of desire and identification. In my research, this was a very important methodological and theoretical contention in understanding the identity with which African students would want to ally themselves, and thus perform. Moreover, given the pressure of North American hegemonic representational discourses, especially the different forms of media representation, African youths find themselves in a social space where they are to become Black. This means learning Black culture and language as they are accessed in and through Black/popular culture. Here, music is crucial, especially rap. In the following excerpt, captured as a "natural" interaction one night in the house of one student, the presence of Black-stylized English and rap citation is quite clear.[4]

> **Sam:** (laugh) I don't rap man, c'mon give me a break. (laugh) Yo, a'ait a'ait you know, we just about to finish the tap [tape] and all that. Respect for my main man. So, you know, you know wha 'm mean, 'm just represenin Q7. One love to Q7 you know wha 'm mean and all my friends back in Q7. Even though you know I haven't seen them for a long time, you know, I still I got love for them you know what 'm mean. Stop the tapin boy.
> **One male voice:** Kick the free style. [boys are talking in Somali]
> **Sam:** So, yo you want to record again?
> **Awad:** I don't want it, I don't want it.
> **Sam:** Why not?
> (20 minutes of Gangster rap music; Cool J; Boys II Men; Brandy. Jamal performs as DJ: while songs are playing, he repeats and emphasizes expressions, lines or notes.)
> **Jamal:** Kim Juma, live put the lights on. Wordap. [boys speaking in Somali] Peace out, wordap, where de book. Jamal 'am outa here.
> **Shapir:** Yo, this is Shapir. I am trying to say peace to all my niggers, all my bitches from a background that everybody in the house. So, yo, chill out and this is how we gonna kick it bye with that pie. All right, peace yo.
> **One male voice:** Peace and one love.
> **Sam:** a'ait this is Sam, repres'in AQA where it's born, repres'in you know wha 'm mean? I wonna say whassup to all my niggers, you know, peace one love. You know wha 'm mean. Q7, repres'in forever. Peace!

Of interest in the excerpt is the citation of the Black-stylized English: "Respect to my main man" "repres'in Q7," "kick the free style," "peace out, wardap," "I'm outa here," "yo, this is Shapir," "I am trying to say peace out to all my niggers, all my bitches," "so, yo chill out," "and this is how we gonna kick it'," "peace yo," "peace and one love'," "a'ait, this is Sam repres'in AQA," "I wonna say whassup to all my niggers." These boys are undoubtedly influenced by rap lyrics, syntax and morphology and, in particular, gangster rap style. In rap lyrical style, by and large, one starts his/her performance by checking the microphone: "One two, one two, check check mic check." Then, the rapper either will cite an already composed lyric or "kick a free style" (i.e. be spontaneous). The rapper usually begins the public performance by introducing him- or herself (yo this is Shapir) and thanking his/her "main man" (best friend, who often introduces him/her to the public). In gangster rap, however, one represents not only oneself but a web of geo-physical and metaphorical spaces and collectivities, which are demarcated by people and territorial spaces ("represenin Q7," "a'ait, this is Sam repres'in AQA"). At the end, when the citation or the free style is completed, one again thanks his/her "main man" and "gives peace out" or "shad out" (a shout) to his/her people.

Rap for these boys is a "language" that expresses the human and cultural experience of diasporic North American Black peoples, and their identification with it is related, first, to their stage of life (youth) and, second, to their lived experience (such as police brutality, human degradation and racism). Listen to Jamal reflecting on how African students relate to Black popular culture and rap in particular:

> Rap is created to self-express. It is for this reason that rap, Black Americans created the rap to self-express, how do I say it? Their ideas, their problems. But, if we are influenced by rap it is because we are young.... If we could integrate ourselves into rap, it is because they [rappers/Black Americans] speak about or they have the same problems we have.[5]

Obviously, we need to engage with all forms of appropriated and cited language in a critical manner. Some of the language used by these boys is certainly horrifying and shocking. The boys not only used language violently; they also abused it. As well, they posited a problematic category of masculinity in which the latter is equated with how tough one can or should be. The sexist term "bitches," which has been challenged by female rappers like Queen Latifa or Salt 'N Pepa, is indeed a product of a public space that is predominated by men (Rose 1994). It appears that some African boys take up this language unproblematically, but it does not always go unchallenged. As one sixteen-year-old boy put it, "Occasionally, rap has an inappropriate language for the life in which we live." One fourteen-year-old girl observed, "You know, some rappers are like so rude." A seventeen-year old girl commented: "Ok, hip hop, yes I know everyone likes hip hop. They dress in a certain way, no? The songs go well. But, they are really—they have expressions like 'fuck,' 'bitches,' etc. Sorry, but there is respect."

These deconstructions of gender, sex, language and age are very important in understanding who learns what and how. Despite the ambivalence of some girls towards rap, all African students demonstrated a desire for and identification with Blackness and Black cultural forms. This identification influenced African students to various degrees, with the boys and younger girls probably more apt to perform rap and fully "take up" hip hop identity. This is linked to the notion that being Black in a racially conscious society, such as Euro-Canadian and American societies, means that one is expected to be Black and act Black, and so be the other (Hall 1991). Being Black plays a vital part both in how students are positioned inside and outside Marie-Victorin and in how they position themselves. How students are positioned inside and outside the school is one of the determining factors in their political, linguistic and cultural choices (Foucault 1977; Labov 1972).

The notion of positioning is spoken of eloquently in Fanon's *Black Skin/White Masks* (1970). Fanon (cited in Hall 1991) talks about "how the gaze of the Other fixes him in an identity." When the child pulled her hand and pointed at him, saying "Look, Momma, a Black man," Fanon writes, "I was fixed in that gaze"—the gaze of otherness (Hall 1991).[6] But this example is probably too graphic, given the subtle and subconscious nature of the net-like representational discourses within and through which identities are formed.

Nonetheless, based on Foucault's (1977) notion of how people are positioned and constructed within and through discourses, the shift from what can loosely be called "home cultures" (Somalian or Haitian) to hip hop is a result of students' Blackness. Through very complex social mechanisms, such as race and racism, continental African students' range of choice is in fact limited to Black culture and discourse and, in rare and extreme cases, White dominant culture. The difficulty with taking up White cultural and linguistic practice is that it attracts accusations of "race treachery" (Feagin et al. 1996). As one male student commented about hockey, "*Je n'ai rien à investir là-dans*" ("I have no interest in investing in it"). Given the dominance of Blackness in basketball, however, this student had every reason to invest in it, or so he mentioned later in the discussion. The expense of hockey equipment, in addition to its association with Whiteness, deter him from seeing hockey as a site of identification. Students in a focus-group interview stated that, because some girls dress in garments which are considered "White" dress, they as criticized as "race traitors."

Taking up, identifying with, imitating or citing hip hop as an identity means learning the cultural as well as linguistic practices that are introduced to continental African students through Black popular culture. They enter the representational discourses of Blackness and hip hop by learning a new style of dress and new ways of walking and of talking. Students thus enter a null curriculum, with which they do identify; a curriculum that, at least partially reflects their own subjectivities; a curriculum that influences who they are and how they see the future.

Closing Comments

> Anti-racism education focuses on an explication of the notion of "identity," and how identity is linked with/to schooling. Anti-racism education recognizes that students do not go to school as "disembodied" generic youths. Therefore, it is important for educators to understand how students' racial, class, gender, disability and sexual identities affect and are affected by schooling processes and learning outcomes. (Dei 1996a: 31)

The issues at stake in this chapter are how on-school and off-school formed identities enter the schooling processes, how these identities can be engaged in classroom practices and activities and how critical educators and anti-racism curriculum practitioners can bring student-based and student-produced knowledge into the classroom, not to be consumed but rather critically engaged. This raises questions of voice and experience. How do we acknowledge previous experience as legitimate content and yet challenge it at the same time? How do we affirm student voices while simultaneously encouraging the interrogation of such voices? And, finally, how do we avoid the conservatism inherent in simply celebrating personal experience and confirming what people already know? (Giroux and Simon 1989a)

It is now known that students do not come to classrooms as generic disembodied subjectivities. On the contrary, racial and gender identities formed outside the classroom are crucial in the learning processes. More specifically, however, this chapter shows the ways in which Black popular culture (defined as a null curriculum),[7] as a curriculum that is unauthorized and often negated by the school system, is and can be an on-school and off-school site where learning can and indeed does take place. The notion of learning and worthwhile knowledge needs to be problematized and broadened to include a variety of forms. Accordingly learning can mean learning cultural and linguistic practices that are not valued by the dominant culture. This raises the question: Why do students choose practices that are marginalized by the dominant group's narratives and cultures? The answer lies in what can be called the politics of positionality of Blackness, that is, how students are positioned as "Blacks" by hegemonic discourses.

This positionality needs to be deconstructed and new formulations that link on-school and off-school identities to classroom praxis need to be articulated and re-articulated. Within the previously outlined anti-racism curriculum, for example, there is an urgent need for praxis that links "formal" education/learning with the popular "informal" one. If those "who have been denied their primordial right to speak their word" (Freire 1993: 69) are ever to speak it, their world has to be linked to their word. I am suggesting rap be incorporated into the classroom, particularly English classrooms and especially English as a Second Language classrooms. There, rap can be studied as a genre, style and content, or it can be used simply to expose students to different linguistic variations and accents.

Rap and Black popular culture in general can create safe spaces where issues of oppression based on gender, race, class and ability are brought to the fore. Rap as an aesthetic and oral narrative performance could be a curriculum that brings students' concerns about sexuality, police brutality, racism and sexism to the centre. Also as a space for knowledge production, rap can be envisioned as a borderland which creates a language of critique that goes hand in hand with a language of possibility and hope (Anzaldua 1990; Giroux and Simon 1989a, 1989b; Simon 1992).

I end this chapter with a hope that those who do not see themselves represented in the curriculum, those who cannot relate to the curriculum, those who are wittingly or unwittingly kept silent may find a subject matter to which they can relate and with which they can identify, a subject matter that brings their experience to the forefront so that it can be valued and not uncritically engaged.

> By ignoring the cultural and social forms that are authorized by youth and simultaneously empowering or disempowering them, educators risk complicitly silencing and negating their students.... This is unwittingly accomplished by refusing to recognize the importance of those sites and social practices outside of school that actively shape student experiences and through which students often define and construct their sense of identity, politics, and culture. (Giroux and Simon 1989a: 3)

The issue at stake, for Giroux and Simon (1989a) as it is for me, is not only to motivate and empower students but, more importantly, to enable them to locate themselves in time and history and, at the same time, critically interrogate the adequacy of that location.

Notes

1. To illustrate the difference between race and racialized identity, I take the Black example. The category Black is socially constructed and historically specific, and its meaning changes depending on the historical moment, nation and narration. Race and racialized identity can be equated to being and becoming Black. Elsewhere (Ibrahim 1998), I argue that being is an already formed identity but

becoming means that the self is going through social processes, such as racism and marginalization, whereby it becomes aware of its Blackness.

2. Within an anti-racism framework, I use pedagogy, curriculum and praxis interchangeably to address the philosophy, discourses and practices that link off-school students' formed identities with on-school/classroom activities and pedagogies.
3. All interview tapes and transcriptions have been kept private.
4. All names were altered. Sam is a nineteen-year-old boy from Djibouti. He is the rapper of the school and the "Jordan" of the basketball court. Shapir is a twenty-year-old boy from Djibouti. He has a very enlightened political discourse. Jamal is almost twenty years old and comes form Djibouti. He volunteers as a DJ at CIUT, a local radio station, where he airs rap in French and English.
5. This is a quotation from a focus-group interview with the boys. It was conducted in French, and this is my translation.
6. See Hall 1991 for an excellent discussion of how the other can be hated and at the same time desired.
7. The term "null" does not suggest to me that the subject matter is null; it is null in its non-existence in the curriculum. My research has shown that non-classroom sites can be learning sites, and thus are not null (as in zero) curriculum.

Chapter Four

Rethinking Access:

The Challenge of Living with Difficult Knowledge

Carl E. James and Joy Mannette

From a liberal perspective, education is an important mechanism for promoting social justice, enhancing equality of opportunity and providing citizens with the knowledge and skills that enable them to participate effectively in Canadian society. However, research shows that social stratification, supported by classism, sexism, racism and ethnicism, operates as a major barrier to educational access and participation of particular groups of Canadians (Fleras 1996; Henry and Tator 1994; Chilly Climate Collective 1995; Haggar-Guenette 1994; Anisef and Bellamy 1993; Bellamy and Guppy 1991; Carty 1991a; James 1990; Gaskell et al. 1989; Anisef et al. 1985; Special Committee on Visible Minorities in Canadian Society 1984). Publicly funded post-secondary educational institutions across Canada, conscious of shifts in law and custom around questions of cultural diversity (e.g., federal and provincial human rights and equity legislations, Section 35 of the Canadian Charter of Rights and Freedoms), have responded by initiating access programs to address the needs of historically disadvantaged groups who were not gaining access to post-secondary education (Allen 1996; Chilly Climate Collective 1995; James 1994a). As articulated by Dr. James Hall, Jr. in his 1990 keynote address to the Conference on "Strategies for Improving Access and Retention of Ethno-Specific and Visible Minority Students in Ontario's Post-Secondary Institutions":

> The challenge ... of diversity ... is upon us.... There are four things that I identify, four reasons that motivate institutions to do something about this diversity.... It is good for education, it is the proper Christian thing to do, it is mandated ... it is good economics.

An examination of access programs across the country indicates that they vary considerably in terms of how they define and operationalize access.[1] While all programs speak to the issue of systemic barriers, there are ambiguities in their construction and implementation. In this chapter, we examine post-secondary educational access programs. We do so by using two interconnected approaches.

The first approach documents the stories of those students from historically disadvantaged groups[2] who have entered university through access programs. Following the work of Canadian First Nations writers (Brant 1994; Keeshig-Tobias 1990; King et al. 1987), we suggest that stories of access experiences be understood as analogous to theorizations, meaning that within the constructs imposed by the tellers, stories seek to make sense of social phenomena. We are suggesting here that the stories that students tell signify the extent to which access programs have come to represent racial change in universities and colleges where undeserving "others," who bear both cognitive and cultural deficits, are "given" entry to scarce educational resources (James and Mannette 1996). While universities tend to target many historically disadvantaged groups, it is, as Grayson and Williams (1994) and Grayson, Chi and Rhyne (1994) found, those university applicants who are willing to categorize themselves as racial minorities or people of colour who will favour and use "affirmative action" programs as a means of gaining access to educational opportunities.

The other approach of this article explores the ideological perspectives that seem to inform the roles, expectations and strategies of both post-secondary institutions and students. The explanations and theorizations offered by those who have experienced the university through an access initiative, as well as the strategies and programs of the university, provide opportunities to enrich and complicate what we suggest is a story of living with the ambivalence embedded in difficult knowledge.

Writing from a psychoanalytical perspective, Britzman (1996: 42) suggests that "difficult knowledge" is experienced when persons externalize conflicts: "It is this splitting—of putting good inside and bad outside—that renders engaging ambivalence intolerable." To move beyond this impasse, Britzman (1996: 44) recommends that "the study of ambivalence—where love and hate co-exist and are directed at the same object—must also be tolerated, not encrypted." What makes the stories of access experiences difficult knowledge is a recognition of the limits of "telling story" and of the ambivalences and tensions within the storytellers as they encounter what is unsettling. For these storytellers this difficult knowledge is demonstrated in their struggles to reconcile their expectations with their alienating experiences within the university.

The following italicized quotations come from students who were enrolled in a southern Ontario university faculty in which an access program exists. This access program targets First Nations, persons with disabilities, persons of colour and refugees. The students volunteered their reflections in video- and tape-recorded group discussions. Students also made written reflections in the forms of response journals for course purposes and in notes and e-mail. Also, we conducted a focus-group interview with ten African Canadian students (five males and five females). Eight were in their final year of university, and two had graduated earlier that year. Their ages ranged from twenty-four to twenty-nine years, the average being twenty-five years. The focus-group participants were not pre-screened to establish who entered the faculty through the access route; however, during the discussion, eight of the ten participants said that they had "applied through access." The selection of African Canadian respondents is based on the fact that, compared to other "racial minority" applicants, Black people, including those who exceeded the basic requirements, were twice as likely to apply through the access program. This is important to note because middle-class Black students believed that applying through an access admission process would enhance their chances of being accepted into the program. We have interpreted this as an indication of the lack of confidence of such students that their class can mitigate against structural racism. Further, as students within the particular faculty, they were more often identified as "access students" by their peers and course directors (see James 1994a). It also suggests something about what Blackness signifies in southern Ontario (Walcott 1996).

Access: Mediating Systemic Barriers?

> *You know there are systemic barriers in society so you want access to give you that chance.*
>
> *I think that one of the major problems with [universities] is policy, and I said ... it is easier to write a policy; it is easier to write down what you're supposed to do and what's going to happen in the event of this. But it is very hard to carry it out.*

We enter "telling-story" (Battiste 1986) with the concept of policy. As Silver (1990: 19–20) puts it, "[t]he study and analysis of policy are concerned with its formation and formulation, its contexts and constraints, its implementation and evaluation." So, let us examine the context in which universities today have initiated access programs and explore the nature of the "chance" that historically disadvantaged students have been given through access initiatives.

In the 1990s, particularly in Canada's large urban centres, there has been a marked demographic change.[3] Historically disadvantaged groups, particularly women and "racial minorities," now constitute a substantial portion of the population from which universities and colleges recruit students.[4] This population challenges educational institutions to provide education to students who differ in preparation and culture from those the institutions have traditionally served (Feagin et al. 1996; Stewart 1994; Richardson and Skinner 1991; Ahamad 1987).

Embedded in the protocols of Canadian post-secondary access programs that are based on the liberal ideology of multiculturalism is the concept of "voluntary marginal differentiation" (Burnet 1981, cited in Peter 1981: 56–67). This practice means that, to enter into access initiatives, members of historically disadvantaged groups must "consent" (Hall and Jefferson 1976) to their insertion into such processes. Post-secondary access initiatives, then, can be understood as liberal "quests for social justice" (Orris 1990) within the context of what are seen as "essentially reformable social systems" (Burton and Carlen 1979).

In this way, post-secondary educational institutions are seen as responsive to those historically disadvantaged populations who signify social change. Post-secondary educational institutions are also able to instruct the polity by their well-publicized example. What is key, however, is that post-secondary educational institutions, within their own relevances,[5] have been able to define what social justice might entail (e.g., facilitating equality of opportunity at the point of admission) and how it might be accomplished (e.g., reforming admission processes).

Silver (1990) warns us that policy analysis has been contaminated by its inability to forge analytically adequate connections between grand theories, such as political economy, and accounts of educational experiences. To move beyond this lacunae, we suggest that access policies be conceptualized as expressions of "official discourse" (Burton and Carlen 1979; Mannette 1988). According to Burton and Carlen (1979) official discourse is one moment in hegemonic renegotiation following ideological disruption, which has jeopardized the fragile and necessary "consent" of subordinate factions on which hegemonic elaborations rely (Hall and Jefferson 1976). Access programs are often understood to be post-secondary institutional responses to the ideological disruption to the university ethos posited by other critiques (Chilly Climate Collective 1995; Bannerji et al. 1991a). These critiques have challenged notions of universities' neutrality and objectivity and have suggested that, rather than a meritocracy, universities produce and reproduce the gender, ethnic, race and class hegemonies characteristic of a particular historical period. Certainly, students who enter universities through access programs tell of *"the pressure they [communities] brought to bear"* on the reform process within educational institutions. However, while important components in post-secondary educational reform, these activities, and other related social movements, form only part of the process. To invest them with the social power to effect institutional change is to deny the flexibility of hegemonic elaborations and their essentially processual nature.

As noted, hegemony is fragile and in constant need of renegotiation (Hall and Jefferson 1976). We suggest that post-secondary educational reform (e.g., access initiatives) developed to enhance the presence of historically disadvantaged groups, is but one moment in hegemonic production and reproduction. Official discourse in the form of policy documents serves to assign blame in terms of the temporary failure of essentially reformable systems. So, for example, at York University's faculty of education, we find that the access initiative program emerged out of the 1995 fact-finding mission and report of the Anti-Discriminatory Advisory Group (ADAG).

> Guided by community involvement and the knowledge that discrimination is often systemic to institutional policies and practices and processes, ADAG established the Access Initiative (AI) Program. This

> Access project was designed to encourage targeted groups and recruit them into the Faculty and the University. This was to ensure that the teacher candidates more closely reflected the population of Metropolitan Toronto schools.

Emphasis on human fallibility often reinforces the notion that, had universities adequately discharged their functions, the critique that occasioned the hegemonic renegotiation would have been averted. As noted in the 1989 Dalhousie University *Report of the Task Force on Access for Black and Native People*:

> To the extent that those we spoke with did blame the universities, it was for inadequately preparing prospective teachers and counselors to work with students of different ethnicity or race. Insofar as teachers and counselors behave in ways which are insensitive or racist, Faculties and Schools of Education are said to share the blame. (xvii)

Once the institution has been seen to take charge publicly and authoritatively in the assignment of blame, the institutional process of official discourse instructs on the kind of institutional change required to obviate the problem (Mannette 1990). Thus, official discourse, in the instance of post-secondary access policies, transforms an ideological phenomenon (e.g., claims that erode confidence in the neutrality and meritocracy of post-secondary education) into material events (e.g., the initiation of investigation into such claims, the production of a fact-finding report, the elaboration of recommendations, the implementation of access initiatives). Interestingly, the representative individuals from hitherto excluded groups, who animated the critique through claims of institutional bias, get invited to participate in the fact-finding, report-writing and ongoing administration of access programs.[6]

To fine-tune the essentially reformable system and to be seen to ensure equality of opportunity, post-secondary institutions target particular historically disadvantaged groups for access. In most cases, Canadian institutions name "racial minorities," people of colour, women, Aboriginal people and/or people with disabilities as their targeted communities. It may be argued that it is these groups who have been able to mobilize politically to bolster their claim for entry into hitherto culturally privileged institutional life (Feagin et al. 1996; Chilly Climate Collective 1995; Bannerji et al. 1991a; Calliste 1996a; Allen 1996; Harkavy and Puckett 1994; Thompson and Tyagi 1993). In many ways, however, access initiatives also further monitor and limit the rate of cultural change within post-secondary educational institutions. For example, we can see how, at Dalhousie's law school, Black Nova Scotians and Mi'kmaq people are considered for admission only under the access program.

Getting "Access-ed": Negotiating Entry

> *They don't have to like me; they don't have to like my personality or the way I look, but I just don't want my opportunities to be limited and that's it. You don't have to like me but just don't block me from doing what I need to do. Don't maliciously take away what I have a right to....*

Typically, "access applicants" are expected to provide educational information (including grades), indicate their "target group" membership and provide information about themselves that demonstrates difficulties they might have had in acquiring the necessary educational qualification for university entry.[7] According to the students who applied through the access route, this was one of the most stressful demands of the entry process. They recalled how they had struggled with this final demand in the absence of a clear rationale for the requirement. Not only were many of them uncomfortable with having to declare their identity to fit any or some of the ascribed, homogenizing labels, but they also were not sure what the university expected and to what use the institution would put what they wrote.

Nevertheless, many believed that their experiences counted and that autobiographical information required in the access application offered the hope that they would not be judged on marks alone, since, as they asserted, the grades students get are not isolated from their experiences and from what they had to endure in their educational process (Fine 1987: 137). On this basis, they suggested that the autobiographical information presented them the opportunity to "discuss" the reasons for their grades. But they felt a tension between wanting to tell their stories and giving the impression that they are incapable, hence jeopardizing their chances or, conversely, gaining entry out of sympathy. What this shows is the respondents' distrust of the institution and the rules under which they were expected to operate. This also shows that institutional policies, such as access initiatives, appear to legitimate notions of systemic barriers while continuing to privilege certain notions of success (e.g., grades, writing skills, etc.).

The main question for access applicants, it would seem, was whether to write about their circumstances or to write about how they dealt with those circumstances and how the experience affected them. In other words, these students engaged in internal struggles to mediate the tensions occasioned by being required to be simultaneously victims and survivors. It is crucial to point out, however, that autobiographical accounts violate a clear precept of what counts as legitimate knowledge in the academy, which privileges "stories" that have been arrived at through the applications of disciplinary-bound methodological protocols (Brookes 1992; Belenky et al. 1986; King et al. 1987). Access respondents felt this prohibition.

Universities have always claimed to be objective and culturally neutral

(Chilly Climate Collective 1995). Universities have tinkered with admissions processes, creating the access ghetto while leaving the admissions process intact. They invest in both regular and access admissions with notions about the integrity of their process and the sanctity of academic standards. Given the universities' ambivalence about singling out demographic variables to facilitate entry, access programs are still troubling to universities' sense of themselves. In a sense, the access solution, seemingly in response to charges of universities' cultural privileging, also highlights that privileging. We suggest that this posits an ideological disruption for university actors, which is manifested in many ways, including the questioning of merit, qualification and standards (Schenke 1993; Sleeter 1994a). However, this helps to explain why deans of faculties with access programs will speak of the progress that has been made through such initiatives and will contend that such programs will be unnecessary three to five years hence. However, it is important to note that, thirty years later, Dalhousie's Transition Year Program not only continues but has now been complemented by the Indigenous Black and Mi'kmaq Program (IBM) at its law school.

"Race-ing"[8] Access: Experiences and Consequences

> *There are low expectations set for people of colour and so, therefore, when you start to—it's not even defying the odds—because there is this whole mentality that you must be stupid; you must come from this colonial "yes, massa," type of attitude that you can't excel and if you do excel it's probably because somebody showed you how and so you did not do it on your own steam.*

In relating their experiences within the university, respondents reported that they were perceived as "access" because they were Black. This stereotyping and the resultant behaviours towards these students by both professors and peers contributed to the frustrations and sometimes anger that they felt in the university. Sometimes they would take actions and raise the issues that they perceived needed to be addressed, but they were usually dismissed as trouble-makers.

The idea of trouble is a key component in how access students are understood and perceived, regardless of what they may or may not say or do:

> *All students have to, in a way, look at what they are writing; but … because of our colour, we have to be extra careful and probably not, say, talk about racism.… Nobody wants to speak about these kinds of issues. There are certain things you just have to let lie low because you want to go through. So you play the game.*

Trouble also comes from other students, who refer to access programs as "reverse racism" and constantly query the "unfairness" of targeting some groups for admission. With considerable irony, one access student noted in response, that "there already is an access program for White people; that's the regular program." In discussing specific experiences in some of their university classes, access respondents talked repeatedly of intimidating and disrespectful ways in which they were treated by professors who had low expectations of them and doubts about their ability to do well academically. For example, one student observed, "They don't seem to expect much from us." Another related that he was called into a professor's office to answer questions in order to verify if he had written his essay himself; it was considered to be too good for him. These experiences are not dissimilar to those of Carty (1991a), who also attended a southern Ontario university. She writes that she was told by a professor, who did not know her since "he had never granted [her] the opportunity to speak in his class" and hence had no basis on which to judge her capabilities, "that the argument [in her paper] was so very lucid, the paper so well researched and written, that it was apparent to him that [she] must have received help with it since it would be rather difficult for a student at [her] level to present work of such calibre" (Carty 1991a: 14).

The respondents often connected the feelings engendered by this treatment to the resentment that they felt from some of their professors and peers. They pointed out quite often how frustrating it was to be perceived as unqualified for university, or, in their own words, to "be seen as access" both by some of their peers and by professors who based their perceptions solely on the colour of their skin. This represents, in effect, the racialization (Grayson and Williams 1994; Hatcher and Troyna 1993) of access students; that is, they are being socially constructed as persons whose abilities, achievements, possibilities and actions are determined primarily by their race. It also posits the racialization of access policies and programs which produces a "peculiar eclipsing" of the access logic and the presence of other targeted groups.[9]

Many of the informants indicated that underlying the doubts about their qualifications to be in the university was the question of merit. This question led to much of the anxiety and tension they experienced both within themselves and with their peers and professors. They saw the institution as giving credence to the meritocratic myth (Mazurek 1987) while failing to acknowledge the existence of the structural barriers to their participation (e.g. racism, sexism, etc.). As a result, they developed a lack of trust in the fact that they would be judged on their abilities and work (see Hammonds 1993). In light of this, most students said that they tried to do well, working "twice as hard as everyone else just to show that [they] were capable" because they did not wish to validate the stereotypes that were held of them, primarily by their White peers and professors. In writing about this question of merit, which plagued "racial minority" students, Schenke (1993: 27) points out that "the belief that being properly qualified equates with high academic standing and individual achievement, regardless of social difference, obscures the recognition of institutional racism and historic and systemic practices of exclusion." This issue of qualifications is quite significant since it brings to the fore how the perception of not being "qualified" hinders full participation by these students and is perpetuated by the institution.

The perception of how the existence of an access program contributes to both the labeling of some "target group members" within institutions and the existence of tensions are corroborated in the American context[10] by Christine Sleeter (1994a). She tells of "White" students' objections to "an alternative certification program for prospective teachers of colour" at the teacher education program in which she teaches. The White students in the regular education program saw such initiatives as "racially biased and wrong"; they were unwilling to engage in any discussion that would provide them with information about the need for such a program; and, according to Sleeter (1994a: 8), they wanted "validation that the program was unfair toward Whites." In a similar discussion, James (1995a) writes that, in a Canadian faculty with an access program, White students tended to see such programs as "reverse racism" and contrary to the principles of meritocracy. Sleeter sees such reactions as premised on their liberal notions of colour blindness and their support for equal opportunity, truly the multicultural social democratic perspective. Sleeter also sees White students' reactions as "White social bonding," a process by which the students affirm "a common stance on race relations issues, legitimizing particular interpretations of groups of colour, and drawing conspiratorial we–they boundaries" (1994a: 8).

Beyond the interpersonal tensions that access programs inspire are the structural tensions that they articulate for post-secondary educational institutions. As mentioned above, access policies/programs are troublesome signifiers of the challenge to universities' ethos. Further, the perception among some faculty and administrators that such policies/programs are an anathema to scholarship and quality of programming generates additional sites for conflict in varied venues from committee work (e.g., hiring and tenure) to boards' and senates' allocation of such systemic irritants to the purview of presidents (James and Mannette 1996). Further, there is the cultural shock of the presence of hitherto excluded populations and what they signify from a psychoanalytic perspective (James 1981). In this sense, bodies that are different from the normative construct are, in themselves, disruptive (Walcott 1996). As well, these bodies frequently carry consciousnesses, such as anti-racism, feminism, etc., which propel their bearers to disrupt the canonical discourses (Feagin et al. 1996; Chilly Climate Collective 1995; hooks and West 1991). So, while the process of hegemonic renegotiations is engaged, it is engaged uneasily, and, clearly, some notions of change (e.g., multiculturalism and liberal feminism) are more malleable than others (e.g., anti-racism as theorized, radical feminism and queer theories).

Internal Tensions: Living with Difficult Knowledge

> *Last year I ended up being the person that everybody from every side of the coin would come to talk about issues because I wouldn't yell at people even though I thought they were being racist. I remember spending a good two-and-one-half hours with this woman over an argument she had in class and she could not understand how she was being racist. I kept showing it to her and showing it to her and at that point you have to ask yourself this ... where do I stop saying she is just ignorant; where do I draw the line?*

Many of these "perceived access students" talked of the conflict within that they experienced in the university. Usually, these conflicts were seen to be caused by external forces rooted in the institution. Further contributing to this conflict, as in the above quotation, was their continued investment in liberal enlightenment notions of learning; they tended to expect that their discussions with peers and professors, their articulateness and intelligence demonstrated through high grades, would convince people of their worthy presence within the academy.

These tensions also leave students feeling diminished and paralyzed by imposed and structurally real victimhood, puzzling over "when to speak," how to "censor their writing" and how to avoid further victimization. This reflects the dilemma regarding particular experiences of racism that may be considered "legitimate" and therefore worthy of sharing and those that may be challenged as non-racist. One respondent recounted this dilemma in a particularly powerful way:

> *I guess that understanding is that you can't bring up those issues in your class because of fear of getting a bad grade or something like that. But in my first year ... we were doing one workshop and there was a very racist comment made and all the Black people in the classroom, obviously, it hit them too. My friend, we looked at each other and, you know, we kissed our teeth and all that. But, I mean, it was a White girl that stood up and put the other girl in her place and, you know, brought the issue to light and made us work with it. I think, you know, sometimes that's what you gotta do at the risk of whatever, you know, because, after that, I kinda wished I had done that because I think that was something I should have done.*

At the heart of this dilemma is the epistemological question of what counts for knowledge and how it should be encoded and decoded (Mannette forthcoming; Monture-Angus 1995a, hooks and West 1991) and what is the cost of going against the grain. Since post-secondary educational institutions are, by societal definition, the keepers of legitimate knowledge, the question of historically disadvantaged groups inserting their hitherto excluded and devalued stories is a difficult one. But this is not how universities perceive themselves. As one university administrator, Milton Orris (1990: 8), articulated in his opening remarks to the 1990 Conference on Strategies for Improving Access and Retention of Ethno-Specific and Visible Minority Students in Ontario's Post-Secondary Institutions:

> My hope is that as we approach these questions [access, retention, successful completion] we do not surrender to a completely instrumentalist outlook. In the final analysis I, and I hope you, do not want a university completely subservient to social pressure. As the distinguished historian of education Diane Ravich recently observed, and I quote, "True believers in all societies have never been comfortable with the kinds of ideas and activities found in the university. They have seen the university as a citadel of doubt, scepticism, non-conformity, unorthodoxy and dissent; a place where young people learn to question the faith of their elders. A safe haven for those who question the conventional wisdom," and she concludes, "and so it should remain." And with that I conclude with the observation that it is my hope that at the end of the day our universities in Ontario will be more accessible, more equitable, and leaders in the exploration of our remarkable pluralism, but every bit as saucy and intellectually independent as they presently are.

But the view of the university as a "safe" place where professors' curricularly articulated knowledges can be challenged was not shared by the students with whom we spoke. In fact, they were very concerned about issues of safety; a concern that Patricia Monture-Okanee (1995: 18), a Mohawk woman and educator, also talks about in her essay "Surviving the Contradictions: Personal Notes on Academia." She points out that she risked this safety and attempted to influence the content of her course on Aboriginal people but was unsuccessful. She writes that, while in university, not only were some of her courses about Aboriginals taught by non-Aboriginals, but in some cases, as in an anthropology course on Aboriginal Peoples of Canada, "all the materials used in the course were written by non-Aboriginal people [and] all the guest speakers were non-Aboriginal people." After a number of students "confronted the teacher" and expressed their concerns, they were "excluded, denied and marginalized."

The tremendous tension that some Black students experience as they negotiate the conflicting interpretations of who/what they are is further increased by the common perception that, because they are Black, they must be "access":

> *You don't want to hear, well, she got in with access. She really didn't have the qualifications but because of access they took her. So, it's as if you have to work twice as hard as everyone else, just to show everyone, that look, this is not the way it is. I am capable; I can do this stuff.*

This raises the intriguing question of why these respondents so compellingly identify as African Canadians. We would like to introduce a structural explanation rooted in Smith's (1984) notion of "textually-mediated reality." According to Smith's theorization, the essence of school knowledge is encoded in key documents, such as grade reports, etc. Having "chosen" to name their access category as "visible minority—Black," these access students come to be administered on that basis. Thus, their lives as "access students" are articulated in terms of what that naming signifies. While Smith (1984) emphasizes the structural effects of the insertion of lived experience into "textually-mediated" ways of knowing, we would like to suggest what such naming signifies for those who have "colluded" in this self-identification. Having rationalized their access application as members of the targeted population (visible minority) and within the context of the connotation of "visible minority" as skin colour, it may be contended that these students who entered the university through an access program participated in producing the social relations of their designation. This is a textually based application of the structural hegemonic thesis. Indeed, Smith's (1984) contribution as applied here may be understood as an exemplar of the kind of operationalization of structural analysis in schooling that was advocated earlier by Silver (1990).

Expectations and Promises of Multiculturalism and Anti-Racism

> *They are speaking about multicultural and anti-racism education … and diversity and inclusion and giving us so many ideas … but at the same time they're telling us you can't really go changing things.*

A number of the students with whom we spoke felt that the existence of an access program meant that the university was committed to equity and social change. They expected to be exposed to transformative education that acknowledged their presence through content, pedagogy and structure. They expected to have voice, both in their classes and in the university generally. And, given the racial and ethnic diversity of their classes, they had assumed that discussions of race, racism and oppressive structures in society would have been openly encouraged, even though they were not part of formal lectures. Influencing their perceptions and expectations were their multicultural schooling experiences and anti-racism, which for them has become the paradigm of transformation.[11]

In fact, the students disparage multiculturalism ("Yeah, we'll bring in certain types of food") and privilege anti-racism but know from their own schooling that anti-racism is deeply contested:

> *I don't think [the universities] will meet anti-racist education with open arms for a number of reasons: things that are not considered normal, things that challenge them to look into their own position.... People are quite comfortable the way it was.*

But the way in which universities have developed and implemented access programs is based on the liberal framework of multiculturalism[12] and the corresponding traditional values of the institutions, which view higher learning as apolitical (Fleras 1996). As Karl Peter (1981) so cogently said of multiculturalism:

> What is presented here as a liberal policy, that individuals are free to graduate into mainstream Canadian society if they so wish, is in fact a policy of "ethnic group containment." Ethnic groups are steered away from any contact with political and economic powers and are neutralized in their role as providers of individual satisfaction, adding a touch of colour to the otherwise drab Canadian socio-cultural scene.

Within this context, participation in post-secondary education serves an important function in the production and reproduction of the currency of citizenship. Thus, a key structural component is not only in the containment but also the eradication of difference. This ensures that those who are different may enter into the intended ideological and practical homogenization imagined as the university experience (James and Mannette 1996). In this sense, access programs could also be seen as one more assimilationist institutional strategy.

The university enables the transformation of those from "targeted" historically disadvantaged groups into students who are able to use the cultural capital offered by the university education in their aim to become effective participating citizens. It is important to note that this citizenship effect is not only about the realization of individual aspirations and fulfilment, the so-called liberal dream of "making it." It is also the requisite of the social system producing and reproducing itself through securing the "consent" of those with the talent to succeed. There is no need, therefore, for institutions to transform themselves as long as they appear to be providing opportunities to those who have agitated for space and voice within the institutions.

Evidently, this is contrary to many of these African Canadian students' concepts of the opportunities that they expected once they entered the university. As one person commented, "We believe that if you have access in principle, it's supposed to be working to change the curriculum. That's not happening. So, I believe that's where the problem is." Access, then, is more than just gaining entry into university; for, once in university, students must be provided an academic environment in which the curricula, pedagogy and social relationships are conducive to their learning, welcoming of their participation in all areas of university life and responsive to their needs, interests and expectations. This means that universities must move beyond providing equality of opportunity—a tenet of multiculturalism—to ensuring equity. As Evans and Davies (1993: 23–24) argue:

> Equality in education has been defined purely as a technical concern with the distribution of opportunities amongst different social groups.... Equity "gauges the results of actions directly against standards of justice." It is used to determine whether or not what is being done is just. It is critical to uphold a distinction particularly between equality of opportunity and equity because the achievement of the former is no guarantee that the latter is also evident.

The anti-racism perspective recognizes that universities operate like "corporate businesses" (Newson and Buchbinder 1988), based on Eurocentric, middle-class and patriarchal curricula (Henry and Tator 1994; Ng 1994; Thompson and Tyagi 1993; Carty 1991a). Proponents of the anti-racism perspective, with the understanding that post-secondary education is overtly political, interrogate the ways in which educational institutions perpetuate cultural hegemonies; and they argue for action to produce social change (Dei 1995b, 1996a; Fleras 1996; Troyna 1987). Further, this paradigm advocates that universities recognize that racism, classism, sexism and others operate within their structures, and hence they must be active agents of progressive social change; they cannot pretend to be neutral sites of intellectual discourse, education and societal socialization.

Within the anti-racism paradigm, access initiatives recognize the socially constructed "multiple identities" of individuals and groups (Dei 1995b, 1996a; C. James 1996; Walcott 1994). These "multiple identities" of gender, ethnicity, race, sexuality and others are understood to be relational as well as complex, contradictory and shifting (Walcott 1994). Further, as Walcott (1994) points out, effective anti-racism strategies must "take seriously *the politics of difference;*" that is, they must be concerned with all forms of oppression and domination both individual, institutional and structural. Difference, then, is not merely variation but deviation (see also West 1993a). Within the academy, therefore, gender, ethnicity, race, class and other factors must be seen to be salient in the construction of "privileged meanings" (Hall et al. 1981) of what constitutes knowledge, the principles of merit and the subjective experiences of all who participate. Further, individuals' multiple characteristics cannot be reduced to a single category, such as Blackness, femaleness, sexual orientation, etc. To do so, as Walcott (1994: 13) argues, would be to legitimate "the neglect or exclusion of other important variables of social difference."

Further, anti-racism posits that students' differences must also be acknowledged not in terms of their merely having a voice, but as Mohanty (1993: 61) suggests, "the sort of voice one comes to have as the result of one's location—both as an individual and as part of collectives." Hence, post-secondary institutions should be ready to give space and to respond to "active, oppositional and collective voices" that seek to transform colonializing educational practices into those which provide empowerment (Mohanty 1993). On this basis, post-secondary institutions must engage in what Thompson and Tyagi (1993) call "the politics of inclusion." This means that institutions that undertake to develop and implement access programs must be willing to examine their practices and accept accountability for the structural factors that mitigate against full participation of a diverse population of students and faculty. As Thompson and Tyagi (1993: 90) explain, "the politics of inclusion allows for the development of an 'informed consciousness' that provides the impetus for long-term educational change." What we suggest is that hegemonic elaborations cannot take up these demands and remain within the hegemonic logic; in Williams' (1981) typology, anti-racism is oppositional, not merely alternative, as is multiculturalism.

It is not entirely clear how these respondents understood anti-racism. On the one hand, it is fair to say that they did not conceptualize anti-racism in as complicated a way as anti-racism theorists did (Dei 1996a; Desai 1996; C. James 1996; Lee 1994; Bannerji et al. 1991a; Troyna 1987; Thomas 1987). As well, they seemed to engage less in reflective personal critique (see Dei 1996a) than in critiques of the social and educational structures.[13] This seeming preoccupation with structure appears to be based on the tensions and conflicts, indeed, their ambivalence about pursuing a post-secondary education in an institution where their expected systemic changes were not evident and where racism and discrimination were constant reminders of the barriers that inhibit needed changes. Racism and racial identity seemed paramount to the students, so that the complexity of these factors and their interconnections with other oppressive forces (related to class, sex, gender, sexuality and disability) got lost. Our reading of the students' reflections suggests that they did not necessarily recognize that the hoped-for change could be internal as well as external, personal as well as structural.

Understandably, the students expected universities to "walk the talk"; they inferred that if universities had access programs, they must be committed to systemic change. They felt that while the access initiative was a potentially good step, given that it "helped" them "to get into university," they were disillusioned that such initiatives are not accompanied by the university's commitment to addressing structural barriers, specifically racism and discrimination. We suggest that much of their disillusionment is an artefact of their lingering liberal notions of the university, what the taking-up of anti-racism must mean and their partial understandings of the anti-racism perspective. The key issue with the anti-racism politics is that, unlike multiculturalism, its ethos cannot be renegotiated or accommodated in and by the hegemonic elaborations and discourses (of class, gender, ethnicity, race, etc.) that currently characterize the fabric of these institutions. Indeed, we find that, where anti-racism has been taken up in post-secondary educational institutions, it is practised by relatively isolated individuals, and/or it has been selectively and partially institutionalized devoid of its activist theory and political action.[14] As such, we find it unlikely that even a depoliticized anti-racism will be "honoured" with the institutional ghettoization, which has been the effect of anti-sexism's recasting as women's studies.[15]

Conclusion

> *It's not about getting a few visible minorities in a program. It's about educating whoever's there.*

We have discussed two stories of living with difficult knowledge. For the universities, this is expressed structurally and interpersonally. Structurally, the hegemonic ideological disruption, signaled by other charges of bias, resulted in university-defined and driven activities which were designed to mediate the disruption and name and redress the problem. The scrutiny of universities and whom they serve contributed to the writing of reports with recommendations and the creation of access initiatives. All of this was accomplished with the support and effort of hitherto excluded populations. However, as Henry and Tator (1994: 86) suggest, "the university has generally used the same approach as other liberal institutions by initiating conservative actions which do little to change the status quo." This inability to implement programs that appeal to these historically disadvantaged students is particularly perplexing since, as McCombs (1989: 130) argues, it is within universities that issues of racial, sexual and class "oppression, dominance, and inequality are most clearly articulated and researched."

In the wake of access initiatives, the institution remains unsettled. Now access programs serve as a reminder of implicit threats to passionately held values of scholarship, integrity, excellence, etc. Further, the residual unsettling was structurally unanticipated in that the renegotiation process was intended, in the short term, to allay doubt and thus restore confidence in institutional integrity. In a sense the hegemonic tool has produced another kind of disruption, particularly in terms of the "visibility" and consciousnesses of the newcomers. This gets played out in various ways, ranging from canonical critiques to confrontations between professors and students, among professors and among students.

We see in this period of history a significant rise in hitherto excluded populations participating in institutions, having thrown off the material (e.g., colonialized status) and psychic (e.g., colonized mentalities) manifestations of skin-colour race relations hegemonic domination. So, in the case of these African Canadians, they are prepared to seize spaces made available to them through their struggles and hegemonic negotiations of those struggles. One such space is access initiatives in post-secondary education. Structurally, their presence signifies change, both within the institution and in their homes and communities. This is sometimes a comfortable signifier but, more often, it is not. Within themselves, this is manifested in their doubts about their abilities, tensions concerning when/what to speak and a debilitating sense of disillusionment. However, the disillusionment could become an enhancing experience for the "accessed students" in that they are forced to confront their ambivalences which occasioned extravagant expectations for change. Following our earlier qualifications of what hope entails, we suggest that hope can be premised only on what is, which is opposed to ideological obfuscation of what is desired. Further, an examination of how and why utopian desire has been created in the minds of these historically disadvantaged students is an important political project for themselves and for communities.

This leads to another crucial realization in the difficult knowledge that we, as researchers, also find in this work. What makes the knowledge difficult is not just the "trigger," for example, the presence of visibly different bodies or the outsider critiques of the canon. For the university or, more appropriately, those advocates of the traditional university privilege, it is not merely the presence of visibly different bodies that is unsettling. It is what those bodies signify to those with university privilege. For example, one participant recalled:

> *I had one professor who told myself and a group of friends—we were very verbal in his class—that he had had our type in his class before, and that he thought that we should withdraw from the course because we weren't going to pass; and he doesn't need our type around here to give him problems.*

Many other students told similar stories. What troubles them is not so much the disrespect from others, annoying as it might be. It is the doubts that are created within themselves, which are triggered by this disrespect, that make the situation unbearable. And it is the "desperate blank pages" (Tynes 1992) of Black history that haunt them as they encounter canonical knowledge that does not even place Black people in footnotes. It is the residual effects of colonial history, what Battiste (1986) has called "cognitive assimilation," that has also created this tension in them.

Universities must make structural changes if they expect to make their resources and services fully accessible to historically disadvantaged students. In demonstrating their commitment to access, universities, and faculties in particular, must engage in a review and re-evaluation of their policies and practices, particularly those concerning established entry requirements, merit, pedagogical practices and course content. These reviews and evaluations, and whatever changes may result, should not be based only on the need to recruit or on the presence of historically excluded students. Indeed, *all* students stand to benefit from inclusive recruitment strategies, curricula and pedagogy. Also, academic freedom (see Lamy 1994; hooks 1988), the most often cited reason for maintaining the status quo, must be examined to ensure that it does not interfere with equitable treatment of students, particularly those who were hitherto excluded. We concur with these students' arguments that it is indeed important that historically disadvantaged groups are now able to gain access to post-secondary institutions. However, merely gaining entry does not necessarily represent the university's commitment to equity. If equity is to be achieved and full participation realized then historically disadvantaged groups must be able to work and learn in an environment that respects their talent and welcomes their contributions. It is this difficult knowledge with which universities must learn to live. In living with this difficult knowledge universities are finding themselves expressing discursively through policy and protocols what are at the very least uneven, and at their worst, contradictory imperatives. It is unclear whether universities will resolve the tensions inherent upon wanting to be "enlightened," wanting to increase enrollments through "minority recruitment" and wanting to maintain what have traditionally been considered academic standards, which are of course racialized, etc. For those whose admission to universities is through "access," difficult knowledge entails two separate yet connected dimensions. They must live both with the idea of hope grounded in the possibilities for institutional change in universities and with the unsettling thought that the change they seek may be more elusive than imagined.

Notes

1. For example, at the University of Toronto there are undergraduate and professional programs to prepare students for regular degrees. In terms of special programs, there is found a non-degree "pre-law" program at the Saskatchewan Indian Federated College, which attracts Native law candidates from across the country. The University of Western Ontario's Graduate School of Journalism offers a communication program for Native students. Native studies programs were found at Trent University and the University College of Cape Breton. Some universities (e.g., the University of Toronto and the University of Manitoba) had support systems for minority students in regular degree programs. These programs are relatively recent, although the transition year programs at Dalhousie University and the University of Toronto date from Black and Native human rights struggles in the 1960s and '70s (Calliste 1996a; Inglis et al. 1991; Mannette 1990; Moore 1980).
2. We are borrowing here from the South African context in which those who have been historically excluded from decision-making and full participation in social

and institutional life are known as historically disadvantaged groups. This naming recognizes the social and political nature of historical disadvantage; the need for historical compensation and reconceptualization; and the complex nature of historical disadvantage in ethnic, race, gender and class terms. This naming also seeks to move beyond the dominant Canadian construct "visible minority," which obfuscates the relational nature of the social dynamic of inequalities and postulates that the "visibility" is something that resides within "other" rather than an ideological construct of ethnicity, race, gender and class privilege.

3. According to Samuel (1992), the number of racial minorities in Canada was 1.58 million or 6.3 percent in 1986 and 2.58 million or 9.6 percent in 1991. It is projected that by 1996 and 2001, the numbers will increase to 3.94 million or 13.4 percent and 5.68 million or 17.7 percent respectively. About half of the racial minority population lives in southern Ontario (Kalbach et al. 1993). Samuel's estimates have been supported by the recent 1996 census information, which reveals that racial minorities make up 11.2 percent of the Canadian population and 32 percent of the Toronto population (Mitchell 1998: A1).
4. Burke (1994: 36) reports that "of the 310,884 children expected to immigrate to Canada between 1990 and 1995, 73% (222,945) will be aged 5–14, and the remaining 27% (83,939) under age 5." She (Burke 1994: 36) estimates that 55% of all immigrant children—coming primarily, according to Badets (1994), from Hong Kong, China, India and Africa—will live in Ontario. We think that it is important to note that, as post-secondary educational institutions continue to experience fiscal crisis, the entry of the "culturally dissimilar" is more about attracting potential client markets than it is about civic responsibilities.
5. Dorothy Smith (1974) argues that what occurs in complex organizations is a kind of ideological circle in which what "counts" and how it is encoded into text are shaped by the organization's structural relevances, that is, the social relations (of power, etc.) animating the organization.
6. We suggest that this representative inclusion process is a way in which institutions negotiate hegemony and mediate the tensions between themselves and students. Internal post-secondary institutional studies and committee work that resulted in access initiatives defined the problem of post-secondary education for historically disadvantaged groups as one of gaining admission (J. Hall 1990; Orris 1990). On this basis, access programs, so-constituted, have tended to emphasize recruitment and entry activities.
7. "Appropriate qualifications" tends to refer to a particular grade point average, such as B+ or A-. This grade point average is assumed to signal the mastery of certain skills of oracy, numeracy and literacy. Writing style is highly valued. Other appropriate qualifications, depending on the discipline/field, may include relevant experiences and excellent letters of reference, which speak knowledgeably of the accomplishments that make the applicant suitable for admission and/or likely to succeed in the field (see James 1994a).
8. The term is borrowed from Toni Morrison (1992b) *Race-ing Justice, Gendering Power* in which contributors, with reference to the Clarence Thomas chief justice appointment hearing, discuss the ways in which justice in America is influenced by skin colour and gender.
9. It would be an important comparative study to examine experiences of other targeted groups. What we suggest here is that the extent to which access signifies

Blackness must be read in the context of what Blackness denotes in the sub-region (e.g., a meter of racial change in the society, popular condemnation of immigration, the conflation of immigrants with people of colour, the overdetermination of Blackness with criminality, the extent to which Blackness subverts the moral order, articulation of Black people as state clients as the state downsizes, etc.). Following James (1981), we suggest that, coterminous with the class imperative for Blackness as labourers and servants, is a powerful ideology of skin-colour race that constructs Blackness at the level of the unconscious and that is given expression in the binary oppositions of Western thought in terms of "darkness and death, evil and decay." However, while Blackness may be "fearful" in this sense, it is also "fascinating" (James 1981) and alluring—alluring to explore what liberation from the constraints of (Western) culture(s) may be effected through intercourse with the (possibly contaminating) other.

10. In the American context, state supported "affirmative action" programs help to influence universities' initiatives and students' responses.
11. We suggest however that their knowledge of anti-racism is largely based on how it has been taken up in their schools and communities.
12. This is based on the Multiculturalism Act (1988) of Canada which claims that the government of Canada recognizes the diversity of Canadians and "is committed to a policy of multiculturalism designed to preserve and enhance the multicultural heritage of Canadians while working to achieve the equality of all Canadians in the economic, social, cultural and political life of Canada." This ideology of cultural democracy presupposes that the norms, values and principles by which the state operates are neutral and fair, and therefore citizens are able to participate fully in the society and institutions, uninhibited by cultural barriers. Multiculturalism, then, is seen as a viable, progressive and fair way in which to address the multi-ethnic constituencies within Canada (James 1995b: 35).
13. We suggest that part of the struggle for the students is their difficulties with their ambivalence. We raise this point cautiously since we are very aware of the ways in which such notions have been/will be taken up in "victim blaming." However, we feel that this is an important analytical and strategic idea that fleshes out our sense of what living with difficult knowledge entails.
14. This is very true of the institutionalization of anti-racism practice in public schooling (see James 1995b).
15. Women's structural relegation to the domestic sphere and exclusion from privileged institutions has only relatively recently been mediated by renegotiation of gendered hegemonic elaborations, and the so-called progress of women continues to be mediated by patriarchy as well as skin-colour racism, classism, ageism, etc. (see Jordan and Weedon 1995; Bannerji et al. 1991a: Chapter 6).

Chapter Five

Black Women Teachers' Positionality and "Everyday Acts":

A Brief Reflection on the Work to Be Done

Annette Henry

> Creating a society that can be judged favorably by the way it treats the women of its darkest race need not be the work of black women alone, nor will black women be the exclusive or primary beneficiaries of such a society. Such work can be engaged in by all who are willing to take seriously the everyday acts engaged in by black women and others to resist racism and sexism and to use these acts as the basis to develop ... theories designed to end race and gender subordination. —Paulette M. Caldwell, 1997

Some years ago, while teaching at a faculty of education, I worked with Dan,[1] a White male secretary who had a short-term assignment in our department. One morning, I went into the department specifically to discuss a number of duties that I had given him and that he had not carried out accurately. When he saw me, he fled down a flight of stairs. At the bottom of the stairwell were three public telephones. He picked up the receiver at one of the booths and called the police, claiming that his life was in danger and that I had tried to physically assault him. The chairperson of my department dealt with this incident by warning me to never touch anyone ever again. Furthermore, Dan, who used to share an office with two women of colour, was moved to private space in another office. At the end of his temporary assignment, he took a job in another building working on a prestigious project by a scholar noted for his left-wing politics and social justice activism. When I expressed to my colleague that, indeed, "Whiteness is the consolation prize" (see Harris 1993), he retorted, "What's the matter, do you want Dan to be out of a job?"

The chairperson of my department and an assistant to the dean dealt with this incident as an "unfortunate" occurrence rather than one of a continued legacy of racism and sexism in the institution. They failed to see the connection between this story and other stories of my experience as the sole Black female faculty member. In fact, my chairperson said that "if it had been the other way around, it would have been racism." Her comment left me speechless. She was probably referring to my "superior" position as a professor. Indeed, Dan was a secretary, but his Whiteness and his maleness gave him power and credibility—

so much so, that he wrote a five-page letter, which he presented at a meeting with senior administrators, questioning my curricular activities and my commitment to "multiculturalism." Although the assault story was untrue, I was reprimanded, and Dan was moved to another work space where he would not have to suffer the emotional harassment of dealing with a supposedly hostile, violent, dangerous, Black female professor.

The plot thickened in ways that space and time do not permit here. However, this story illustrates how a faculty of education—which had a mission statement to serve its teachers, students and the largely Black urban schools in the university neighbourhood and a faculty that gave lip service to recruiting "minority" professors and students and which had the responsibility to prepare elementary and secondary teachers for work in multilingual, multiracial environments—had failed to acknowledge and deal with some of the political issues implicated in its mission statement when faced with an "everyday act" such as I have described.

I began to think about and make connections with other instances in the lives of Black women teachers. I agree with Patricia Caldwell, who argues that we have to be willing "to take seriously the everyday acts engaged in by black women and others to resist racism and sexism and to use these acts as the basis to develop ... theories designed to end race and gender subordination" (1997: 304)

At this time, with increased cultural and racial diversity, many ministries of education, faculties of education and school boards are seeking to hire faculty and prepare and hire teachers who are representative of diverse multiracial and multilingual populations and to develop and implement anti-racism (Dei 1996a). By looking at these "everyday acts" in which Black women find themselves in struggle, I want to briefly examine how Black women teachers are positioned in their training and professions. I present two short vignettes, the first with teacher candidates, the second with a veteran teacher. I want to discuss their accounts in tandem with some literature by Black feminist theorists who write about Black women's lives and experiences. My aim is to explore the meanings and contradictions of anti-racism from the experiences of Black women. I conclude by stressing that an analysis of these "everyday acts" can show areas where some serious political work needs to be done regarding anti-racism.

Two Variations on a Theme

First Story: "They'll probably send you to Hamilton Heights"

> *"Why her?"*
> *"Why now?*
> *"Was this special treatment?"*
> *"Wasn't there a White woman or White male more qualified?"*
> *"Can she teach?"*
> (Linda S. Greene)

Arlette, Keisha and Camille were three vibrant Black women in their late twenties. They had just completed their last class in a bachelor of education program at an urban university in southern Ontario. It was a warm, sunny day in June. It should have been a day of celebration and ceremony. It wasn't. I could sense their pain as I drove into the parking lot where they were standing.

We stood talking in the parking lot for about forty minutes. Brows knitted, Keisha and her friends shared how certain instructors in the program had treated them. For example, they complained that they had consistently received Bs and Cs on assignments given by a particular instructor, Rich Thompson, while most of their classmates always received an A. They did confront their teacher, but he failed to adequately explain their lower marks. Furthermore, Rich Thompson and another instructor, Fred McBride, often belittled their presence in the program. They endured the following comments from their instructors such as "You'll get jobs" or "The board will hire your kind" or even "They'll probably send you down to Caledon Heights. You'll get a job over there!"

In an economic climate in which many graduates could not be assured of a teaching job, their instructors insinuated that these three Black women would be hired because of their race, and pressed into doing the work that no else wanted to do—teach in Caledon Heights, a Black area. Mr. Thompson and Mr. McBride did not consider that Keisha, Camille and Arlette might have aspired to teach in Caledon Heights or in other areas with a large Black population. In fact, as activist, anti-racist teachers, Keisha and her friends chose to work in areas like Caledon Heights and envisioned their future vocation as a means to create communities of caring and resistance for Black children rather than perpetuate an educational system that alienates pupils of African descent.

Arlette, Keisha and Camille were being initiated into the (White supremacist) culture of employment, one which connotes Black inferiority and unsuitability ("Oh you'll get jobs" and "The board will hire your kind"). The instructors also hinted at the false argument of "reverse racism" (see James 1995a). As the above quotation from Linda S. Greene implies, there is necessarily and always controversy, or "pedagogical politics," when a Black women is hired. Interestingly, at this large urban university, many initiatives have been set in place in the name of anti-racism, including a program to recruit and support teacher candidates from underrepresented groups. However, this official discourse did not engender enabling practices here.

The actual practice of anti-racism was not created in this forum in which students felt that they could not challenge problematic practices, attitudes and behaviours in their pre-service program. Returning to Caldwell's (1997) argument in the introduction, the everyday experiences of Black women could help develop a theory and practice relevant to their concerns and beneficial and relevant to the concerns of others.

Second Story: "You'd better handle it!"

> They cannot recognize the ways their actions support and affirm the very structure of racist domination and oppression that they profess to wish to see eradicated. (bell hooks 1988)

Viv, an African Canadian teacher in her fifties recalled her teaching days in Montreal in the 1960s. With great animation, she told how White male colleagues feared Black male youth. Thus, administrators often called upon her to intervene in situations perceived to be volatile. "That's why the principals used to like me so," Viv chuckled. "I used to go out and face the boys head on! They [the principals] used to say, "Oh Viv! You'd better handle it!"

Viv's brief account, which is similar to the previous story, reveals the power of dominant discourses routinized in everyday practices. Lest we think that things have changed since the 1960s, there are a number of research reports that remind us of the ideological construction of Black women in contemporary Canadian society, women constructed as a service class of caregivers, servers and helpers (Brand 1987, 1988; Calliste 1991, 1993; Carty 1994). In fact, research across disciplines shows that Black women professionals are in tenuous positions socially, politically and economically, consigned to arduous work duties, less than favorable conditions, biased performance evaluations, dismissals due to racism and sexism and a myriad of other injustices (Allen 1997; Calliste 1993; Cooper 1991; hooks 1993; Kirby and Hudson 1993; Silvera 1983; Snapp 1992). Black women professionals know too well how, historically, their race, gender and class backgrounds have structured them in the workplace "to clean up everyone's mess" (hooks 1981: 154). Black women teachers, once hired, are often expected to do the "hands on work" and the less intellectual work (Bangar and McDermott 1989; Collins 1990; hooks 1993).

Viv's story raises questions about the purposes and intentions for which Black women teachers may be hired. This story points to the positionality of Black women in White institutions. Black women teachers often find themselves having to provide the curricular diversity and attend to the "special needs" of Black students (Allen 1997).

What might it mean for teachers, like Viv, in school boards striving toward anti-racism? Will it require Black women to always be the ones to deal with Black students, who are often stereotyped as "problem kids?" The "You're Black!—You deal with it!" damage control approach that administrators impose on Black colleagues can often signify a lack of political will to create fundamental changes in existing school relations and institutional structures as well as a lack of political will to examine the structural and political dimensions that cause Black students to fail, drop out and become discouraged or angry. Instead, many a Black teacher (both male and female) is hired and told, "You'd better handle it!" As Black women teachers point out (Allen 1997; Bangar and

McDermott 1989), they are often expected to oversee myriad areas—managing "Black Studies" curriculum development, mounting Black history month activities, counselling Black students. What might be the emotional and physical toll placed on teachers like Viv who are positioned as "mammies" and "maids"?

Concluding Questions

> The presence of Black faces does not change the essential nature of an institution nor does it alter its ethos. (Evans 1988)

In each of these three stories, the status quo regarding relations of power and subordination on the basis of race and gender was kept intact. There were no concrete institutional strategies that had been implemented. These Black women were in positions where they were isolated and bore the political responsibility of raising the awareness and consciousness of the White people in their work environment. Yet again, it becomes the job of the "oppressed" to teach White people about their power.

Anti-racism, by definition, is political, transformative and oppositional (Brandt 1986; Dei 1996a; Kailin 1994; Lee 1989). Developing "anti-racist" curriculum and hiring initiatives is not enough. Acknowledging the need to recruit "visible minority" teachers is not enough. The everyday acts mentioned here underscore that, even with a commitment to anti-racism, institutional climates may be hostile or slow to change and, indeed, race, class and gender locate and inscribe Black women in inequitable positions. Despite structural and institutional constraints, Black women must take difficult transformative stances so that the current processes are not maintained. Importantly, as Paulette Caldwell (1997) reminds us, it should not be the political realm solely of Black women but of all of us to critically reflect upon these everyday acts of power and subordination and to use them to develop theories and workable strategies to end inequality.

Note

1. All names are pseudonyms.

Chapter Six

Mapping the Unknowable:

The Challenges and Rewards of Cultural, Political and Pedagogical Border Crossing[1]

Evangelia Tastsoglou

This chapter focuses on "boundaries" and "border crossings" in classrooms, and maps the field for a critical pedagogical practice of egalitarian border crossings. There are several points of departure. First, there is the sociological premise that social differentiation, classification and group formation are features of social life; at the same time, there is a radical vision of a society of democratic polyphony (Mouffé 1988; Giroux 1993: 81), where dialogue and equal participation across borders is not only possible but indeed the only way toward emancipation. Second, there is Henry Giroux's notion of critical pedagogy as an aid to students who engage knowledge as a "border crosser" (1992b: 22, 29, 169). Finally, there is Elizabeth Ellsworth's argument that, since oppressions are contextual and classroom political dynamics *a priori* "unknowable,"[2] critical pedagogical practice cannot be anything but contextual (1989: 323) or a "pedagogy of place" (Giroux 1993: 77–78).

The chapter is divided into three sections. The first section deals with the questions of boundaries and border crossings through a review of selected literature in sociological theory and research. Visions of egalitarian border crossings and challenges to their realization are especially highlighted. The second section unpacks specific borders in classrooms and carries over the implications of, as well as challenges to, the sociological vision of (egalitarian) border crossings in critical, feminist and anti-racist pedagogical practice through reviewing the literature on educational theory and narratives of educational practice. The third section examines self-reflexively the constitution of boundaries and border crossings within this writer's narratives of pedagogical practice and "educational life history" (Middleton 1993) in an attempt to illustrate the issues of boundaries and border crossings but, most importantly from the point of view of political pedagogical practice, to map the "unknowable" politics of her classroom by at least "situating" herself.

By focusing on the individual self, this chapter in no way attempts to divert attention from the larger social structures (for example, the institutionalization and even the systemic character of certain borders) and, therefore, from the need for collective struggles in society and in education in order to make egalitarian border crossings more possible. This chapter merely assumes that borders are also internalized and that for an effective practice of critical, feminist and anti-racist pedagogy, the constitution of various borders within the educator needs to be understood as well. It may not be possible to know *a priori* what a critical, feminist and anti-racist pedagogical practice will (or should) be like in the context of a specific classroom, since such practice has to be "situated" (Ellsworth 1989). However, it is crucial to have a well-grounded understanding not only of the borders—and their cross-sections—likely to be encountered in such a classroom but also of those contributed by the educator her/himself.

Boundaries and Border Crossings

Boundaries in Sociological Theory and Research

From the inception of the sociological discipline, sociologists have been fascinated by the concept of "boundary"[3] and the questions to which the concept gives rise: what holds a society together; what binds a social group together, separating it at the same time from other groups or people (i.e., what are the co-ordinates around which boundaries are erected); how social groups emerge (i.e., how boundaries are constructed); what purposes the distinctions between groups serve (i.e., what the functions of boundaries are); how rigid such distinctions or boundaries are; under what conditions and with what consequences boundaries can be crossed. The language used and the formulation of the problematic of boundaries has varied by sociological tradition. In the contemporary world, we witness both increasing tendencies toward elimination of certain boundaries (i.e., globalization), as well as tendencies toward making boundaries more distinct and rigid (i.e., inequality among and within nations, ethnic and racial conflict). Therefore, I argue that it is a particularly urgent task to understand the nature and dynamics of boundaries.

The tradition of functionalism deals primarily with the question of "what" boundaries are (defined in terms of what boundaries "do", i.e., their functions). In this sociological tradition, boundaries have to do with classifications, which human beings create through contrast and inclusion. Social groups structure their common social life by creating distinctive spaces (i.e., the "sacred" and the "profane") and, further, by establishing elaborate rituals for passage from one space to the other (Durkheim 1965; Durkheim and Mauss 1963). For symbolic interactionism, on the other hand, the key question deals with "how" boundaries are constructed and perpetuated. Erving Goffman (1963) argues that boundaries are primarily symbolic representations that most often take the form of a stigma. For Howard Becker (1963), boundary-creating deviant acts exist only insofar as they are defined as such. Finally, for the Marxist tradition, the key question refers to the functions—often confused with causes—of symbolic boundaries. Marxists, regardless of the degree of autonomy they cede to the political and ideological spheres, argue that cultural or symbolic boundaries exist as a result of domination and to serve the interests of the ruling classes by justifying an existing unequal distribution of resources (Lamont and Fournier 1992).

Opposing both the objectivism and subjectivism of previous sociological traditions, Pierre Bourdieu proposes a political economy of symbolic goods through his "structural constructivism" (1989) and asserts a single, overarching objective space of "distinction" based on social class. For Bourdieu (1984), the "logic of distinction" is a principle of organization basic to all forms of social life, creating boundaries that are not only symbolic but also political. In his attempt to rebut Bourdieu's objectivism, John Hall (1992: 259–60) juxtaposes his own vision of "cultural structuralism" by suggesting not a single field of distinction but "multiple and overlapping institutionalized cultures, described as cultural structures, and heterologous 'markets' and 'currencies' of cultural capital."

Contemporary empirical research addresses the earlier questions of "what", "how" and "why" in regards to symbolic boundaries in ways that cut across the various sociological traditions and attempt to bridge the gap between inequality studies and culture and symbolic boundaries. Lamont and Fournier (1992: 1–17) group such research into three large streams. First, the stream dealing with the cultural aspects of inequality and identifying the symbolic dimensions along which distinctions are made, such as types of activity (high culture, cuisine) and categories of persons (gender, ethnicity). This research was developed in response to the economic focus of inequality of the 1960s and 1970s by structuralists and Marxists. The second stream of empirical research identifies the processes by which boundaries are constructed as (i) institutionalization over time of cultural categories; (ii) mobilization of "cultural repertoires and contexts of interpretations"; and (iii) exclusion, based on the "nature" of boundary itself and, especially, on the politics of institutions involved in its management. The third stream, dealing with the question of "why" there are boundaries (what their origins are, which functions they play), identifies the social groups constructing them (for instance, women or "ethnic cultural capital") and the relations of domination that are maintained by enforcing boundaries through politically-laden discourse or through threat of punishment in case of boundary transgression (Lamont and Fournier 1992: 11–12).

Toward a Vision of Border Crossings

One crucial question in regard to symbolic boundaries is whether human social relations are possible or even desirable without boundaries. Are boundaries to be discarded because they can politically reflect, re-create, justify or perpetuate inequalities? The answer, according to practically from every school of sociological thought, as well as historical analysis, is that the rise and fall of various types of boundaries is "the very story of human civilization" (Oommen 1995: 251) and that a richly textured social life necessitates exclusions, demarcations, boundaries and memberships (Wolfe 1992: 311–12; Cohen 1985). Furthermore, reflecting on the experiences of societies with religious fundamentalist or secular totalitarian ideologies which have tried to merge different spheres of social life into a single, one-dimensional reality, Oommen argues that in such societies the individual is "a mere spark in the collective current of social life" and that human life is "nasty, brutish and short" (1995: 251–61). Be it, at the very basis, the nature of social life, a "logic of distinction" (Bourdieu 1984) or the need for boundaries as referents of identity (Cohen 1985: 117–18), boundaries continue to provide the framework for ordering the social world, constructing identities and excluding and discriminating by creating barriers.

How should we weigh then, in a normative sense, the principle of a democratic commitment to the universal rights of citizens (i.e., tearing down the limits to inclusion imposed by barriers/boundaries) against the usefulness or even necessity for boundaries? A first step is to recognize that boundaries are constantly in flux, shifting and changing in historical meaning. When certain types of boundaries become contested, de-institutionalized or "desacralized," others are constantly configured and constructed in a process of "fission and fusion" (Oommen 1995: 252–53) or of "construction, destruction, and deconstruction of civic solidarity" (Alexander 1992: 289). The second step is to recognize that, at a given historical moment, not all boundaries have the same (discriminatory) effect (Wolfe 1992: 312), which means that we have to gain a historically grounded understanding of the function of specific boundaries and to identify those kinds that are being used as a basis for discrimination and against which we should fight. Wolfe's liberal guidelines to the dilemma of boundaries involve respecting those that are not imposed by power-holders as well as those that are the product of a "moral passage" (1992: 320), that is, of an informed choice taken after considering options. The problem of such a position is that it assumes that subjects are "rational," equal and equally informed about reasonably equal options. In reality, groups on either side of the border are not "equal," various degrees of "imposition" go into the social construction of specific borders, and real "border crossings" on an equal basis on both sides are rare (hooks 1994a: 5–6, 1994b: 131).

Wolfe sees social differentiation as a continuous process evolving from the pre-modern societies of "mechanical solidarity" to the post-modern societies that strive to "abolish" all boundaries, and he recoils from both extremes. He is rather in favour of striking a balance between "inclusion" of all citizens (or "the principle of democracy") and "exclusion" (or "the basic social and sociological principle of boundaries"). Recognizing the complexity of the issues, he expresses caution before any mechanistic formula of balance and suggests that the meta principles guiding how we resolve the polarity between "democracy" and "sociology" be determined "by the specific kinds of moral controversies with which we are confronted" (Wolfe 1992: 323).

Focusing on the concrete expression of the same problem on the level of law and social organization, Oommen (1995) identifies as the greatest challenge of contemporary society that of balancing (individual) equality, identity and pluralism. Contesting boundaries is a prerequisite to equality; yet it erodes identity and, consequently, cultural heterogeneity. Oommen offers a generic blueprint as to how to achieve such a balance, on the "world society" level only, by distinguishing between, on the one hand, the utopian ideal of certain universal political rights, which should be guaranteed to the citizens of a "world society", ("equality of opportunity, accessibility to justice and institutionalization of democracy and human rights") and, on the other hand, "specificities of particular societies and civilizations" that originate in the geographic, historical, cultural, political and economic conditions which should also be protected (1995: 266–67). The challenge of concretely balancing individual versus group rights, which is the challenge of democratic inclusion versus social exclusion in complex, heterogeneous and democratic societies, is however far greater, as the whole debate on multiculturalism attests.

Both Wolfe's (1992) liberal "solution" to the dilemma of boundaries ("democratic inclusion versus sociological exclusion") and Oommen's (1995) broad blueprint make no attempt to overcome the polarity of inclusion/exclusion. Henry Giroux's (1991a) post-modernist position, on the other hand, strives to overcome that very dualism. For Giroux, post-modernism aims at "abolishing" borders by acknowledging that their shifting character proves that they are constructed and by making space in society for oppositional and submerged voices and practices and, therefore, allowing "a series of referents for rethinking how we are constituted as subjects within a rapidly changing set of political, social, and cultural conditions" (1991a: 233). Like Laclau and Mouffé's vision of "radical democracy" (1985; Mouffé 1988), and in the tradition of African American feminist writers, Giroux articulates a vision of "a radical democratic culture and society" (1991a: 240, 1993: 80–81) that preserves multiple but flexible borders, in the sense of reaching out and positively appreciating differences (Lorde 1984: 111-12) as well as striking alliances among individuals or groups in a "politics of solidarity forged through diverse public spheres" (Giroux 1992b: 32).

bell hooks fleshes out the implications for individuals of such a radical "solution" to the dilemma of borders in her theory of "marginality as a site of choice" (1990: 150). Starting from an acknowledgment that borders, stemming from and contributing to inequalities, do exist, while contesting such inequalities, bell hooks conceptualizes the "margin" as "a site of radical openness," a "site of resistance," "a central location for the production of a counter-hegemonic discourse" (1990: 148–53).[4] Choosing to be "on the margin" enables the subject to "cross the border" and to see reality "from the outside in and from the inside out" (hooks 1990: 149); it provides the subject with "a mode of seeing" and way of understanding unknown to those positioned at the institutional centres of power. Since "the border crosser is both 'self' and 'other'" on both sides of the border (Hicks 1988: 52; Verdecchia 1993; Kamboureli 1993), living on the border and acquiring the consciousness of borderlands (what Gloria Anzaldua [1987] terms a "mestiza consciousness") means possessing "contradictory knowledges that cut across dualistic thinking" (Anzaldua 1987; Mohanty 1991).

Choosing to be on the "margin" is predicated on an ongoing critical consciousness of the self as "other" on both sides of the border and of the constructed character of the border; at the same time, choosing to be on the margin is a prerequisite for challenging and deconstructing the border (hooks 1990: 149–50). All we hope to achieve is to eliminate the inequalities and shake loose the exclusions of the border, but we "do not need to wipe out the Otherness in order to experience a notion of Oneness" (hooks 1994a: 234). bell hooks' message is that we can find ourselves in the other, because of our differences. At the same time, we can only see and appreciate the "other" if we have learned to recognize and embrace otherness within ourselves. For society as a whole, real "border crossings" should enable sharing of resources and a "culture of communalism and mutuality" (hooks 1994a: 6).

Classroom Borders: The Challenges of Critical, Feminist and Anti-Racist Pedagogy

I would like to turn next to one particular site of multiple and intersecting borders—the classroom—and to examine some of the most important borders and intersections there. I will focus on the power relations across various types of borders, the lived experiences of those on the less privileged site of the border and the challenges and dilemmas of efforts to transcend borders through "liberatory" pedagogical practice. Building on bell hooks' (1994b) notion of critical pedagogy as "teaching to transgress"[5] and Henry Giroux's notion of "radical educational theory and practice" as "border pedagogy" or "forms of transgression that challenge knowledge and social relations structured in dominance" (1992b: 22, 169–70), in this section, I conceptualize a critical, feminist and anti-racist pedagogy as an attempt at genuine border crossings and at the creation of alternative public spaces, and I attempt to unpack various types of social, political, cultural and epistemological borders in education and discuss their challenges through a critical review of the literature on educational theory and narratives of educational practice.

Toward a Vision of an Alternative Classroom

I am starting from the assumption that classrooms are political and cultural sites "that represent accommodations and contestations over knowledge by differently empowered social constituencies" (Mohanty 1990: 183). They are microcosms that mirror but also reconstruct the divisions, inequalities and struggles of the outside society. In the "traditional" classroom, what Paulo Freire calls "the banking system of education" (1972: 58–59, 149), power hierarchies are left unchallenged and "disruptions" of the status quo (institutional, class, gender and ethnicity/race-based) are minimal. Even the "disruptions" of the liberal classroom are not seriously threatening. As Chandra Talpade Mohanty has shown, in the multicultural, liberal classroom, where lip service is paid to diversity,[6] histories of dominance are being individualized and "coagulated into frozen, binary, psychologistic positions" by uncritically accepting "experience" (1990: 195).

In contrast to traditional liberal curricula and pedagogical methods, critical, feminist and anti-racist pedagogies purport to "disrupt" the canon of the academy to bring about social change (hooks 1994b; Giroux 1992b; Mohanty 1990). Such pedagogies highlight "subjugated knowledges" (Foucault 1972: 81–82) and "alternative histories" (Mohanty 1990: 185), as well as ways of knowing that have traditionally been invalidated, for example, experiential knowing or knowing arising from socially marginalized positions (Giroux 1992b; hooks 1994b; Mohanty 1990; Dei 1993; Manicom 1992; Higginbotham 1990). The objective here is to enable students to shift from being passive receivers of knowledge to becoming actively engaged in the dynamic process of learning, where they are "actively transforming knowledges" (Mohanty 1990: 192), and in the process change themselves (hooks 1994b: 202). Furthermore, the purpose of a critical or a "liberatory border pedagogy" is political (Giroux 1993: 79, 1991a: 245–46) and emancipatory. By challenging knowledge and social relations structured in dominance, "educational struggles [are connected] with broader struggles for the democratization, pluralization and reconstruction of public life" (Giroux 1992b: 22, 1993: 81).

According to some writers, there is a distinction between "critical" and "feminist" pedagogies, with the critical ones emphasizing more "the collective analysis of oppression" and the feminist ones focusing on personal feelings and experiences" (Maher 1987, cited in Sleeter 1991: 20-21). While this point is debatable, I am arguing here for a pedagogy that is critical and feminist and anti-racist. Combining ideas from all three liberatory pedagogies, such a pedagogy starts from the experiences of marginalized groups and aims at developing a collective, "integrative" analysis of oppression(s) (Dei 1993 and 1995b; Calliste et al.[7] 1995). Furthermore, it strives to make the links between experiences of oppression and the interlocking, oppressive structures of race, ethnicity, class, gender and sexuality (Ellsworth 1989; Giroux 1991a, 1992b). Finally, the purpose of a critical, feminist and anti-racist pedagogical practice is activist (Giroux and McLaren 1986: 213–38; Giroux 1992b: 22, 1993: 81; Dei 1993: 38; Briskin 1990: 20, Manicom 1992: 367) and geared especially toward the development of a "multi-centred politics" for social change (Miles 1996). The critical pedagogical aspect in particular calls for "a politics that reasserts the primacy of the social, incorporates multiple struggles, builds alliances and recaptures the concept of solidarity" (Giroux 1993: 78).

An additional element of a "liberatory border pedagogy" that merits special emphasis is best captured by what bell hooks (1994b) terms "engaged teaching." An "engaged teacher" is actively, critically and self-reflexively "engaged" in the process of learning by grappling with difference as a basic condition for understanding oneself and others. Such an educator is in the process of becoming a "self-actualized" person. From such a state of mindfulness one can be always "present" and thus aware of the classroom's fluid dynamics (hooks 1994b: 86, 167). Furthermore, the pedagogical practices of engaged teaching also enable students to become self-actualized individuals; through providing the students with new ways of knowing, engaged teachers "enhance their capacity to live fully and deeply" (hooks 1994b: 22).[8]

What are the specific practices of an alternative classroom in which a liberatory border pedagogy is practised? According to Giroux, such a classroom is (or should be) a borderland (1992b: 28). Educators and students become "border crossers," "moving in and out of borders constructed around coordinates of difference and power" (Giroux 1991a: 248, 1992b: 22, 29, 169, 1993: 78). A liberatory "border pedagogy," as a "decentring" of "dominant configurations of power and knowledge" (Giroux 1991a: 246), involves certain pedagogical conditions and/or outcomes. First, it enables students to engage multiple cultural and experiential references, including their own, and to treat them as socially and historically constructed. Second, there is a central concern in the classroom for understanding how all learners are affectively invested in the "master-narratives of domination" (Giroux 1991a: 247, 249–51, 1992b: 29, 32). Third, educators strive to challenge authority while, at the same time, they insist on relations of authority[9] that allow as many voices as possible to speak (Giroux 1991a: 252), particularly voices that are dissenting.[10] This strategy also requires a critical questioning of the omissions of the "master narratives"—"the discourse of singular generics" (Traweek 1992: 446)—that make up the official curriculum (Giroux 1992b: 33). Fourth, educators analyzed racism[11] not only in structural terms but also in its multiple, historically specific and everyday-life manifestations. Anti-racist pedagogy arises out of specific settings and can be only a situated political practice (Giroux 1991a: 252; Ellsworth 1989: 308). Fifth, educators understand how socio-cultural realities outside the classroom produce "the multiple and contradictory subject positions" that students express inside the classroom (Giroux 1991a: 253). Finally, educators are (or must be) aware both of how their own narratives are affected by their location and of the need to open these narratives to ongoing debate (Giroux 1991a: 253–54, 1992b: 34–36).

Classroom Borders and the Challenges of a Critical, Feminist and Anti-Racist Pedagogy

We will move into our exploration of specific borders with the first major "border," which is the gender border erected around the male/female sexual coordinate and carried over to the classroom as male and female students enact their society's gendered subjectivities built on the basis of unequal power relations. Such a border presents special challenges to the critical, feminist and anti-racist educator. The first and direct form of challenge is the general male resistance to feminism. Less expected and more insidious challenges are posed by female students who resist speaking out in the classroom and may even assume nurturing and protective attitudes toward the male students, whose "feelings" may have been "hurt" by the material presented. What are the bases of such "resistances"? It is well-known cultural knowledge that women who speak "too loudly" or are "too present" (Griffin 1981, cited in Lewis 1990: 481) end up being alone. Within the terms of patriarchy, women have had no choice but to care about the "feelings" of men on whose approval and well-being women's self-esteem and livelihood may depend (Lewis 1990: 474–82). Furthermore, sexuality is an organizing principle of the mixed-gender classroom, deeply affecting how young men and women come together in the process of learning. At the same time, compulsory heterosexuality remains a salient systemic feature constructing heterosexual attractiveness. For these reasons, female students may not feel "safe" in giving voice to their experiences even, and perhaps especially, in the classroom where they are invited to do so.

The pedagogical dilemmas we are faced with here, as Magda Lewis (1990) succinctly articulates, are how to engage female students caught up in the double bind between needing to speak and to remain silent at the same time, and how to speak to men about male domination effectively, making possible a measure of change that would in turn render the classroom a safer place for different voices. Words must be chosen carefully and analyses negotiated step by step. Lewis urges the treatment of "women's resistance to feminism as an active discourse of struggle derived from a complex set of meanings in which women's practices are invested" (1990: 486).

Another major border in the classroom is that of race/ethnicity. Racial and ethnic/cultural minority students are not necessarily the "natural allies" of the critical, feminist and anti-racist educator and may systematically resist efforts at "border crossings" by being silent or by speaking an "encoded speech" (Ellsworth 1989: 313). Such students will not "talk back" (hooks 1988: 8) about their experiences of oppression inside and outside the classroom because they, too, do not perceive the classroom as a "safe" environment in which to do so.[12] Even the feminist and anti-racist classrooms are not necessarily united on the side of the "oppressed" because the "oppressed" are many and too fragmented. Participants occupy multiple and contradictory subject positions among their classmates and within themselves. Because of such positions, participants/subjects have different experiences of, and perspectives on, racism, sexism, classism and other forms of oppression. Students assess, consciously or subconsciously, the risks of disclosing their understandings of themselves and of others in the specific circumstances (Ellsworth 1989: 313–16). Elizabeth Ellsworth articulates the pedagogical dilemma in asking by what practices, in class and perhaps outside, can the dominant discourse be disrupted, so that the class does not actually reproduce the existing power relations and so that alternative and oppositional voices can genuinely be heard (1989: 314–24).

It is in the same context of lived experience of racial/ethnic inequality inside and outside the classroom that minority students, to the extent that they are willing to speak out, make two kinds of "essentialist" arguments from their own experiences of oppression: first, "I know because of who I am as a racialized (and/or gendered) subject"; and second, "I speak in the name of the group (race/ethnicity/culture/gender and intersections thereof) of which I am a member." From where do such arguments stem, what are their inherent risks and dilemmas from the point of view of critical pedagogy, and what are the critical pedagogical strategies necessary to effectively deal with identity politics?

Although the first type of argument may be a "reality check" or a "survival tactic" to counteract "normalized" mainstream discourse (hooks 1994b: 83; Ellsworth 1989: 317, 302), it poses distinct risks or traps. The first trap, the liberal[13] trap, posits that everybody is entitled to naming their experiences and that all experiences are equally valid and should be allocated equal space in the classroom. Problems of such pedagogical practice include "an attitudinal engagement with diversity that encourages an empty cultural pluralism and domesticates the historical agency of Third World peoples" (Mohanty 1990: 191), and the trivialization of difference (Yudice 1988). The second trap, the conservative trap, posits that the minority experience has to be "rationally debated" and evaluated on the basis of the validity claims of mainstream group "knowledge." The problem of a pedagogical practice that falls into such a trap is that it forgets that the mainstream discourse is also a partial narrative, which has, however, become "naturalized" and hegemonic and has the luxury of advocating "rational debate" for that very reason (Ellsworth 1989: 305). The task and challenge for a "liberatory border pedagogy" here is to devise appropriate strategies that will help the students to understand "experience" and "difference" in historical and social rather than individual terms and to critically examine the production of individual "experience" by historical structures of domination (Mohanty 1990: 194–96, 199; Giroux 1992b: 170).

The second kind of "essentialist" argument ("I speak in the name of the group of which I am a member") has its origins in the sense of empowerment which group membership provides the individual. Both minorities and majorities speak in the name of respective groups (Ellsworth 1989: 318). The difference in the terms of their talk lies with the fact that the majority does not need to invoke its own group; it simply speaks as "we" or in impersonal terms implying "humanity" as the subject. Such difference reflects the majority's hegemony and the subjugation of minority groups. Minorities more often explicitly invoke the group they "represent," so that they do not appear as isolated atoms in the universalist mainstream discourse. In these days of multicultural education such invocations are no longer necessary. Minorities are "nativized," constructed as "native informants" (hooks 1994b: 44) in the anthropological sense, that is as representatives of "cultures" and "races." The risk of such construction, besides the obvious stereotyping and ghettoizing of individuals, is that it resorts to reductionism; entire cultural histories are collapsed to individual experiences. Although the latter are organized and shaped by historical group experiences, specific individuals partake in too many groups and therefore occupy unique locations, so that we cannot consider their experiences to be identical with those of any particular group. In addition, as even Marx himself knew only too well, social–historical position does not mechanistically lead to one kind of individual politics. Reductionism is not only a cognitive problem of logic; it has political implications as well. Here, it results in a "depoliticization and dehistoricization of the idea of culture and makes possible the implicit management of race in the name of cooperation and harmony" (Mohanty 1990: 195).

A third important border is that which is created between (and among) students in the classroom and the institutionalized authority of the academy, represented in the classroom by the "canon" of academic knowledge (content, teaching practices). Such a canon is political *par excellence*, in the sense of legitimating particular ways of life, as Gayatri Spivak has pointed out (Giroux 1992b: 89–90). In the critical feminist and anti-racist classroom, the authority of the academic canon is subverted by the educator who, although occupying the position of institutionalized power, at the same time tries to alter the rules of the game. What are the students' reactions under such circumstances? As the students are divided along gender, race, ethnicity, class and perhaps other lines, their reactions are mixed and contradictory. On the one hand, some students may "resist" the academic canon and institutionalized authority (Giroux 1983: 107–11), (which are the power structures that marginalize them as subjects) through practices that reaffirm their subjectivities. Critical pedagogy emphasizes that student "resistance" to institutionalized education "is forged from the contradictions they perceive between the dominant discourse of school knowledge on the one hand and their own lived experiences of subordination on the other" (Lewis 1990: 471). In such a case, the critical educator may find a very receptive ground "for teaching to transgress," though the mere fact that s/he teaches "to transgress" does not bring her/him into the same camp with the "resisting" students (see below). Nor does the fact that s/he is in the same camp with the students necessarily mean critical thinking on the part of the students, who may be slavishly adopting alternative approaches as the new orthodoxy, identified with the teacher as a figure of power.

On the other hand, students may resist when the content of the curriculum and the methods of teaching are different from the canon, when the philosophy and the practice of teaching is "to transgress." Some students may resist curriculum that challenges the status quo, be it political, economic or cultural, because they identify with the latter (Solomon 1995: 59). bell hooks (1994b: 32) talks, for instance, about "the sheer terror that inspires in classrooms any de-centring of Western civilization." Even when students do not identify with the status quo, they may still resist curriculum that makes them feel uncomfortable because they reflect on their own particular forms of oppression. Other students may perceive the alternative curriculum chosen by the instructor as "arbitrary," reflecting the instructor's subjective choices and priorities and increasing her/his power. Finally, students may resist the insecurity of "unorthodox" teaching methods, especially the volatility and unpredictability of the classroom dynamics, the relentless questioning of issues, the oppositional voices and the teacher's passion (Hoodfar 1992: 312; Schuster and Van Dyne 1985: 162, 170; hooks 1994b: 40). On a more utilitarian note, some students may resist critical feminist and anti-racist pedagogies because they perceive them as yet another imposition on their limited time, which may be of essence for students who want to graduate and get jobs. Willingness or ability to study critically here becomes a class issue as well (Hoodfar 1992: 310).

One of the most complex border "intersections" is the classroom of the female, cultural or racial minority instructor.[14] Such an instructor stands on the privileged side of the institutional power divide but on a less privileged location than a gendered and racialized subject. It is well documented (Ng 1994; Hoodfar 1992) how students (male and female, White mainstream and cultural or racial minorities[15]) resist the authority of such an instructor. The female, cultural minority instructor cannot lay claim to the authority of the teacher in the same way that a White female instructor does or that White males usually do (Hoodfar 1992: 310). The knowledge she transmits is suspect, tainted by her specific "interest group" position (Ng 1994: 41–46; Ashrawi 1995: 28–30). Moreover, if she experiments with a different pedagogy, she is seen as lacking experience in controlling a class or as someone too lazy to deliver conventional lectures. The pedagogical dilemma here might be as follows: By what practices does the teacher claim a space of her own in the classroom and reassert part of her alienated authority without shutting out any social oppositional groups and without relinquishing her own unique cultural identity, which is necessary if she is truly to become "self-actualized" (hooks 1994b; Hoodfar 1992: 314)?

The last type of "border" that I will deal with is that between the classroom and the outside world, a highly permeable one where larger institutional structures of domination affect, control and "resist" what happens in the classroom in the best spirit of "engaged pedagogy." The institutional structures in place differ, naturally, by educational institution, and they mirror differences in the geographic, economic, cultural and social milieu where the institutions are located. Such an institutional and social "environment of resistance" is felt as a "chilly climate"; a political environment of backlash against feminism[16] and multiculturalism; a climate of inadequate resources for education, misallocation of existing ones and redefinition of higher education in ways that promote corporate agendas (Newson and Buchbinder 1988). It is ultimately an environment of limited space for alternative voices and democratic participation in education (Reyes and Halcon 1988; Mukherjee 1994: 201–07), of lack of institutional support for change (Smith 1987a; Ng 1994), and of "friendly fascism" of claustrophobic and formally homogeneous societies that are friendly toward minorities as long as the latter do not act in ways and occupy positions seen as contradictory to the very stereotypes that minorities embody. The first major critical pedagogical task and challenge here for "border crossings" is to devise teaching strategies that exemplify how what is happening in the classroom and the university is in fact a product of larger social forces operating outside of it. The second major pedagogical task is to broaden the relationship of the university with public life by encouraging the establishment of new forms of public association by academics who are "informed by and contributing to moral and political commitments" (Giroux 1992b: 106) toward social justice and genuine democratic pluralism.

Toward Mapping the Unknowable

The following is an attempt toward understanding the "limit situations" (or borders) of this writer's pedagogical "generative themes" and practices with the purpose of illuminating their socially constructed character and thereby "overcoming" them (i.e., border crossing) through "conscientization" (Freire 1972: 86–96). Such "limit situations" are systemic in nature, and, as an individual, I have little direct effect on them. I can have an effect, however, on the constitution of such "limit situations" (or borders) in consciousness through conscientization. More specifically, in this section I locate my pedagogical themes and practices into what Sue Middleton calls a contextualized "educational life history" (1993: 12, 30, 62), that is, I ground them within the biographical, historical and cultural circumstances that have made them possible. My pedagogical themes are about various types of boundaries (class, gender, ethnicity and race) and the challenges and possibilities of egalitarian border crossings. The pedagogical practices that I consequently—and consciously—engage, strive to implement in the classroom the content of my teaching, which is critical, feminist and anti-racist pedagogy.

In terms of the format of this section, I illustrate and analyze first the challenges/borders (i.e., "limit situations") of selected pedagogical "moments." The challenges of those "moments" have to do with their pedagogical themes and with my attempts to implement a critical, feminist and anti-racist pedagogy while constructed not as an individual but as a generalized and stereotyped female instructor and a cultural "other" in an institutional, social and historical context that is officially welcoming of difference but in reality ethnocentric and suspicious in the best of circumstances. I weave the narratives of such "moments" with narratives from my educational life history—the biographical, historical, cultural and cross-cultural circumstances—that generated the moments, or at least my share in their making, that is the part of the classroom political dynamics that may be "knowable" (Ellsworth 1989).

Pedagogical Practice

The Battle of Meritocracy

The first pedagogical "moment" derives from my experience gathered in my few years of teaching in a senior-level seminar on Gender, Ethnicity and Migration at a Maritime university. The seminar aims at understanding the connections between and among class discrimination, racism and sexism in the migration, settlement and integration/ethnic formation processes in the context of Canadian capitalist state development. Starting from the lived experiences of immigrant, ethnic, visible minority and Aboriginal women and men in those processes and within specific areas of social life, the course investigates the social organization of such experiences by focusing on the larger "relations of ruling" (Smith 1987b). One of the first issues raised by the students is affirmative action, mostly misconstrued as preferential hiring. Student arguments usually run as follows: "Quotas are a form of reverse discrimination" (the "two-wrongs-cannot-make-a-right" argument); "I understand that historically there has been discrimination against minorities and women, yet at this point in history things have been reversed and I—White, male student—despite my superior qualifications, cannot get a job. It is a bad time for White males" (the myth of equity having gone too far); "The important thing in hiring should be who can do the job best, not who has historically been discriminated against" (the myth of meritocracy).

Although this is a mixed-gender class, the students voicing such arguments are mostly White, working-class males.[17] Such students often find themselves in my course by necessity in order to graduate, secure employment—preferably with the Royal Canadian Mounted Police or the fire department—and start repaying their student loans. Some of these young men may already have been rejected in their search for employment, while others simply feel threatened. Thus, they come to my class carrying beliefs fuelled by vested interest, personal experience and emotions for which I, the instructor, serve as the catalyst. In the classroom they are faced not only with a theoretical confrontation to their experiential beliefs but with the very embodiment of what they perceive as threatening their social mobility: a female, cultural minority instructor, who is the likely product of affirmative action herself. Although I understand their anger as grounded in the historically high levels of unemployment and migration in Maritime working-class communities and in the fact that affirmative action programs do not specifically address class inequities, I am faced with an explosive situation in the classroom, which I struggle to transform into a critical learning environment. Little "rational" discussion can take place. Statistics about the "success" of minorities seem to be meaningless. "Group rights" and "equity" are outlandish notions in the dominant individualistic ideology of the "free" market, where people are supposed to be rewarded according to the effort they put into acquiring necessary skills and according to their native talent as proven through fair competition.

What would egalitarian border crossings look like under these circumstances? I have taken several paths in struggling to redefine the situation and to take action in class while allowing for respect, ownership and yet critical engagement with "experience" and enlarging the oppositional space. Outcomes have been of varying success, often involving trade-offs. Yet, I believe that a more effective alternative classroom necessitates first a better ad hoc balancing of the following strategies.

> a) The *deus ex machina* strategy. Teacher "authority" is invoked to end a discussion that excludes and "interrupts" relations and ideologies of domination (Manicom 1992; Lather 1991). Another aspect of the same strategy involves assuming the impersonal teacher style and presenting the experience of ethnic minorities as a matter of fact without mentioning personal experience. The outcome of this particular aspect of the *deus ex machina* strategy is, I feel, like a double negation, first, of the students' agency and, secondly, of my own.
> b) The "post-modernist" strategy of "equal" narratives. Students vent their feelings, while I encourage as many voices as possible without privileging any and censor myself so that I am not perceived as "biased."
> c) "Community alliance" strategy. Guest speakers from the ethnic communities expand and strengthen the oppositional space in the classroom.
> d) Field projects in the ethnic communities. Students have direct, personal contact with members of ethnic communities, which helps to lower stereotypes, though it does not prevent a certain degree of exoticization with racist overtones (as does strategy c).

In addition, a more effective alternative classroom would necessitate modification of some of the above strategies. First, a better implementation of a "politics of solidarity" in this instance would involve not only a "community alliance" strategy but an ad hoc alliance of various "other" marginalized voices in the classroom into a "culture of dissent" (Mohanty 1990). A precondition for this alliance, however, would be to ensure that such voices are nurtured and heard in the first place (especially those of the mostly silent female students). The challenge here would be empowering the "other" students while acknowledging the male students' voices (without validating the sexism and racism of their positions). A possible strategy is to define the range of debate from the beginning of the course through explicit "working assumptions" (Tatum 1992) and "ground rules" (Cannon 1990) for discussion (that is, confidentiality, respect, listening and speaking from one's own experience).

Finally, the post-modernist strategy of equal narratives should be redefined in the sense of Giroux's post-modern critical pedagogy, insisting on placing "experience" in social and historical context and on the politics of solidarity. A more effective implementation of critical pedagogy in this specific instance would be to guide students in seeing how traditional hiring practices and workplace environments have been designed with the skills and needs of a very particular (e.g. White, male) worker in mind. Discussions about the historical basis of this arrangement, as well as the contemporary impact on local communities, might also be useful in bringing students to an understanding of the relevance as well as the problems of affirmative action. The goal and challenge here would be to get working-class males to understand how allying themselves with people of colour, immigrant and women workers might transform work environments and create better work opportunities for them as well (Bell et al. 1996).

The Old New War of the Sexes (Anti-Feminist Backlash) or the Violence of "Family Violence"

My second pedagogical "moment" derives from teaching a large, elective, undergraduate course on the Sociology of Kinship and the Family. This year-long course was taught from an integrated feminist and anti-racist perspective, with a major unit focusing on violence against women in the family. The following two vignettes have been excerpted from my edited after-class notes.

> (a) Instructor's statement in teaching on violence in the family: "Three in ten women have experienced at least one incident of physical or sexual violence at the hands of a marital partner, according to Stats Canada national survey on Violence against Women."
> Student's question: "Are you saying that three in every ten of us will be beating up or will sexually abuse our women?" (sic)
>
> (b) Instructor's statement: "The vast majority of homicide victims murdered in a family context are women. The majority of 'violence in the family' is directed against women."
> Student's question: "Are you saying that the majority of us are violent?"

Leaving aside the (unintentional? mis)reading of statistics, I want to comment on the attitude I sensed behind the question and on the classroom dynamics in this situation where the (White) male canon was ostensibly offended. First, the attitude was defensive; the student personalized the general statement and then attempted to clear his reputation as a male. Second, he did so in a manner that challenged my position by "daring" me to repeat his statement with him (or the class) as subject(s), so that I could be subsequently confronted by the collective outrage of all the White male and female students in the classroom. Third, he was confrontational and attempted to discredit my knowledge (implying that "things have changed" and I simply am not well informed and up-to-date with the modern world) and subvert my authority by making me sound beyond any doubt "biased" (other male students repeated variations of these questions subsequently).

What is even more noteworthy here is the female students' reaction or lack thereof. Some displayed a nurturing attitude toward the hurt male egos. They attempted to "rescue" the men, by stating that the men whom they knew (fathers, siblings, boyfriends) were clearly different. Personal experience, though valid as such, was interpreted in an individualistic way, devoid of critical analysis, understandably validating their current efforts and expectations. The majority of such students seemed to believe that they themselves would escape the fate of "those" women (the "victims") due to their education, intelligence and self-confidence, implying, if not openly stating, that battered women are pathological cases. Finally, mature female students were more understanding and progressive; yet they often displayed an attitude of resignation ("Why bother?", "These are kids; we know better.").

An effective critical pedagogical practice here for egalitarian border crossings to take place is an ad hoc, skillful and delicate balancing act of messages, strategies and techniques, which I learn gradually by trial and error and, often, *a posteriori*. It consists of talking about the horrors of violence against women in the family without diluting the facts and without having to relinquish one's own gendered identity (and so speak as a fictional, generic "human"); of encouraging students to speak from experience; of re-affirming that experience; of assisting students to integrate it with a theoretical understanding of its social and historical context; and of providing a safe and nurturing atmosphere for multiple voices and the critical assessment of everybody's experience. An effective critical pedagogy involves talking about the role of violence in maintaining patriarchal systems and yet not imposing "victim" notions that disempower female students and provoke anger in male students, causing the female students to come to their rescue. Finally, it consists of talking about the systemic character of violence as well as resistance and individual agency but without imposing "liberating" ideas, since any imposition, any forcing of others to jump to our hard-won experiential knowledge and analysis, has the effect of stunting the slow, unique, individual process of developing the critical agency of all students in the classroom.

Toward an Educational Life History

Since systemic obstacles and borders have been tackled in detail earlier in this paper, the remainder of this section focuses on shedding light on the instructor's share in the very making of these "moments," that is on the part of classroom political dynamics that may be "knowable," in an attempt to map the pedagogical terrain for the future. This is accomplished by selecting narratives from the instructor's "educational life history"[18] and attempting to place in biographical, historical and cultural context the above storied pedagogical "moments." In terms of style, I weave my analysis with chronologically and thematically diverse entries, written in a stream-of-consciousness way to capture the rhythms and disruptions of a contextualized "educational life history" (a technique borrowed from Middleton 1993).

A Formalistic Education in Individualistic Capitalist Patriarchy

> Athens, Greece, Fall 1976: First day for the incoming Law School, Section of Law, class of about 800 students. Well-groomed, proud of their success in the highly competitive, state-wide entrance exams, humbled by the weight of history of this University and overwhelmed by their families' expectations and the meaning of University education—tightly knit with survival—of this culture. Lectures of the first day are in Political Economy, Philosophy of Law and Roman Law.... The curriculum is fixed and everybody has the same heavy schedule every day.... I have no sense of personal connection to the material and neither can I make any connections with anything I learned in high-school (except, perhaps, some Latin terms).... I know practically no one else and I am, like everybody else, trying to frantically take notes of everything. During lectures, there is a sense of ceremony and slow movement like the re-enactment of a ritual that thousands of others have also partaken of before; everybody stands in awe listening to the vernacular (male) names and the ultimate legal truths, clapping their hands in the end of the lecture; no questions asked (I do not know what I am supposed to know already and what is legitimate to ask about). In the days that follow, the daring few who raise their hands are given the treatment that dissuades the masses from repeating their *faux pas*.... Students who talk in public do so as representatives of political student organizations and carry behind them the clout of such organizations.... There is of course the other side of formal University culture, that I immediately sense; the grafitti on the corridor and outside walls, the lively political debates in the tiny cafes around the University, filled with smoke, the leaflets and student newspapers, overall too much to process from the perspective of an incoming student overwhelmed with the sheer volume of material to go through and remember and the formal culture of the University.

My immediate meta-lessons of my law school experience were consolidating a schooling in formalistic education, as described above, and individualistic work ethos; sanctioning the drive to "succeed" professionally as indicated through excellent marks in formal examinations; and entrenching a gut-level knowing and recognition of professional and gender hierarchy and deference.

The political processing of these lessons, rejection and dialectical transformation into liberatory pedagogical themes and practices has been a struggle ever since. More specifically, the necessity for the educator to acknowledge where students are, intellectually and emotionally, before s/he starts building bridges to the "new,"[19] the need of students to ask questions and have the intellectual space to reformulate what they are taught, the need for everyone to start from personal experience, the freedom to deconstruct authority and the willingness to acknowledge complicity in constructing power relations, I would only derive several years later after the "culture shock" experienced from living and receiving a formal education in North America, described below.

Encountering the "Other" and the Beginnings of a Long "Epoché"

> Boston, Massachusetts, Fall 1981: There are fewer than a hundred continuing students in the three graduate programs in Sociology here, about eight entering students, including two international students on scholarships. Professors and graduate students seem to know one another quite well, are dressed casually and actually TALK like old friends. I reluctantly share the limelight with the other international (Japanese) male student and I have difficulty talking to anyone.... I do not have questions about anything in particular, because everything is so foreign to me. Everyone is disturbingly helpful and suspiciously friendly, urging me to ask questions and I have no clue what I can legitimately ask about.... I am advised to talk to my professors before making any course decisions and I do it ritually. I register for the courses of those instructors who make me feel more at ease ... and do not even dream of dropping any, despite the alienation from total lack of context I feel (I was able to figure out the context for some of these courses many years later).... I have trouble crossing the distance of culture, educational/social status, and age and addressing my profs by first name.... I consciously bring myself to but often fall back into what comes naturally to me, i.e., "Professor X." I have trouble remembering my classmates' first names since I am not used to addressing people by first name. I read about "culture shock" and, reluctantly, I decide I have one, but I begin to suspect its true dimensions after I have started naming the cultural practices of my country of origin as such and not as my own human nature. In fact, it has taken me about three migrations, more than a decade of traveling every year back and forth, many hours of anthropologically observing the reactions of numerous North American friends visiting with me in Greece, and numerous symbolic "border crossings" to do so.

Encountering the cultural "other" in Boston started for me a slow process of learning to move beyond the cultural differences toward discovering the common humanity. During that process, and as I was identifying the other, I started identifying myself and my own practices as cultural practices. I also learned not to pass quick judgment but to give the benefit of the doubt and always search for the connection between human actions and social environments. These lessons translated into a sensitivity toward, and fascination with, the relationship between human agency and social structure; different cultures and the different human beings they help produce; how difference itself is defined and constructed within various cultures and societies, including the role of power relations in such construction; what the implications of marginality for individuals and societies are; how difference can be transcended; and the stimulating challenges and bittersweet rewards of cultural, political and pedagogical border crossings.

Crossing the Boundaries of Legal Formalism and Starting with the Lives of Real People: An Epistemological and Educational System Shift

> A term paper on rural women in Greece that I undertake to write becomes an investigation of the legal framework of rural wives and women in Greece. My female (consciously chosen as a role model) supervisor comments on it: "OK, but what is women's real life like?" Comment lingers for a long while in a disturbing way: I was unable to undo the semi-permanent damage of learning to operate from a legal framework and reducing reality to legal texts. Neither did I want to let go of my hard-won legal, formalistic frame of mind, with an immense yet flat grasp of ill-connected, unquestionable "facts," the proud success of all my prior education. It was with deep sadness when I realized I had to and struggled for a long time with the uncertainties of the alternative ... (which translated into the very real practical problems of neither being "given" a curriculum, nor research questions, and ultimately being "left alone" in the States amidst plenty of exciting "options," in a manner much more terrifying than in Athens). This is not denying the pleasures of critical learning and thinking, choosing issues that are relevant, creatively synthesizing across domains of knowledge ("divergent production" as opposed to "convergent thinking"[20]) bringing experience in, going for depth rather than breadth.... It is merely pointing out the difficulties of any "unlearning," especially of ways of thinking and forms of knowledge that one has mastered to perfection. One has to be constantly alert to a possible— even subconscious—slip.

It took me an even longer while to realize that such "unlearning" is not really about "forgetting" but about learning more; that the "system" of which I had become so critical during my graduate school years (top-down, valuing a broad range of knowledge fields but at the expense of deeper connections) may have just been the caricature of educational principles that should not really be evaluated on the basis of their distortions; that in reality I had experienced and was taught two different learning styles, which were both equally capable of distortion (and I got a sense of what the other "system's" applied, market-tailored distortions may look like later on in my teaching experience in Canadian institutions of higher learning). Both "systems" and respective "mindscapes" are inscribed in me and have been struggling toward a balance in my teaching practice. Having lived on both sides of this epistemological border—as well as of the cultural one—has been essential in critically assessing them and has provided me with a new appreciation for the satisfaction and challenge of so delicate an undertaking.

On Strategy: Grappling with the Imposition of "Rescue"

> Toronto, Canada, Fall 1990: I sit in this crowded seminar on Feminist Aesthetics and Pedagogy and feel very conscious of the space that I am taking. I have just finished my Ph.D. and I am trying to heal from the process by immersing myself in a private dialogue with feminist texts which I have recently discovered. I speak little in class and, being in the amphibian status of a visiting scholar, I make few contacts with either graduate students or faculty. Everybody asks me where I am "visiting" from, a normal question to ask a "visiting scholar," but not someone who is settled in the city of the institution "visited".... In one of the last meetings, a student who is also a published poet and whom I have come to like for her "disruptions," verbally assaults the instructor, accusing her of the very elitism, classism and racism that the class had been so critical of throughout the semester. As examples she cites "those voices that were hardly ever heard in the classroom." I have a vague sense she includes me in her fictional plural, but I am embarrassed at the disruption of my privacy to confront her right away.... The instructor and others are, it seems, equally embarrassed at what they see as "betrayal," "unfairness," policing for "political correctness," etc. I confront her in the break saying that I did not need any defense, I did not feel like speaking very much for my very own reasons that had nothing to do with how comfortable I felt in the class. She is quick to add she was not referring to me and the discussion ends like a stillbirth.... It took me time to admit that we were both "right," in different ways. It took me time to learn to speak in public places and not be embarrassed by my visibility, the sound of my voice, and culturally-specific styles of expression (gender, class and ethnicity issues).

I have obviously little control over my various social constructions as other (woman, cultural minority, and so forth). Even when I am "problematizing the experience" of my White, male students, it is clear whose side I am on, not only because I am constructed as other but also because I choose to be. What I can affect much more significantly, however, is how I respond to and use such constructions to debunk them. Despite my reading in critical pedagogy, feminism and anti-racism, I am finding my way in the classroom by groping in the dark, an education through trial and error and self-reflection. What I have learned that absolutely does not work in struggles toward pedagogical "border crossings" is the imposition of labels, theories, messages[21] that negate students' subject positions. I have personally reacted strongly against and rejected such impositions on me, unless and until I was ready to form my own counter-narratives. Critical, feminist and anti-racist pedagogies are about affirming agency *par excellence*. Yet, in practice, there is a critical distance between our need to exuberantly convey the "truth" and the slow, painful groping that the birth of a (conscious) subject involves, as well as the patience, intuition, experience and skill such birth requires of the educator in the role of a "midwife." We often prefer numbing unconsciousness and "forget" our experience of the slow and painful process of learning to view the world differently from the mainstream, the process of overcoming our "culture shocks" and of crossing/transgressing our personal, educational and biographical boundaries.

Epilogue

I started this exploration of border crossings with a critical overview of the sociological literature on boundaries and border crossings, which I found necessary to enlarge and cross-fertilize with selected post-modern ideas, radical political philosophy and African American feminist writing. The latter helped to flesh out the rather abstract discussion on group boundaries by stressing the necessity for egalitarian border crossings (including a politics of solidarity) in order to achieve a radical democratic—truly participatory and equitable—society. I proceeded to examine specifically the constitution of various social, cultural, epistemological and political boundaries in classrooms. From the first theoretical exploration of boundaries, I carried over the implications of egalitarian border crossings in education and I conceptualized a critical, feminist and anti-racist pedagogy as an attempt at egalitarian border crossings in the school and in the process of "learning for citizenship." At the same time, I examined the challenges to such crossings for the critical, feminist and anti-racist educator. Shifting levels and crossing a border of "voices" in writing, I focused self-reflexively in the last part of the chapter on the constitution of boundaries and challenges to border crossings within personal pedagogical practices. As it has been stated throughout, a critical, feminist and anti-racist pedagogy can only be contextual because the politics of the classroom are *a priori* unknowable. When it comes to implementing such a pedagogy, apart from the general pedagogical principles and an understanding of the possible boundaries, no prescription can be offered. The only knowledge that might help then, to map the field of practice, is self-reflexive understanding of what we carry into the classroom as educators and located human subjects. Thus, I have located my class "moments" and practices in a contextualized "educational life history," as a way of mapping the "unknowable" politics of the classroom to make the actual practice of a critical, feminist and anti-racist pedagogy effective as well as truly liberatory.

Notes

1. Two earlier versions of this chapter were presented respectively at the XXXII World Congress of the International Institute of Sociology (Trieste, Italy, July 1995) and at the expert seminar on "Socio-Cultural Problems in Border-Crossings: Comparing Perspectives in East and West" (University of Joensuu, Mekrijärvi Research Station, Finland, March 1996). The author is grateful for critical comments from Dr. Maureen McNeil, Lancaster University, United Kingdom; Dr. Pirkkoliisa Ahponen, University of Joensuu, Finland; and five anonymous sets of reviews from this book's reviewers. Ultimate responsibility lies with the author.
2. According to Ellsworth, the classroom political dynamics are *a priori* "unknowable" because: (1) one's politics are not entirely "determined" by one's social location as a racialized, gendered, classed, etc. subject. There are personal commitments to struggles that do not fit the stereotypes; (2) we all occupy too many, and too different, subject positions, so that groupings along any single line are almost impossible and certainly unpredictable; (3) alliances among different groups and individuals are therefore situational, shifting and contextual (1989: 323).
3. Etymologically, the term "boundary" refers to that which binds, which holds together (J.B. Jackson, cited in Buijs 1993: 1). In contrast, "border" refers to that which separates, which divides. These are the two aspects of the same phenomenon; both, boundaries and borders can, and often do, result in "barriers."
4. Social scientists have focused for a long time on the unique qualities and special politics that a "border" position makes possible. Feminist Jean Bethke Elshtain comments on how exclusion from institutional power may provide women with space for critical reflection and make challenge to that power more likely (1992: 119). Anthropologist of science Sharon Traweek analyzes the exciting possibilities for creative physics research, at the "borderland" of Tsukuba Science City, in a community of scientists marginalized by the restrictive and hierarchical Japanese academic establishment (1992: 457–58). Classical sociologist Georg Simmel (1950: 405) comments on "the Stranger's" unique position on the borders of society and the exceptional freedom of spirit and judgment that such a position affords its occupants.
5. "Transgression" is defined as "a movement against and beyond boundaries" (hooks 1994b).
6. Henry Giroux calls such pedagogy characteristically a "pedagogy of normative pluralism" (cited in Mohanty 1990: 195).
7. In the anti-racist literature, such analysis is termed "integrative anti-racism" because race is the "point of entry" through which the varied and interlocking forms of social oppression "can and must be understood" (Dei 1995b, Calliste et al. 1995: 5).

8. According to John Weaver's (1995: 174) reading of bell hooks, "engaged pedagogy" is even more demanding than conventional critical or feminist pedagogy because it emphasizes well-being and teacher self-actualization.
9. The use of power is not always counterproductive (see example in Lewis 1990: 480).
10. As C. Talpade Mohanty states, a border pedagogy aims not only at demonstrating the social–historical construction of difference as devalued "otherness" but at creating "public cultures of dissent" (1990: 207).
11. I would add here sexism, classism, heterosexism and other forms of domination.
12. Linda Carty talks about the "outsider-within" status of Black women students and analyzes the ways in which they are silenced even if they are willing to "talk back" when not supported in public by like-minded classmates (1991a: 15–29, 36).
13. Identical with one interpretation of post-modernism.
14. See Carl James (1994b) or R. Patrick Solomon (1995) for male, racial minority instructors' special pedagogical challenges and the classic study of Jessie Bernard (1964: 257) and more contemporary analyses (Sheila McIntyre 1987/88: 376–77, 391) for female instructors' pedagogical challenges. Marilyn Schuster and Susan Van Dyne write about the inherent contradictions (e.g., masculine "authority" versus feminine "nurturing") by which the role of female instructors is fraught in patriarchal society (1985: 165–68).
15. The specific dynamics of resistance are different for White mainstream and minority students. Differences in the minority teacher–minority student interaction have been observed in different classrooms (James 1994b: 135–37; Hoodfar 1992: 314). Such differences may be partially explained by the instructor's gender, but, generally, they speak to the classroom political dynamics as being "unknowable" and, therefore, to the need for critical pedagogical practices to be contextual (Ellsworth 1989: 323).
16. In her analysis of her encounters with blatant sexism and anti-feminism in the law school at Queen's University, Sheila McIntyre writes, "I hope we will stop interpreting individual incidents of sexism and anti-feminism as anomalies or as proxies for other institutional problems" (1987/88: 373).
17. Interestingly, most female students do not take part in the discussion though some are supportive of the male students' point of view.
18. An educational life history brings together the analytical concepts of "human agency" and social structure(s) and shows how inseparable they truly are.
19. I am speaking here of the need to cross the border between the intellectual/emotional development of the teacher and of the students.
20. G.P. Guilford, quoted in Susan Takata (1991: 253–54). "Convergent thinking" forces the student to "converge" on the right answer. It is a characteristic and a consequence of what Freire (1972) calls the "banking system of education."
21. An imposition even in the name of emancipation does not "guarantee an emancipatory outcome" (Acker et al., quoted in Lather 1988: 576).

Chapter Seven

Why Write Back to the New Missionaries?

Addressing the Exclusion of (Black) Others from Discourses of Empowerment

Handel Kashope Wright

> [The] theoretical encounter between black cultural politics and the discourses of a Eurocentric, largely White, critical cultural theory ... is always an extremely difficult, if not dangerous encounter. (I think particularly of black people encountering the discourses of poststructuralism, post-modernism, psychoanalysis and feminism.)—Stuart Hall

> Liberation is a social act.... Even when you individually feel yourself most free, if you are not able to use your recent freedom to help others to be free by transforming the totality of society, then you are exercising only an individualistic attitude toward empowerment or freedom. —Paulo Freire

> I'm saying something now that you don't need deconstruction to know—that the only way to work with collective agency is to teach a persistent critique of collective agency at the same time. You cannot not want it and at the same time you do a critique of it. It is the persistent critique of what one cannot not want. —Gayatri Chakravorty Spivak

Specific Examples from the Larger Context of the Marginalization of Black Others

Few would deny that there are ways in which non-Westerners in general and people of colour in particular have been and continue to be rendered marginal in academic discourse. Examples of this phenomenon abound in all academic fields. Two concrete examples, one historical and specific to the discipline of anthropology, the other contemporary and specific to the field of history, will illustrate this point. The classification of humanity into discrete, so-called "races of man" was an integral part of the development of the discipline of anthropology. Before the intervention of White anthropologist Franz Boas at the turn of the century, such classifications were inherently racist. With his insistence that such markers of "race" as phenotypical characteristics ought to be considered quite separately from and not as determinants of such things as intelligence and morality, Franz Boas (1940, 1969) is credited with having made a crucial intervention in taken-for-granted racist anthropological conceptions of race. However, the Black intellectual W.E.B. Du Bois, who produced similar work, had received short shrift by both Boas and mainstream anthropology until recent rehistoricizations of his contributions. As Faye Harrison (1995: 54) puts it, "Through correspondence and shared participation at conferences, Boas was aware of Du Bois's work; yet Boas did not cite it. Consequently, Du Bois was erased from the discourse that became anthropology's mainstream." Similarly, the work of figures like Deloria, "one of Boas' indigenous field assistants, who offered a critique of Anglo-Texan racial supremacy" were, until recently, not acknowledged in mainstream anthropological discourse (Harrison 1995: 53–54).

While the example from anthropology might suggest that the problem of marginalization is a historical one, one could point to numerous recent examples of the marginalization of African Americans to illustrate that the problem is ongoing though often more subtly in contemporary times. While the historical problem was one of simple occlusion, contemporary examples are rather more complex. Karen Winkler (1998: A13) points to such an example by wondering aloud why Robin Kelley, an African American professor of history and African studies, who is an exemplary and prolific academic by all accounts, has not had his work reviewed in *The New York Times*: "Is the American press—and the public it serves—interested in the diversity of African-American thought, or just in a few media stars? How much do black scholars have to do to prove themselves?" Kelley appears to have been given his due in academia; he is the youngest person to be promoted to full professor at NYU, has garnered several prestigious awards for his books and is on the editorial board of several journals. However, these well-deserved indications of success are undermined by colleagues who suggest, for example, that his success is somehow due to unearned privileges stemming from affirmative action and, therefore, that his work is not as good as his accolades would suggest. This tainted affirmation and recognition constitutes, in fact, a form of remarginalization of the African American academic. Furthermore, Winkler's point about media stars is an indication that we have moved from wholesale marginalization to a system of tokenism whereby a very select few African Americans are held up as exemplary in their field. It would appear that this informal quota system is to be maintained such that even when others of equal prowess arise, they cannot be accorded equal stature and recognition.

This academic marginalization of the others is not of course about personalities per se, nor is it only about discrimination against individuals nor even groups of people based on race. Such discrimination is linked to the power hierarchies that exist between Eurocentric knowledge and knowledge production on the one hand, and "other" knowledges on the other. Edward Said (1993: 51) put the matter cogently when he pointed out that part of his inspiration (or instigation, if you will) to write *Orientalism* was what he saw as the systematic, taken-for-granted marginalization of others' knowledges and bodies of work by a globally dominant Eurocentric knowledge production system:

> What partly animated my study of orientalism was my critique of the way in which the alleged universalism of fields such as the classics (not to mention historiography, anthropology, and the sociology) was Eurocentric in the extreme, as if other literatures and societies had either an inferior or a transcended value. (Even the comparatists trained in the dignified tradition that produced Curtius and Auerbach showed little interest in Asian, African, or Latin American texts.)

Biting the Hand that (Force) Feeds You

As a progressive continental African male working in the North American academy, I utilize and am variously influenced by contemporary discourses like post-modernism, post-structuralism, post-colonialism, feminism and Afrocentrism.[1] Generally, I have found them to be potent means of addressing the concerns of marginalized groups, providing common or similar language and sites for progressive people from marginalized and more powerful groups to dialogue and work toward a more just and democratic global and local society. However, there are also ways in which these same "empowering" discourses can themselves become quite oppressive and exclusionary. To further complicate matters, inclusion is not necessarily a panacea for the problem of exclusion, and the politics of certain discourses demand what could be considered "positive exclusion" at certain times and in certain circumstances.

In terms of the specific issue of exclusion, the focus of these progressive discourses is, rightly, on critiquing mainstream, traditional academic discourses and social formations, identifying and addressing the myriad ways in which society in general and mainstream academic discourses in particular operate and so marginalize or exclude certain voices and perspectives. Since much progressive work is focused on critiquing traditional non-progressive work, the articulation of "other" positions and the advancement of *avant garde* theory, not enough of it focuses on introspective, self-reflexive examination and critique of the shortcomings of these discourses themselves. Under scrutiny, it becomes apparent that there are ways in which these same "empowering" discourses can themselves become oppressive and exclusionary. At first blush it would appear that the problem of exclusion demands the simple solution of inclusion and that this chapter would simply exhort progressive discourses to be more inclusive. The situation is rather more complicated. Not only is inclusion not necessarily a panacea for the problem of exclusion, but the politics of certain discourses demand what would be considered "positive exclusion" at certain times and under certain circumstances. In any event, my concern in this essay goes beyond the mere assertion of a charge of exclusion to the identification of different motives for exclusion, the articulation of what I am calling critical skepticism, and of ways of working with and around exclusion in forwarding progressive praxis. It is also worth pointing out first, that this essay is neither simply nor principally about post-modernist, Afrocentric and feminist discourses; and second, that it is not an essay on Canadian anti-racism per se. While I am invested in and draw upon the above-mentioned three discourses in my own praxis, and while I do examine these discourses in this chapter, my intention is not to undertake an indepth examination nor a fully articulated critique of them here. The discourses identified and examined are in fact virtually incidental to the purpose of this essay; they serve principally as illustrative examples. My focus is on the phenomenon of exclusion and marginalization of Black figures at work, its underlying causes and uses, ways of addressing it and ways of working with and in spite of it.

The essay also is intended as an exercise in anti-racist critique of progressive academic discourses in general rather than an example of Canadian anti-racism specifically. In Canada anti-racism has progressed beyond a narrow critique of multiculturalism and an insistence that racism rather than cultural misunderstanding is the central source of discrimination and dissent in Canadian society. Anti-racist discourse is now more nuanced and reflects an acknowledgement that factors such as class, gender, sexual orientation, (dis)ability, culture and geography intersect with and complicate race and racism and therefore ought to be taken into account in addressing social justice. The principal focus in this more nuanced form of anti-racism remains (or ought to remain) on race and racism. It is in this emerging tradition of nuanced anti-racist discourse that I offer an essay that concentrates on addressing the exclusion of "others" (primarily Blacks) from progressive academic discourses as an exercise in the general concerns of anti-racist discourse. I do not focus here exclusively on the marginalization of African Canadians in the Canadian academy. Rather my approach is at once personal and global. I draw on my own identity politics (or politics of identification, if you will) and figures and works from Canada and the United States to England and continental Africa in discussing the issues.

I critically examine the discourses in which I am invested and upon which I draw in my own praxis. I utilize a politics of identity and difference to illustrate how discourses of empowerment have been and continue to be complicit in the very problems they purport to address in mainstream academic discourses.

In undertaking such an examination, I am in part attacking the very discourses in which I am invested and upon which I draw, discourses which sustain me academically and politically. In effect, I am biting the hand that feeds me. However, as I consider how discourses of empowerment set up their own canon, figures and texts outside of which one operates at considerable risk, I am forced to realize that the very discourses that promise to be so liberating can also end up being restrictive and prescriptive. Who dares deride Derrida, forego

Foucault, dismiss Deleuze and still claim to undertake post-modernist praxis? What critical pedagogue feels free to forget Freire, jettison Giroux, slough off Simon?

My point is not to dismiss or undermine the importance of these figures and their works. Rather, I want to draw attention to the fact that these works become, collectively, the principal means through which we can speak to one another. There is of course the very positive fact that these figures constitute a bridge across difference, providing a (common?) language in which White Canadian post-structuralist feminists, for example, can speak to and be understood by Black male Afrocentric post-colonialists. What is ironic for both groups, however, is that having undertaken the arduous, ongoing struggle to throw off the yoke of the hegemonic, patriarchal, Eurocentric academic tradition of Great White Fathers, they now turn to what can be considered a new (albeit more palatable) set of White fathers in order to speak to one another. The pressure that members of marginalized groups put on themselves and on one another to keep up with the works of principal progressive figures and to use their language, ideas and concepts to talk to one another, ironically ends up creating an atmosphere that is hegemonic. Even in these purportedly post-modern times, the discourses of empowerment are not yet so open that a continental African scholar can draw upon the African canon let alone emergent African intellectuals (on a Palmer, an Okpewho, or even an Ngugi or an Aidoo)[2] without in effect ending up speaking to him- or herself. Outside of that sometimes controversial group known as Africanists, few Western academics appear to be engaging continental African intellectuals that have not been sanctioned in some way by the West (e.g., Soyinka because he won a Nobel prize, Mudimbe because he draws so much on Foucault). If, in the spirit of post-modernism, the academy in the West is indeed opening up to "other" voices, that process appears agonizingly slow from where I stand. Like any African attempting to do progressive work in the academy, I know that if I am not to be dismissed or categorized as relying on "obscure figures" if I am to be "understood" and acknowledged, I have to engage the Western progressive canon. As George Dei (the only African Canadian professor at the Ontario Institute for Studies in Education as of 1998) summarized his first few weeks at Ontario Institute for Studies in Education, "All I am asked here is 'Have you read Foucault on this, have you read Foucault on that, have you read Foucault, have you read Foucault, have you read Foucault?'"

The continued pervasiveness of (predominantly White, male) Western intellectual work means that while one might endorse the ideas and politics of Western progressive canonical figures, even though one may be intimately involved in the development of the discourses they engender, and even though one may be allied with them in political struggle, there is also a sense in which one has little choice in the matter. This leads me to wonder at times whether they represent a hand that feeds me or in fact a hand that force-feeds me.

Constructive Skepticism? or Stepping Inside/Outside Empowering Discourses

Given this re-examination of my position in progressive discourses, I situate myself in this chapter, as Bennet (1990) would put it, "inside/outside" several contemporary liberatory and empowering discourses to illustrate that the problem of exclusion is not limited to hegemonic traditional academic discourses and disciplines. Utilizing the politics of identity and difference, I hope to illustrate that when contemporary identity discourses like feminism and Afrocentrism are employed in a critique of each other and of more generalized discourses like post-modernism and post-structuralism, they expose the fact that purportedly empowering discourses have themselves become implicated in the process of exclusion, marginalization and misrepresentation, which they are supposed to address in more hegemonic academic discourses. In other words, ironically, counter-hegemonic discourses can themselves become hegemonic.

Bourdieu believes that "enlightenment is on the side of those who turn their spotlight on our blinkers" (1990b: 16). Similarly, I do not consider my project here as simply one of biting the hand that (force) feeds me. While I am not in pursuit of something as lofty as enlightenment (a rather dubious goal, in any case, in these "post-modern" times), I do hope through this chapter to add my spotlight to those of others who are trying to shine some light on the blinkers of the discourses in which I invest. In other words, my intention is to participate in the ongoing critique of the very discourses that sustain me in ways that would lead to the strengthening and advancement of those discourses, rather than to their demise.

Although this chapter deals with difference broadly defined, I want to take up the intersection of race and gender in general and the exclusion of Black women and men from discourses of empowerment in particular as the themes around which most of my arguments are constructed. Even as I utilize a Black identity politics, I do so with an acute awareness of the incisive and cogent critique Giroux (1993: 92–93) has levelled at traditional identity politics:

> Identity politics ... often failed to move beyond a notion of difference structured in polarizing binarisms and an uncritical appeal to a discourse of authenticity. Identity politics enabled many formerly silenced and displaced groups to emerge from the margins of power and dominant culture to reassert and reclaim suppressed identities and experiences; but in doing so, they often substituted one master narrative for another, involved a politics of separation, and suppressed differences within their own "liberating" narratives.

In particular, I want to avoid contributing to a Black master narrative and to point instead to what I consider a crucial acknowledgement of differences within Black identity politics. While the main thrust of my argument is not one of separation, I believe that the engagement of the multiplicity of discourses at play in today's knowledge production should not be allowed to blind us to the fact that certain groups, e.g., Blacks broadly defined, continue to be underrepresented and their work constructed (both by themselves and more powerful groups) as mainly relevant to their specific constituency, while the works of more dominant groups continues to be constructed as universal. The risk of having my arguments constructed as "polarizing binarisms" is, in my view, worth taking to underscore such points.

Totalizing, Eurocentric, patriarchal, hetero normal worldviews have held hegemonic sway over the production, dissemination and evaluation of knowledge in the West and indeed globally. Masquerading as neutral, universal and enlightening, such worldviews and knowledge forms have been implicated in the colonization, enslavement, oppression, marginalization and exclusion of less powerful groups on a local and global scale. However, hegemony, by its very nature engenders the emergence of counter-hegemony; and on both a local and a global level, "others" have produced counter-hegemonic discourses that have exposed the partial, exclusionary and oppressive nature of hegemonic knowledge forms. Contemporary discourses such as post-colonialism, feminism and Afrocentrism are articulations of the previously marginalized or silenced voices of others. More generalized discourses, such as post-modernism and post-structuralism, insist on the inclusion of such marginal voices in explaining the world (Smith 1991). In collaboration, the two sets of discourses constitute a powerful tool that engenders the emergence of a more inclusive, more egalitarian, more democratic academy and global society. However, when turned one against the other, in what I refer to as critical skepticism, they become incisive, revelatory tools of critique. Before providing examples to illustrate this point, I should explain the notion of critical skepticism.

I identify at least three types of discursive skepticism, and I want to start by saying what critical skepticism is not. It is not careerist skepticism, and it is not blinkered skepticism. What I identify as careerist skepticism involves contributors to a dominant or less dominant discourse staking out that discourse as territory and excluding others from it, ostensibly on the basis that they are not members of the group on which the discourse is based. For example, some Afrocentrists might exclude all non-Blacks from the discourse of Afrocentrism on the basis of their not being Black, or some feminists might ensure that males do not participate in the development and critique of feminism because they are not women. The crucial characteristic, however, is that in careerist skepticism, the real motive for exclusion is to ensure that people who are in do not have to compete with others for scarce academic resources and rewards, such as establishing journals and presses, publishing articles and books, obtaining research grants and presenting at conferences.[3]

Blinkered skepticism could be practised by both powerful groups and marginalized groups. In the case of powerful groups it could take the form of exclusion through "natural alliances." For example, a group of White academics might undertake a book project on critical literary studies and rationalize the exclusion of people of colour by asserting that it is simply a book put together by a number of friends. They just don't have any Black friends or know any Asians working in the area, they might say. Such a project is obviously blind to the fact that it perpetuates the very problems of appropriation, exclusion and disempowerment it purports to address in traditional literary studies. Blinkered skepticism could also involve the exclusion of members of more powerful groups by a marginalized group out of a wariness of the motives of members of the more powerful group who claim to want to contribute to the cause. A classic example of this is the scene in the movie "Malcolm X" (screenplay by Baldwin et al. in Lee and Wiley 1992) in which a White co-ed asks Malcolm, "What can the good White people like myself, who are not prejudiced, or racist, what can we do to help the cause?" After staring at her for a while Malcolm replies, "Nothing!" (Lee and Wiley 1992: 278). Blinkered skepticism also involves an unwillingness to take up the discourses of other groups, such that one's discourse becomes more and more insular. This type of skepticism is negative because, in the case of less powerful groups, it could lead to extreme insularity, minute and ineffective communities, self-marginalization and the restriction of development of the discourse.

Critical skepticism is different from both careerist and blinkered skepticism because it tempers an often quite justified wariness of the motives and actions of others with a willingness to interact with other groups and their discourses. Perhaps even more significantly, it is not merely critical of broader discourses, but in the interaction between two discourses it advances both and in some cases produces a new discourse. Collins' (1990) employment of Afrocentrism and feminism in critique of one another is a prime example of critical skepticism since it advances the discourses of both feminism and Afrocentrism and produces the kernel of an Afrocentric feminist epistemology.

These forms of skepticism should not be thought of as always existing independently of one another. Rather, they often operate in combination. It is often difficult (sometimes even for the skeptic) to isolate which form or which combination of forms of skepticism is at work in a given situation. I believe the usefulness of discerning distinctions between them is to put in place a vehicle for self-reflexivity, which might guide one in thinking through individual and group motives for exclusion.

I now turn to a cursory examination of Afrocentrism, feminism, post-modernism and post-structuralism to illustrate how the utililization of one discourse of empowerment in the critique of another reveals the exclusion of others in discourses of empowerment. I will proceed by identifying a representative rhetorical phrase from each discourse and illustrate how this empowering rhetorical phrase is contradicted in the praxis of the very group that espouses it. I do not intend to make a case here for the full and unreflexive participation of "whiggers" (Black-identified White people), "male feminists," "gay-identified heterosexuals" and other mythical creatures in the movements of their choice. Rather, I am concerned with the exclusion of individuals who, by the very boundaries of identity set up in the discourses in question, ought to be included as full participants. In other words, I am concerned with representation not so much in the sense of how certain groups are portrayed in discourses of empowerment, but rather how discourses of empowerment operate so as to exclude people who ostensibly qualify to be members from contributing to and being taken up seriously within discourses of empowerment. This form of representation involves such issues as who gets to participate in conferences and who gets published, whose vision of the nature and future of the discourse is taken up as valid and worthwhile, who gets to contribute to the theoretical and political development of progressive discourses. It is about who gets to speak and whose voice is marginalized into a progressive subalterndom. What I am concerned about here is the final frontier of representation.

No Matter Where You Come From, as Long as You're Black, You're an African

One of the recurrent problems with African movements from the Negritude movement in Africa and the Caribbean in the 1930s through the Black Power movement in the United States in the 1960s to Afrocentrism has been the proclivity of the (mostly male) intellectuals in such movements to make, as West (1991: 131) puts it, "self-authorizing attempts" to "represent the universal interests" of Black people. hooks (1984: 130) points out another problem: "It may well be that certain efforts at Black liberation failed because they were strategies that did not include space for different forms of self-reflexive critique." Wallace (1990b: 81) points very specifically to the exclusion of Black women from the movement as the reason for the failure of the Black Movement in the United States:[4]

> Perhaps the single most important reason the Black movement did not work was that Black men did not realize they could not wage struggle without the full involvement of women.... By negating the importance of their [i.e., women's] role, the efficacy of the Black Movement was obliterated.

As Afrocentrism emerges as a promising discourse of African liberation (especially in the United States), there are already indications that some of these self-defeating mistakes are being repeated. The movement must respond by making room for a polyphony of African voices and not only tolerating but engendering self-reflection rather than being dogmatic and programmatic. One might start by calling attention to the dangers of such mistakes and reiterating the positions of those who have already begun pointing to those mistakes.

Ostensibly, Afrocentrism is an empowering discourse for all Africans (both continental and diasporic), since it reverses hegemonic Eurocentric worldviews by placing Africa at the centre and insisting on utilizing an African worldview in taking up Africa and the world (Asante 1987, 1990a). Further, Afrocentrism attempts to unite the African diaspora not only culturally but epistemologically through what Asante (1988) has described as Afrology, the systematic study of Africa(ns) broadly defined from an Afrocentric perspective. The notion of Africa as a cultural and spiritual catalyst for uniting Black people all over the world is captured succinctly and poetically in Asante's (1990b: 7) assertion that "Africa does not end where salt water licks the shores of the continent." However, Gilroy (1993) has asserted that the discourse of diasporic Afrocentricity is centred almost exclusively around the Black experience in the United States and fails to deal with what it means to be Black or African in other parts of the diaspora. In fact, Gilroy argues, even the link with the African continent is a claiming of Africa from a particular African American perspective. His conclusion is that "what is known as Afrocentricity might be more properly called Americo-centricity" (Gilroy 1993: 191). Also, some Black feminists (e.g., Collins 1990) have articulated critical positions of difference within Afrocentrism, and in the process, have exposed the fact that because Afrocentric discourse is phallocentric, it is patriarchal, exclusionary and oppressive to them as women and feminists.

Sisterhood Is Global

Feminism is one of the most potent and concerted efforts initiated by women to address the injustices imposed by patriarchy. As far back as the days of slavery, and in what amounts to an early articulation of a politics of identity and difference, Sojourner Truth asked "Ain't I a woman?" (see Gray-White 1985 for excerpts from the speech). Truth was pointing to the life of self-reliance, constant drudgery and physical abuse that she endured as a Black woman and a slave, and she was holding herself up as a living contradiction to the stereotype of the American woman as delicate and helpless. In its stereotype of womanhood, society had excluded her experience, had denied her humanity. On the other hand she was living proof that women could be self-reliant and self-supporting. By titling her first book *Ain't I a Woman? Black Women and Feminism*, hooks (1981) appears to be making the implicit case that, even though women are now articulating their difference in American society through a variety of feminist discourses, the exclusion of Black women's voices, experiences and perspectives still continues. In fact African American women such as hooks (1981, 1984) and continental African women such as Amadiume (1987) have argued that the feminism of the late 1960s and '70s was itself oppressive and exclusionary because, far from representing all women of the world, it represented the worldviews and lived experiences of only White, middle-class, heterosexual women in Euro-America. Of course the multiple discourses of feminism that have evolved over the years have included Black feminism(s). Also, a number of feminist discourses have made concerted efforts to be more inclusive and more sensitive to difference. In fact, anti-racist work and the analysis of Whiteness as a racial category is becoming increasingly important in some feminist circles. However, as Carty (1991b), Razack (1991) and James and Farmer (1993), utilizing their perspective as women of colour, argue, women's studies (which is usually grounded in one or a number of feminist discourses) is still largely exclusionary and oppressive as far as the participation of Black women is concerned. Attempts to rectify this situation have not always been perceived as constructive. James for example "was confronted with assertions by some senior faculty that developing 'Black Women's Studies' and anti-racist organizing with graduate and undergraduate students were 'local turf battles' destabilizing the Women's Studies program" (James and Farmer 1993: 2).

Thus Black women appear to be marginalized traditionally in two discourses that ought to engender their empowerment. Hull et al. (1982) make this point quite cogently in the very title of their work, "All the women are white, all the blacks are men, but some of us are brave."

Challenging the Monopoly of Eurocentric Knowledge: Insisting on a Play of Voices

While the various discourses of post-modernism and post-structuralism characterize the world in a certain way, they do not necessarily constitute a politics in and of themselves. This is in part why Spivak (1990a: 45) declared, "Although I make specific use of deconstruction, I am not a deconstructionist." Similarly, West (1990) has bluntly asserted that Derrida's deconstruction simply has no politics, and Mary Sarup (1989: 104) has declared that "in one of its developments post-structuralism became a convenient way of evading political questions altogether." This is not to suggest that post-modernism and post-structuralism are apolitical. Rather, what politicized intellectuals like West and Spivak are pointing to is the malleability of these discourses, the fact that they can and have been utilized to construct and support everything from right-wing agendas to left-wing agendas, from highly politicized praxis to nihilism. As Lather (1991) acknowledges, one needs to appropriate post-modernism in the service of one's politics, not look upon it as a politics in and of itself.

What all of this means is that the post-modern ambivalence about the ability of rationalism and Western scientifism to explain the world does not necessarily translate automatically to an openness to other voices. Further, while the invitation to include others is, ostensibly, empowering for marginalized groups, sometimes some members of marginalized groups view the intersection of post-modern and minority discourse with considerable suspicion as a hybrid discourse that ends up being counterproductive to their causes. Stuart Hall (1992a), for example, has characterized the intersection of Black cultural politics and what he describes as the Eurocentric, mainly White discourses of post-structuralism and post-modernism (among others) as "always an extremely difficult, if not dangerous encounter" (254). Post-modernism has as one of its tenets a rejection of the presumption of the superiority of Eurocentric, patriarchal knowledge forms (Giroux 1991b) and an openness to the suppressed and marginalized voices of history (Smith 1991). Thus it is supposed to be empowering for marginalized groups; it is supposed to assist in what many (e.g., wa Thiong'o 1993; hooks 1984) have expressed as an urgent need for marginalized peoples to move their discourses from margin to centre. Yet some White feminists (e.g., Di Stefano 1990) are skeptical of post-modernism, arguing that adherence to its rigid anti-essentialism would mean the death of feminist politics. It is on similar grounds and with similar skepticism (i.e., the threat posed to Black identity politics) that I have asked, "Can poststructuralism be a Black thing?" (Wright and Walcott 1992).

Another characteristic of post-modernism is its proclivity to obfuscate the boundaries around traditionally distinct academic disciplines. Influenced in part in its development by this post-modernist trait, cultural studies cuts across traditional discipline boundaries to embrace and juxtapose the study of literature, history, film, sociology, sports, anthropology, theatre, political science, art, etc. in its expansive folds. As principal exponents like Hall (1980a, 1980b) and Nelson et al. (in Grossberg et al. 1992) would have it, cultural studies is not a discipline but an anti-discipline. As a discipline, or rather, an anti-discipline, cultural studies is producing exciting new knowledge and freeing up scholars to be eclectic and imaginative in the issues they take up and the knowledge they produce. However, in mapping its own history, cultural studies traces its origin to a notion of culture put forward by Raymond Williams (1990), a notion which, as Gilroy (1991) points out, is not only narrowly Anglocentric but also erases Blacks in its failure to take up their perspective on and experience of nation and culture in Britain. Also, the failure of cultural studies theorists (with the possible exception of a few Black British theorists like Hall, Gilroy and Carby) to acknowledge C.L.R. James as an early cultural studies innovator is at best bewildering. Ironically, Marxism, which post-modernism would dismiss as a totalizing grand narrative insensitive to difference, claims C.L.R. James for itself while cultural studies, which insists on sensitivity to difference and the voices of others, traces itself back to what amounts to a narrow Anglocentric origin.[5]

What is implicit in these examples, of course, is that exclusion in these discourses does not operate in isolation but rather is intricately linked either as a cause, a result or an associated phenomenon with much more blatantly violent and oppressive factors, such as institutionalized and societal racism, sexism, ethnocentrism and homophobia. What we must keep in mind is that Said's (1985) comment on the worldliness of texts is equally applicable to academic discourses; neither text nor discourse exists in a hermetically sealed cosmos. Rather they are in the world and hence worldly. Thus, in their theoretical and practical development and application, discourses are not only a microcosm of society but are affected and in turn affect society. Rich (1979: 306) captures the link between racism in society in general and the exclusion of women of colour in the concerns of White feminists thus:

> I believe that white feminists today, raised in a white racist society, are often ridden with white solipsism—not the consciously held belief that one race is inherently superior to all others, but a tunnel-vision which simply does not see nonwhite experience or existence as precious or significant, unless in spasmodic, impotent guilt-reflexes, which have little or no long-term, continuing momentum or political usefulness.

What Rich's statement reveals is that, because we are dealing with people who genuinely want to work for social justice and with discourses developed to serve such ends, we should not necessarily look for overt forms of exclusion and oppression in the praxis of empowering discourses. Rather than overt racism, therefore, we are more likely to find White solipsism; instead of blatant homophobia we would find what Britzman (1993) among others refers to as heteronormativity; instead of explicit sexism and misogyny we would find patriarchal condescension. Finally, the ubiquitous staple of all discourses of empowerment is, of course, tokenism.

Why Write Back to the New Missionaries?

Given this situation, it is tempting to characterize proponents of discourses of empowerment as the new missionaries. When missionaries set off to far-off places in colonial times, they were concerned with helping the natives, and they brought the Word of God, which would civilize the natives and save their lost souls. In the process, however, they ended up participating in colonization, attempted cultural genocide, etc. Similarly, more powerful groups come equipped with the virtually religious words of post-modernism and post-structuralism, intent on empowering the marginalized. In the process they have participated in the exclusion and attempted political genocide of such groups. Why should marginalized groups take up these discourses? If they want to reject these discourses, then why should they spend the time and effort to resist them? Echoing Salman Rushdie, Ashcroft et al. (1989) declare that the empire writes back to the centre. The question, however, is why write back?

So why should marginalized groups write back to the new missionaries? The answer is because things are not so simple, not (dare I say it?) so Black and White. Difference does not operate in separate, clear-cut ways but simultaneously involves race, class, gender, sexual orientation, ability etc., in a system of interconnected and layered discourses, which include and empower one in some cases and exclude and disempower one in others. Thus, there is a sense in which we are all both victims and perpetrators of the very problems I have addressed here. We position ourselves and are positioned as subjects of a variety of discourses such that we are always simultaneously both missionaries and natives. It takes only a shift from one discursive perspective to another for the indignant letter one would write to the oppressor to become a note from one's conscience to oneself.

However, I am not suggesting a level playing field of oppression here, nor am I issuing an invitation for all to join me in the immobilizing dualism of *"j'accuse"* on the one hand and *"mea culpa"* on the other. On the contrary, I wish to deal with the issue of subjectivity and power dynamics and to point to ways in which we can operate within and utilize various discourses of empowerment to work toward a more just political praxis. I will therefore overtly reinscribe myself into my text to address ways in which I have acted in and been acted upon by various discourses in order to reveal what has and has not worked for me and what I have discovered to be the pitfalls and spaces of possibility.

Getting Personal

As a Black person and as a continental African, I have to contend with the widespread but often unstated White, Eurocentric fallacy that Black people do not or cannot do theory. On the other hand, I also have to contend with the notion that practice is what Africans should concentrate on since the continent is faced with such a myriad of practical crises that theory is an ostentatious and self-indulgent activity, which the African intellectual can ill afford. Both these perspectives are based on an endorsement of the false, rigid dichotomy between theory and practice. If not doing theory means not engaging theory as an end in itself, then I agree; I do not do theory. If not taking up theory means not engaging in what Christian (1990) disparagingly refers to as the Eurocentric "race for theory," then I plead guilty to not taking up theory. However, if the inextricable links among theory, politics and practice in the development of praxis are acknowledged, then I would insist that I do take up theory.

My insistence on dealing with praxis rather than practice is in itself a political act, designed to counteract the pervasive exclusion of Blacks in general and continental Africans in particular from the process of theorizing. I have often been told by Africans and non-Africans alike that there are pressing, practical problems facing the continent and that my energies would be better spent addressing them. At the very least this attitude betrays a gross underestimation of the power and politics of theory and theorizing. As Spivak (1990a: 6) says of Derrida, "He will not allow us to forget the fact the production of theory is in fact a very important practice that is worlding the world in a certain way." My response, therefore, to those who would eschew theory in the name of practice is that, while most African economists and sociologists have been relegated or have relegated themselves to testing and applying theories of development conceptualized in the West, those same theories are producing strategies such as structural adjustment programs, which serve the interests of Western capitalism and are antithetical to the development of African communities. I take my cue from the Chinweizus, Aidoos and Soyinkas of literature, the Asantes and Amins of political science and economics, the Amadiumes of sociology. These are continental Africans who insist on theorizing rather than being relegated to practice and who also insist on utilizing theory in the context of praxis rather than as an end in itself; women and men who repudiate the false dichotomy created between theory and practice and elect to engage in developing and promoting African praxis in the face of hegemonic, exclusionary, Eurocentric "hyperdisciplinism."

Even as I situate myself as a victim of exclusion who has to offer resistance by inserting and asserting myself in the academy, I am also aware that as a heterosexual male from a middle-class background, and as an academic, a university professor and a researcher, I am privileged and/or have power over others. In my attempts to contribute to the evolution of a just society, I must be constantly vigilant about the danger of appropriating the discourses and voices of others. In the past I simply avoided addressing gender issues. However, I have come to realize that this is a cop-out, not only because of the obvious fact that I am gendered but especially in the face of exhortations from African feminists like hooks (1988) and Aidoo (1992) for Black men to address gender issues and become involved in feminist discourse. While I am supportive of African feminist discourse in particular because it intersects with general Black liberation discourse, I am acutely aware that as a man I cannot and should not wish to claim feminism as an identity politics. Thus, I try to be careful to speak about gender issues but not for women. I believe that to move from speaking about women and gender to speaking for women is to step from the cutting edge into the abyss of appropriation of voice. This is not to say that taking up feminist discourse and gender issues is unreservedly positive. Potentially, each time I speak to these issues, I take up space that a woman, especially an African woman, could have used to speak to them. As a person with privilege, I am learning that it is also necessary at times to step back, to allow others to speak for themselves rather than show my "sensitivity" by taking up that space myself. Thus I attempt to practise a politics that includes what could be considered positive self marginalization.[6] If all of this sounds as if it is grounded in the feminist post-structuralist notion of being "self-reflexive," I freely acknowledge the debt, especially to the work of Lather (1991) and Britzman (1990). While I have strongly advocated self-reflexivity throughout this essay, I also want to stress that self-reflection should not be allowed to become an immobilizing factor or an excuse for not taking action. As Lather (1991: 20), an enthusiastic proponent of self-reflexivity warns: "In an era of rampant reflexivity, just getting on with it may be the most radical action one can make."

I have had to deal with conflicting messages inherent in the different discourses I utilize. For example, I have been very bothered by the need to do

Black identity politics on the one hand and the danger of committing the post-structuralist sin of being narrowly essentialist on the other. Afrocentrism virtually demands that I be essentialist while post-modernism demands that I be resolutely anti-essentialist. The feminist and Black criticisms of the dangers of anti-essentialism, and Fuss' (1989) illustrations of how strategic essentialism operates in minority discourses, have endorsed and made me more comfortable with my basic position on this dilemma, namely to hold these competing discourses in tension, applying, as it were, strategic essentialism mitigated by post-modern critique and post-modern perspectives grounded and politicized through Black identity politics. Spivak (1990a: 45) probably explicates and justifies the notion and utilization of strategic essentialism most cogently when she declares:

> Since one cannot not be an essentialist, why not look at the ways in which one is essentialist, carve out a representative essentialist position, and then do politics according to the old rules whilst remembering the dangers in this? That's the thing deconstruction gives us; an awareness that what we are obliged to do, and must do scrupulously, in the long run is not OK.

Finally, I wish to stress that I have found collaboration with others essential to my politics and praxis. There is still much truth in the tired old saying "united we stand, divided we fall." But unity should mean neither an assumption of nor a search for homogeneity. I do not believe that understanding other people's causes and perspectives and collaborating with them in a democratic fashion to bring about social change could be accomplished as easily as Giroux's (1992a, 1992b) notion of border crossing would suggest. However, I wholeheartedly endorse his crucial point that in a time when we are all busy articulating how we are different from one another, we must find ways to come together to work for social justice. I believe we must start with the development of a serious attitude of not only listening but hearing one another. I suppose what I am advocating here is a politics of identification as opposed to a politics of identity. A politics of identification produces coalitions which create community. The communities produced are of course what Anderson (1991) would describe as "imagined communities," but, like nations, they can be sustainable communities nonetheless.

For me, the aim of collaboration is not necessarily the achievement of consensus among various groups. Consensus is often too illusionary, impractical and coercive, especially in these times of identity politics and the purported post-modern condition. Rather I want to work with others toward solidarity around issues. As Welch (1990: 133) points out:

> Solidarity has two aspects ... (1) granting each group sufficient respect to listen to its ideas and to be challenged by them and (2) recognizing

that the lives of the various groups are so intertwined that each is accountable to the other. These forms of recognition assume working together to bring about changes in social practice.

This Is Not Necessarily a Conclusion

Even as I speak of collaboration and solidarity, I feel that those of us attempting to undertake progressive praxis should continually reflect on how power operates within and among the discourses of empowerment. There is both "good" and "bad" exclusion and all of us engaged in progressive work in the academy need to be self-reflexive about which is in operation at particular junctures and not assume that inclusion is a panacea for addressing exclusion and related problems.

My point here is not about maintaining self-reflexivity and allowing for a polyphony of voices only within individual discourses, however. Attempting to achieve coherence and alliance among disparate discourses and movements is such a struggle that there is always a temptation to frown on critique of the often frail alliances we create. As Spivak (1990a: 93) reminds us, however, even though we desperately want to establish and maintain alliances across difference, "the only way to work with collective agency is to teach a persistent critique of collective agency at the same time." I want to end therefore by pointing to the continued marginalization of Third World intellectual work and to the ways in which attempts to include marginalized groups in mainstream progressive discourses can end up being quite problematic. In my opinion, there is too much business as usual in relations between the powerful and the less powerful. I once declared (Wright and Walcott 1992) that the Yoruba god of communication, Esu, is the original post-structuralist. I did so ostensibly because, with Esu, meaning is constantly differing and deferred. For example, Esu is sometimes female, sometimes male and sometimes androgynous, thus emphasizing yet obfuscating gender and producing indeterminacy of meaning in supposedly fixed notions of gender and sex. My more crucial objective, however, was to undermine the practice of fixing the origin of the notion of difference in particular and other discursive concepts in general in Eurocentric and academic knowledge production. Where do "new" concepts originate is a question too glibly answered by looking not just to the academy but to the European academy specifically. When C.L.R. James wrote *Beyond a Boundary* (1963), a work in which he juxtaposed cricket, history, literary criticism and cultural analysis, can he be said to have read Stuart Hall? When Chinweizu, Jemie and Madubuike developed bolekaja criticism is it because they had read Terry Eagleton?

Too often, attempts to take the work of Third World academics and writers seriously results in tokenism, condescension and appropriation. Why, for example, must Soyinka be referred to as the Bernard Shaw of Africa, and why are the myriad schools of literary criticism produced in Third World countries homogenized in literary history and criticism texts as Third World or post-colonial criticism while those produced in the West are regarded as distinct schools and approaches? Let us by all means examine the finer points of exclusion, but at the same time let us be clear that those who have been marginalized so long in the academy need the space to speak out and deserve to be heard, and those who have held hegemonic sway need to listen more. For all our talk about empowerment, there are still too many Spivaks waiting to translate too many Derridas for their intellectual praxis to be acknowledged, too many Soyinkas waiting for their Nobel Prize in order to be read at the centre, and too many who continuc to murmur:

> I would have liked to tell you
> the story of the nightingale who died
> I would have liked to tell you
> the story…
> Had they not slit my lips. (Samih al-Qassim)

Notes

1. It is possible to view post-modernism and post-structuralism as progressions from modernism and structuralism. There is, however, a sense in which they constitute radical breaks from these older discourses, to the extent that they could be viewed as paradigmatic shifts, which potentially constitute them as emancipatory, counter-discourses in relation to these established hegemonic discourses. It is in this latter sense that I employ them here. As I shall argue later, however, while they can be taken up as counter-hegemonic and emancipatory discourses, they do not necessarily constitute a politics in and of themselves.
2. All the references here are to African writers and literary critics. Eustace Palmer (1972) is one of the first African critics to write sustained literary criticism of the African novels produced in the early 1960s and was head of the department of English at Fourah Bay College at the University of Sierra Leone in the 1970s and 1980s, yet he is hardly acknowledged outside African literary circles. Isodore Okpewho's (1992) African literature, *Backgrounds, character, and continuity*, could be considered a definitive text on African orature, yet the hyperliteracy of Western literature and the fact that his work is about African literature specifically have ensured that he remains obscure in Western literary circles. Ngugi wa Thiong'o (male Kenyan novelist and critic) and Ama Ata Aidoo (female Ghanian playwright, novelist and critic) are more widely known but, again, almost exclusively as African writers and critics rather than simply as writers and critics of literature in general.
3. Of course careerism does not apply in the case of radical (i.e., separatist) feminists and Afrocentrists. Such groups do advocate complete separation from dominant groups but do so on the basis of their politics rather than out of careerism. The strict exclusion of non-group members (men in the case of radical feminists and non-Blacks in the case of radical Afrocentrists) is an inherent factor that in fact defines the politics of these groups.
4. Wallace has been critiqued for making the simplistic assertion that Black women

were completely excluded from the Black Movement. In *Invisibility Blues*, Wallace (1990a) amends her position and makes the more complex point that, while there were some women who participated, the Black Movement was dominated by men and the orientation, discourse and perspective was not only male but overtly macho.

5. There is even a Marxist C.L.R. James Society, complete with a C.L.R. James journal.
6. I should add what I consider the important caveat here. A Black South African feminist colleague, Nombuso Dlamini, has cautioned me that positive self-marginalization should not be allowed to become a euphemism for immobility or an excuse not to undertake political action around gender issues.

Chapter Eight

Anti-Racist Organizing and Resistance in Academia[1]

Agnes Calliste

In February 2000, an Ontario Human Rights Commission (OHRC) investigation committee found that Dr. Kin-Yip Chun, a world-renowned Chinese Canadian physicist and research associate at the University of Toronto was wrongfully denied a tenure-track position in four separate competitions between 1987 and 1992 because of racism and cronyism in the hiring practices of the University of Toronto's physics department. He was also subjected to a series of reprisals or a "poisoned work environment" after he began to complain to the university administration of unfair treatment by the department. These reprisals culminated in his wrongful dismissal in 1994 (Canadian Association of University Teachers 2000; Keung 2000; Ontario Human Rights Commission 2000; Schmidt 2000). The OHRC committee concluded that the "power imbalance inherent in the dynamics of an 'old boys' network effectively screens out racial minority persons ... who are unable to tap into this network" (Keung 2000: A1). It recommended that the Commission establish a board of inquiry to settle the dispute under the Ontario Human Rights Code.

The university administration rejected the OHRC's report and "recommended" that the case should not be sent to a board of inquiry (MacPherson 2000). The administration, like many other employers in similar situations, blamed Chun for his problems by focusing on interpersonal dynamics such as "personality problems" (see Calliste 1996b, 2000a, 2000b; Das Gupta 1996; Doris Marshall Institute and Arnold Minors and Associates 1994). It argued that Chun's contract was terminated because he failed to obtain "overhead" funds[2] as part of his major research contract and because of his "increasing unsuitability" as a colleague due to his "deteriorating mental state" and "irrational behaviour" (Canadian Association of University Teachers 2000: 4; Schmidt 2000: A5).

An internal investigation committee at the university acknowledged that Chun was exploited during his nine years there,[3] but it denied that Chun was a victim of discrimination. However, the OHRC's investigation committee found that the university committee's report was flawed because it proceeded on the mistaken assumption that discrimination must be intentional instead of investigating the adverse impact of the physics department's discriminatory hiring practices and harassment on the complainant as well as the administration's role in his marginality and exclusion[4] (see Keene 1992 for a discussion of racial discrimination). Moreover, the OHRC committee argued that an "employee's angry reaction to discrimination does not justify the termination of an employee" (Canadian Association of University Teachers 2000: 4;). Chun thinks that his case "may just be the tip of the iceberg" with respect to the university's unfair hiring practices (Keung 2000: 1). He has sued the University of Toronto for wrongful dismissal (Schmidt 2000).

Chun's case is not unique. In a 1976 racial discrimination case against Dr. Briggs, Principal, and Algoma University College in Ontario, the OHRC found that Dr. Singh, a Canadian of Pakistani origin, was wrongfully denied a tenure-track position in the department of sociology because the college administration did not want "too many Pakistanis in the Department" (Ontario Human Rights Commission 1976: 13). Witnesses testified that the principal voiced concern that hiring a third Pakistani in the department would jeopardize the "Canadianization" and "immaculate community image of the College," which might result in declining enrolment (Ontario Human Rights Commission 1976: 14). The board of inquiry decided that Dr. Singh was discriminated against on the basis of his country of origin, not on the basis of his race. It ordered the college to compensate the complainant for lost wages and expenses incurred. The complainant also had the right to apply for the tenure-track position, which was still open for 1976–77. If he failed to get a position for the year due to lateness, the college would be obligated to pay him for that year (Ontario Human Rights Commission 1976: 23–26).

The principal's blatant discriminatory arguments in Singh's case reflected the social constructions of the Canadian citizen as White and Whiteness as immaculate (Dyer 1997; Hall 1998). Since such overt racism is no longer acceptable, it is being replaced by a much more subtle ideology of cultural inferiority, which is very insidious and much more difficult to prove (Gilroy 1991). There have been several informal complaints against universities who reinforce the marginality of Aboriginal and racialized minority faculty and students by denying their experiences of racism and reprisals and blaming them for "their" problems rather than seriously investigating the problem of racism.[5] Scapegoating minoritized faculty and students diverts attention from a critical analysis of the structures and practices that treat them inequitably and try to make them appear crazy while justifying the status quo. As bell hooks (1992a) points out, people in power tend to label as crazy those whom they perceive as a threat to the status quo. Hopefully, Chun's case will encourage more faculty, staff, students, anti-racist activists and their allies to organize and demand institutional and systemic change to address racism and the interlocking systems of social oppression (such as sexism and classism) in their respective universities and colleges, as well as at the local, national and international levels.

This chapter focuses on anti-racist organizing and resistance in academe in two Nova Scotia universities—Grand Bras and Paradise universities[6]—from 1987 to 1999. I adopt an eclectic theoretical perspective, which includes anti-racism, feminism, social closure and cultural Marxism, to develop the strongest explanatory model (Belkhir 1996; Brandt 1986; Collins 1990, 1996; Dei 1996a; Glazer 1991; Hick and Santos 1993; hooks 1995, 1997; Lorde 1995; Murphy 1988; Omi and Winant 1983; Parkin 1979; Razack 1998; Roediger 1991; Tomaskovic-Devey 1993). The study treats race, class and gender not as variables but as organizational processes of the university. It examines the conditions under which these anti-racist struggles materialized, the constraints placed upon them and their effects. Blacks and First Nations people remain the most marginalized/excluded groups in academe in Canada. Women, in particular, are denied access to positions of power within institutions and their experiences and perspectives are considered irrelevant (Carty 1991a; Monture-Angus 1995b; Razack 2000). This study focuses on their experiences.

Aboriginal people and racialized minorities are dramatically underrepresented as faculty, and they are virtually excluded from administration. The few who become administrators are undermined by some of their colleagues, faculty and staff (personal communications, June 1999). The Canadian Sociology and Anthropology Association (CSAA) Status of Women Sub-Committee's 1994 survey[7] of sociology and anthropology departments in Canadian universities and colleges illustrates the underrepresentation of Aboriginal people and racialized minorities on faculty. The data indicates that only 5 percent of all tenured or tenure-track faculty in these departments were men and women of colour compared to 30 percent women and 65 percent men not of colour. There were no Aboriginal people within this group. Aboriginal faculty in sociology and anthropology departments comprised only 2 percent of 203 full-time sessionals hired in 1991–94. Similarly, among new hires, 6 percent were men and women of colour compared to 66 percent women and 28 percent men not of colour (Baker et al. 1996: 1–2). Moreover, as Sherene Razack (1998: 206) points out, "the academy is anything but comfortable" for faculty and students of colour, but more importantly, it has become "less physically safe as the number of incidents of Black students and faculty being threatened and assaulted rises." Several Black faculty, especially women, confirm that there is no fundamental difference between racism in the street and racism in their respective universities (and other professional settings) except that sometimes racism in the university may be more covert (interviews July 1997; personal communications 1982, April 1998, February 2000). The middle-class values that the university represents, such as the commonsense appeal to reason, may take "the rough edges off ... but the impact is no less severe" (Carty 1991a: 15).

Study Methodology

My discussion on anti-racism organizing and resistance in universities is based upon data drawn from the following sources. First, as part of a larger study on access to universities, unstructured interviews were conducted in 1997–98 within a sample of thirty Aboriginal and Black students, several student advisors and faculty members, mainly from two universities in Nova Scotia. The sample was drawn through snowball sampling and referrals. The second source of data consisted of participant observation at numerous 1987-99 university committee meetings, such as those on access and equity for Aboriginal and Black students; panel discussions on anti-racism in the university; the Nova Scotia Interuniversity Committee on Access consultative meetings with African Canadian and Mi'Kmaq communities; and local, national and international conferences on resisting professional exclusion and marginality in academe. The primary data are supplemented with documentary analysis of organizational records and other secondary sources. I have gained valuable insights from working closely with Black and Aboriginal students for several years. To maintain confidentiality, I use fictitious names for actual persons and institutions, except those already named in secondary sources. The cases include my experiences and those reported to me by others.

Theoretical Framework

Anti-racism is a critical discourse of social oppressions (such as racism, sexism and classism) through the lens of race. It is also "an educational and political action-oriented strategy for institutional and systemic change to address racism and the interlocking systems of social oppression" (Dei 1996a: 25). The emphasis on racism is not intended to prioritize oppressions. Instead, the anti-racism discourse highlights the fact that, though "race" is a "fundamental organizing principle of contemporary social life" (Winant 1994b: 115) in racialized societies, those in power continually deny that race is an integral part of the ongoing social processes of the university. Access to university education, work and justice are constrained by relations of oppression such as racism and gendered racism (Brandt 1986; Essed 1991). Gendered racism refers to the racial oppression of racial/ethnic minority women and men as structured by racist perceptions of gender roles and behaviour.

The anti-racism theory incorporates many theoretical perspectives and builds on critical race, class and gender studies to provide an integrative understanding of oppression as well as individual and collective resistance (Leah 1995). The theory provokes analysis of individuals' social and political position in society, but it directly confronts issues of racism within society's power structures, encouraging oppressed people to see the source of their oppression within structures. Anti-racism examines historical relations of domination and subordination and places power relations at the centre of its analysis. Anti-racism goes beyond acknowledging the material conditions that structure social inequalities to question White power and privilege and its rationale for dominance (Bonnett 1996; Dei 1996a; Dyer 1997; Frankenberg 1993; Razack 1998; Roediger 1991).

Anti-racism (like feminism and Marxism) questions the role that the state and societal institutions play in producing and reproducing inequalities. It acknowledges that Canada is a capitalist, racist and patriarchal society and that universities, as state regulated and funded institutions, are structured to perpetuate those relations (Carty 1991a; Hick and Santos 1993; Ng 1994; Smith 1977). The university plays an important role in producing and reproducing segments of a stratified labour force (trained personnel) and the structure of labour relations based on race, gender and class positions. Moreover, the university legitimizes the ideological relations that support present-day Canadian society by defining and legitimizing Eurocentric, middle-class and patriarchal curricula while delegitimizing/marginalizing other forms of knowledge and pedagogy through discourse, texts, curricula and assessments (Dei 1995a; Dei et al. 1997; Graveline 1994; Ng 1994). As Leith Mullings (1997: 107) points out, the debates about anti-racism (or critical multiculturalism) and the intellectual canon are not simply about which books to read but "about power and privilege and how they are to be distributed." As an employer, the university also produces, reproduces and utilizes work relations and roles structured by race, class and gender. Anti-racism questions the devaluation of the knowledge and experiences of subordinate groups as well as the marginalization and silencing of certain voices in the university and in society. It recognizes the need to confront the challenge of social diversity and difference in Canadian society and the urgency for inclusiveness and equality in our educational institutions, workplaces and society (Calliste 1996b, 2000a; Dei 1995a).

The anti-racism perspective, like feminism (Armstrong and Armstrong 1990; Smith 1977), acknowledges that the state and societal institutions (such as the university) contain and manage the protests of oppressed groups (for example, by individualizing complaints and by treating racism and sexism as if they reside only in certain individuals) but also that they do not conduct a critical analysis of the structures and practices that treat Aboriginal and racialized minority women and men inequitably nor do they challenge systemic racism and patriarchy, especially racism, unless they are pressured into doing so (Bolaria and Li 1988; Calliste 1996b, 2000b; Henry et al. 1999; Young 1992; Young and Liao 1992). Thus, the university, like the state, responds variably to anti-racist, feminist and other minority struggles (whether it crushes, appeases or co-opts them) in accordance with the groups' economic, political and social power.

Universities have remained bastions of White male power and privilege partly because White males have historically and contemporarily employed exclusionary social closure processes, which preserve their advantage by tying access to valuable academic jobs, and other social and economic opportunities, to group characteristics such as educational credentials, race/ethnicity, gender and ideology. Social closure processes include gatekeeping and sponsorship mechanisms; the application of rules, including seniority rules;[8] and the construction and maintenance of barriers, which make it very difficult for "outsiders" to maximize their potential and to be productive (Breton 1979; Taylor 1994). Parkin (1979: 44) defines social closure as "the process by which social collectivities seek to maximize rewards by restricting access to resources and opportunities to a limited circle of eligibles." Gaining employment and promotions through the ranks to administrative positions is not based just on an individual's academic performance or merit. One must be a member of a powerful and privileged group or at least be perceived as having "personal suitability," being able to "fit in" at the institution and to help maintain the status quo. As Breton (1979: 283) points out:

> One's competitors for scarce resources are not simply other individuals; they are "outsiders," members of another collectivity. What counts in "taking advantage of opportunities" is not so much individual skills ... as the effectiveness of the social organization for the control of [work] domains and of access to them developed by the group with which one is affiliated.[9]

In sum, discrimination in universities, as in other organizations, is partly the result of power struggles and unequal power relations. In capitalist, racialized and gendered societies such as Canada, racism, sexism and classism interact and compound the oppression. For instance, several faculty members in one department acknowledged that occasionally a White "outsider" (male or female faculty) who asserted his or her rights had been treated unfairly by a clique. However, James and Gwen, the two faculty members of colour, have suffered the brunt of gendered racism and harassment. They have been infantalized, inferiorized and humiliated publicly (for example, in departmental meetings) (Howard 1997; personal communications April 1993, November 1994, February 1999). This is particularly true for Gwen, an assertive Black woman who speaks out against racism. She is being harassed because her oppressors are threatened by her assertiveness in resisting the multifaceted oppression and because she has challenged White patriarchal definitions of Black femininity. Her oppressors wish to control her assertive behaviour and undermine her ability to influence others. She has been socially and professionally ostracized, and this continues to the present. Similarly, Marjorie Simon, a Mi'Kmaq and a former faculty member, argues that some members of the academy inferiorized and infantalized her "as if she were a ward of some institution" (Simon 1998). Aboriginal people and racialized minorities are perceived as "outsiders within" the "hallowed halls" of the academy. They are expected to know and stay in their ascribed "place." They must accept their subordination. Most faculty members are silent when their Aboriginal and racialized minority colleagues who "make trouble" are harassed; they fear reprisals, and some are complicit in the oppression of minoritized faculty (Howard 1997; personal communications April 1993). As Sheldon Taylor (1994: 8) argues:

> How is it ... that a qualified Black Ph.D., with seniority within a

> university setting, could suddenly discover that he/she is being overlooked for the teaching of a familiar course, in favour of a junior—not even qualified—first-level graduate student? Protests in such instances when they occur by Blacks, are met either with a wall of silence, more reviews by committees and the usual practice of the professorial closing of ranks.

Social closure theory also postulates that excluded groups or socially defined ineligibles (such as White women's groups and racialized minority men) could resist domination (or White male hegemony) by organizing to maximize their claims to rewards and opportunities. The excluded, in their turn (intentionally or inadvertently) may secure privileged positions for themselves at the expense of some other groups (or close off access to remaining rewards) through subordination of a social category of ineligibles (Parkin 1979). Some privileged or White women faculty members and administrators, in striving for social equality with men of their class, have been complicit in exploiting and marginalizing/excluding Aboriginal and racialized minority faculty members (Collins 1990; hooks 1995, 1997; Lorde 1995; Razack 1998). For instance, some White junior faculty women, including sessionals, have undermined senior faculty women of colour to assert their own social power and skin privilege.

The eclectic theoretical framework is relevant in explaining Aboriginal and Black faculty members' and students' anti-racism organizing and resistance in academe. Aboriginal, Black and other racialized minority faculty members and students (like their counterparts in the United States) have been simultaneously oppressed by racism, classism and sexism (see Carroll 1982; Reyes et al. 1990). Some Aboriginal and racialized minority students and faculty members acknowledge that they experience multiple oppressions in academe. For instance, in 1997, Henry, a White male student, asked Janet, an African Canadian student, where did she steal the new leather jacket she was wearing. She replied: "I did not steal it. I slept with your father" (interview March 1997). However, some minoritized students, faculty members and staff emphasize racism because it is more visibly salient for them. Most of the oppressors of Aboriginal people and racialized minorities in academe are White men and, to a lesser extent, White women (interviews June 1997; personal communications Fall 1999).

Anti-Black and anti-Aboriginal racisms are rooted in historical processes such as the enslavement of Africans,[10] colonialism and the decimation of Aboriginal peoples and appropriation of their land. Slave and colonial relations were characterized by super-exploitation, brutal repression and ideological subjugation of Africans and Aboriginal peoples by Europeans and the subordination of Aboriginal women to both European and Aboriginal men (Amott and Matthaei 1996; Baker 1983; Bourgeault 1989; Churchill 1992; Davis 1981; hooks 1981; Steckley 1999; Thatcher 1986). Although Black female slaves were assigned domestic work, they were defeminized and forced to do the same arduous fieldwork as their male counterparts, work that would have been considered inappropriate for White women. Aboriginal women and men were isolated on reserves or remote settlements. The ideological forms of racism and sexism that Europeans employed to rationalize the exploitation of and domination over Black and Aboriginal peoples stigmatized them as inherently inferior.

Racism interacts with sexism and class exploitation in the labour market. Racially specific gender and classist stereotypes have played an important role in relegating Aboriginal and Black men and women to specific occupations, in barring them from entry into others and in influencing managerial strategies of control (Collins 1990, 1996; hooks 1981). Blacks have been perceived as better suited to unskilled service-oriented jobs and those requiring heavy physical labour, rather than to professional, skilled and supervisory positions (Baker 1983; Calliste 1993, 1996b; Collins 1996; Mullings 1997). Ideologies and images of Black women as "mammies," "Jezebels," "Sapphires" and "matriarchs," like the Black male images of "Sambo" (the Tom), "Buck" and "Rastus" ("the coon"), emphasized physical attributes over mental and social (see Barbee 1993; Calliste 2000b; Collins 1990, 1996; Davis 1981; Fox-Genovese 1988; hooks 1981; Mullings 1997). Sambo and the "mammy" images of loyal and obedient male and female servants were created to justify the economic exploitation of house slaves. While these were portrayed with affection by Whites because they posed no threat to the White patriarchal social order, the image of Sapphire depicted Black women (for example, those who speak out against racism) as evil, treacherous, stubborn and hateful (Collins 1990; hooks 1981; Mullings 1997). These racially specific notions of femininity and masculinity are used to rationalize the marginality and exclusion of Black women and men in the academy.

Racism in Universities

Racism and other forms of domination (such as sexism and classism) are not recent phenomena in Canadian universities. These institutions of higher learning, like their American and British counterparts, have been used historically by the dominant group to oppress and exploit racialized minorities, women and other subordinated groups as well as to rationalize, justify and naturalize dominant ideologies and the status quo (Belkhir and Duyme 1998; Brown 1992). For instance, in the decades before the Second World War, some scientists and social scientists, including academics, promoted theories of biological determinism on genetic racial inequality, namely that racialized minority groups, particularly those of African descent, were less intelligent and more criminally inclined than Whites (Belkhir and Duyme 1998; Fredrickson 1971; McLaren 1990). This persists into the present (Jackson 1998; Herrnstein and Murray 1994; Segal and Kilty 1998; Spence 1999; personal communications January 1992). Moreover, some faculty members were eugenicists, who strove to protect the qualities of "the superior race" and classes (i.e., Euro-Canadian middle-class society) from degeneration by racialized minorities and the lower class. Discussions about eugenics "coloured," classed, gendered and sexualized a range of social policies: intelligence (and mental) testing; Canadian immigration; birth control; and forced sterilization of the "feeble-minded" in Alberta and British Columbia (McLaren 1990).

Until recently, however, allegations of racism were tabooed in the sacrosanct institutions of higher learning, which were seemingly devoted to the pursuit and communication of knowledge and which emphasized complete dependence on the principle of merit. Anyone who dared to allege that there was racism in the university was likely to be deemed "emotional," thus "irrational" and "unprofessional" (personal communication 1977; Reddick 1992). The terms, "racism" and "anti-racism" are still considered "ugly," almost obscene, words in some universities, despite incidents of blatant and subtle racial discrimination and harassment. Typically, these incidents are kept secret or are attributed to individual ignorance or fear of the unknown—the racialized "other" (Anti-Racism Forum 1999; personal communication October 13, 1999).

Recent complaints and research on racism in the academy indicate that academic culture has become a contested site primarily because racial/ethnic and other minoritized groups (for example, women and the working class), traditionally excluded from higher education, are now becoming more politicized and are attending higher educational institutions in increasing numbers (see Bannerji et al. 1991a; Giroux 1994b; Graveline 1994, 1998; Henry and Tator 1994; Monture-Angus 1995b; Ng 1994). These subordinate groups have been organizing and demanding access to educational resources, equity, justice, identity and representation (such as in curriculum content and pedagogy) and social justice.

Racism in universities manifests itself in several ways: through the formal and the "hidden" curricula (such as the climate and tone of the campus, university calendars and recruitment materials); through racial/ethnic slurs, jokes and stereotyping; and through racial harassment of Aboriginal and racialized/ethnicized minority students, faculty and staff. Racism occurs in the formal curriculum in three ways: through invisibility of First Nations' people and racial/ethnic minorities; through the exclusion of these groups from any positive representation; and through the so-called "objective" interpretations and explanations that actually represent the dominant racial/ethnic groups' interests (Carty 1991a). Aboriginal and Black students at Grand Bras and Paradise universities reported finding that both the formal and hidden curricula denied, excluded and rejected the identities, history and contributions of Aboriginal and Black people (interviews April 1 and 23, July 12, 1997; Lavery 1996; see also Nova Scotia Interuniversity Committee 1992). Mary, a descendant of Black Loyalists, discusses the invisibility of African Canadian and Mi'Kmaq history and their contributions to Canadian society:

> I am taking Pre-Confederation History.... The way he [the professor] taught the class [was] as if there were no Blacks and Mi'Kmaq in pre-Confederation history because he never said anything about them.... We did the War of 1812, we talked about the Irish and the Scots, but nothing about Blacks. (interview April 1, 1997)

Although Mary felt that the professor was denying legitimacy to Aboriginal and Black experiences, she said that she did not ask him about the omission because "he was so nice" (interview April 1, 1997). Instead, she asked Jane, a Black faculty member, for references on the Black Loyalists for her term paper so that she could learn about her heritage. Jane encouraged Mary to act on her own behalf. She did go to see her history professor for some sources for her term paper and found him very helpful (personal communication 1997). This indicates that some students need help on how to take action on their own behalf. The class might have benefited had Mary asked her professor about the omission of Aboriginal and Black peoples from the curriculum.

Some students and faculty members in Canadian universities have expressed concern and disappointment that most women's studies programs focused on White women's studies (interviews April 1, 1997; personal communications March 1998, June 1999). This is reflected in the choice of both curricula and faculty. They argue that these programs either exclude or marginalize women of colour by hiring one as "a token"; she is often harassed. Moreover, most of the courses are Eurocentric and middle-class and do not validate the various experiences that different students bring to the classroom (personal communications March 1998; interview April 1, 1997). Mary discusses her feelings of isolation, alienation and invisibility in a family class that did not represent what she knew about Black families:

> We had these discussion groups.... I did my readings but I did not contribute much because I felt out of place.... My course was women's studies. We were discussing motherhood, the changing role of women in the workforce. We never really did anything on Black women ... and all the stuff that we were doing was focusing on what it is like to be a White woman. I did not recognize myself in the material. I knew the work, but what was the point? She [the professor, Sara] could have made me feel a bit more comfortable if she would have included material on Black women. She called me aside and asked me what she could do to make me feel comfortable. I told her that it would help if she called upon me a bit more and she could incorporate some things on Black women. After that, she treated Black women as an add-on. (Interview April 1, 1997)

Instead of integrating Black women into the course, the professor simply moved them from invisibility to marginality. Mary's observations on the family course were confirmed by some White students who also expressed concerns about the Eurocentric focus of many of their courses. For instance, they found that when some faculty included course materials on immigrant women, they were often about European immigrant women and/or they treated First Nations and racialized minority women as add-ons, thereby marginalizing them (personal communications 1997-99). In 1999-2000, however, the women's studies program hired a faculty member who is co-teaching a course with Sara and who integrates anti-racism and post-colonialism in her courses (personal communications March 26, 2000).

Some educators unconsciously (and consciously) produce and reproduce racism, sexism and classism in the classroom by excluding racialized minorities from positive representations. For instance, at a symposium on women's health held in one university in 1996, Merle, a White faculty member, showed an overhead of an angry Black woman (overloaded with books, holding a vacuum cleaner and brandishing a pot in her right hand as if she was about to throw it or strike someone with it) to illustrate anger and stress as risk factors in cardiovascular diseases. It was the only image shown of a woman of colour. Since there was no time for discussions after the presentations, Gail, a Black faculty member, expressed her concerns to Merle privately. Merle apologized to the Black women who attended the symposium for having inadvertently offended them. She claimed that the purpose of the image was to illustrate the effect of multiple roles on women's health and did not seem to recall that the image was that of a domestic worker.

Merle seemed to have missed Gail's point that the racist, sexist and classist representation of Black women—as emotional, irrational and out of control—was not simply a lesson on women's health but also on prejudice and stereotypes against Black women. Behaviours need not be intentional to be racist. The adverse effects of the behaviours also make them racist.

Gail made a number of unsuccessful attempts to counteract this stereotypical representation of Black women and the "subtle" ideology of cultural inferiority in a class discussion. Most of the White students denied that the overhead was stereotypical. Further, they argued that the professor did not construct the images but reproduced them from a text written by an expert; thus implying that the author, a White man, had to be right. Gail, on the other hand, was told that she was "too sensitive" (personal communication 1996). Scapegoating Gail for raising the issue of gendered and classist racism diverted attention from a critical analysis of both the overhead and the Eurocentric, middle-class, patriarchal curriculum and justified the status quo.

Black and some Aboriginal students feel systematically marginalized and excluded. Black students describe some Nova Scotian universities as being "White" institutions ("a White university in a White town") that are unresponsive to their needs. Except as athletes in some universities, they feel invisible

(*Academic Forum* 1999; *Anti-Racism Forum* 1999; interviews April 1 and 23, 1997; personal communications November 8 and 19, 1999). Brenda observed that, at one university, "the recruitment material was all White and, if it included Blacks, it was only [the international students in a Diploma program]. This feeds into the stereotype that all Black students [are in this particular program]" (interview April 23, 1997). What some students find most frustrating is the university's apparent lack of awareness or refusal to admit that there is a problem. Brenda, notes: "I made a comment that the school does not recognize Black students for anything other than for our athletic abilities ... the only picture you see of us is going up for a basket. Someone replied, 'But they are really good at getting those baskets'" (interview April 23, 1997). This illustrates the university's denial of racism. Recently, Grand Bras and Paradise universities revised their recruitment materials to include Aboriginal and racial minority students; however, some students, faculty members and staff find that Aboriginal and Black students are still being marginalized. For example, they argue that Black students at Paradise University are still portrayed predominantly as athletes, are in the background or are presented simply as tokens. Moreover, the discourse on the local Aboriginal and African Canadian communities is patronizing (interview April 23, 1997; personal communications September and November 1999).

Some universities recruit Black students predominantly as basketball and football players, unconsciously (and consciously) producing and reproducing the racist, classist, sexist and sexualized stereotypes of Black students, particularly males, as "dumb jocks" and "happy-go-lucky" people who make "good athletes" but who are less intelligent and less ambitious than White students (personal communications October 1998, November 1999, February and March 2000). Thus, the tracking of Black students into sports in high school continues at the university level (Black Learners Advisory Committee 1994; Dei et al. 1997; Head 1975; Henry 1978; James 1997; Solomon 1992; Spence 1999). Donald (1993: 1), a faculty member, notes:

> I am struck by the smaller number of Native and Black students on this campus ... equally disturbing [is] the visible role of the few Blacks on campus as people with skill to be good at sports.... There appears to be a subtle, disturbing impression around this community (students and non-students alike) that most Blacks on ... [Paradise] campus have been sought by the University first to play basketball.... The smaller number of Blacks on campus and yet their disproportionate number on the basketball team only reinforces this singular image held of them.

Seven years later, David Frank, a high-achieving Black student and football player, expresses similar views:

> White people are very stereotypical in regards to Black students. The first question that comes out of their mouths is, "Do you play football or basketball?" This type of generalization has to stop. It is time for White people to generalize Black students in an academic environment first, and athletics second. (2000: 5)

Athletic scholarships help to provide access to university and opportunities for upward mobility for some Black students. While some "student athletes" (such as Frank) do refute the negative stereotypes by their high academic achievement, the stereotypes seemed to have become a self-fulfilling prophecy for others. They focus excessively on sports, which detracts from study time, and they have unrealistic expectations of becoming professional athletes. For instance, Lloyd, a junior "student athlete," argues that "sports is his life" (personal communications February 26, 2000). He expects to be a professional football player despite the fact that his team won only one game in the 1999 Atlantic University Athletic Association tournament (see Messner 1991; Spence 1999).

In addition to stereotyping Black and Aboriginal students as low achievers, White students are guilty of racial harassment and gendered racism (slurs such as "Go back to Africa where you come from," "squaw" and "nigger") (*Anti-Racism Forum* 1993; personal communications 1989 and April 27, 2000). For instance, Angela, an international student, alleges that in the fall of 1999 she received a harassing phone call from a White male student, telling her to "go back to where she came from." She reported the shocking incident to the residence assistant, who advised her to ignore it but promised to take action if the abuse was repeated. Angela sought help from other university personnel before any action was taken (personal communications October 1999). The two students from whose room the call was made received a letter of reprimand. Residence staff and other student employees on the campus were offered training in cultural awareness, anti-racism and the importance of reporting incidents of harassment and discrimination (personal communication February 2000). The problem was not dealt with satisfactorily because the defendants were not told to attend the seminars, and although the seminar was offered, it was not mandatory. Moreover, these racist and sexist incidents are not as isolated as the university would claim; they are the daily lived experiences of many students (*Anti-Racism Forum* 1993, 1999; personal communications March 28 and April 27, 2000).

In March 1999, James, a Mi'Kmaq student, reported at an anti-racism forum that he was constantly harassed by some White students, who made racist comments and gestures in his English class. He felt so disgusted and frustrated that on several occasions he seriously contemplated withdrawing from the university. In the late 1980s–early 1990s, several Aboriginal and Black students articulated their concerns about the "freezing" and "hostile" climate on the campus; they felt like "outsiders," not like members of the university family (*Multiculturalism Committee Forum* 1992; *Anti-Racism Forum* 1993). At a panel discussion on access to Black students in October 1992, a Black male student said that he felt like an "outsider" every day, as if he was "always standing on a chair" (*Multiculturalism Committee Forum* 1992). As a result of these kinds of concerns, the Multiculturalism Committee recommended in 1992 that the university write a policy on racial discrimination and harassment and take proactive measures (such as anti-racist education) to combat racism among all constituencies: students, faculty, staff and administration.

Aboriginal and racialized minority students' experiences of everyday racism reflect the systemic racism in the university. Thus, it could be argued that the university is being complicit by refusing to address systemic and ongoing racially-based discrimination and harassment, by insisting that these are isolated incidents and by co-opting and redefining students' experiences. The aforementioned racist and sexist telephone call appears to be one of the best kept secrets on campus. I agree with Larry Roper (1990: 13A) that it is time to "face up to racism on campus.... Racism flourishes because of the silence of those who allegedly oppose it. Silence makes people who in their hearts deplore racism co-conspirators with racists." In sum, systemic racism and everyday racism produce and reproduce each other.

This section of the chapter has shown that, while many administrators and faculty members pay lip-service to the need to ensure equality of opportunity for all students, in reality they are more concerned with maintaining the status quo (O'Brien 1990; personal communications February 1998, February 1999).

Harassment of the Faculty

Racial harassment of university faculty members takes several forms: targeting First Nations and people of colour for discriminatory treatment; infantalizing and inferiorizing them as if they are not good enough; giving biased performance evaluation; exercising differential assignment of courses and scheduling; and subjecting them to latent corrosive terrorism. Outspoken racial minority professors, particularly women, may be targeted for differential treatment. This sometimes takes the form of negative documentation (or building a paper trail) for minor or non-existent problems, which can be used against them during evaluation for contract renewal or tenure/promotion. For instance, Marion, an Aboriginal professor, alleged that in 1998 she received a memorandum from her departmental chair because she was a half-hour late for a departmental meeting with students but that a White male professor, who was one hour late for the same meeting, was not reported. The memorandum was placed in her file and used during her evaluation for contract renewal (personal communications June 3, 1999).

Aboriginal and racialized minority professors are subjected to false accusations and blamed for events or actions in which they were not the sole participants. They may be blamed also for conflicts with colleagues and staff, even when they may have been the victims of harassment. For instance, Zanana, an African Canadian faculty member, alleges that she was wrongfully accused by her department chair of hoarding or losing a transcriber. Although Zanana and her research assistants said that the transcriber was returned to the department almost a year earlier, the chair, Roger, insisted that she was responsible for it because the departmental records indicated that she was the last person who borrowed it. After Zanana had received several memoranda on the subject, she decided to telephone the other departments to find out who might have borrowed the transcriber. She found out that a secretary had borrowed it for almost a year and that the department's record was not updated. Zanana claimed that Roger never admitted his mistake. He pretended that the whole incident had never happened. Incidents of false accusation, and attempts to classify courses on anti-racism, Black (and Native) studies under criminal justice[11] reflect the criminalization of Black (and Native) peoples and the racialization of crime. Research (Hall 1998; James 1994c, 1997) suggests that racial minorities will always be located within a set of meanings that are socially situated and defined by systems of cultural representation. Thus, although Zanana is a faculty member, she is not "immune to the stereotypes and concomitant issues and problems that go along with being a racial minority, and a Black [woman]" in particular, in Euro-Canadian society (James 1994c: 51). As Patricia Collins (1996: 40) points out: "Black women have been denied the authority to challenge" powerful White males' definition of Black women as "a negative other, the virtual antithesis of positive White male images." However, Black women's self-defined standpoint and self-valuation have led them to resist the dehumanization essential to systems of domination.

There are several cases of some White professors inferiorizing Aboriginal and racialized minority professors. The race-specific typing of minoritized faculty members, particularly women, as being capable of and restricted to teaching courses on race and ethnicity only is one form of inferiorization and ghettoization (Razack 2000; Reyes and Halcon 1988). For instance, Jane, a Black professor, who was teaching a research methods course, reported that in the 1980s a White male faculty member told a White female colleague, in Jane's presence, that it was unusual for people of colour, particularly women, to teach research methods. However, he acted as if Jane was not even there. She was an "outsider-within" the university as well as in the research methods course because she was seen as teaching in a non-traditional area for her group. She alleged that she was harassed for more than a decade by a clique, mostly Whites, who wanted either to teach the undergraduate research methods course themselves or assign it to a White professor. Research methods, like theory, is regarded as more abstract and rigorous than substantive area courses and thus more prestigious. Social closure theory postulates that the more desirable the job, the more likely subordinate groups (such as Black women) will be excluded, and the more the job is filled by Black women, the more it is devalued and deskilled by employers (Murphy 1988; Parkin 1979).

However, when funding becomes available for research and development projects on African Canadian and other marginalized communities, a benevolent form of racism expresses itself in a different kind of disrespect, one that appropriates the voices of Blacks themselves and presumes to know what is best. This is yet another form of infantalization. Sudden "experts" pop up throughout the university as individuals note that funding might be attached to projects on First Nations, African Canadians and other marginalized communities. Some of the same professors who denied that there was racism or who showed no interest in these marginalized communities now apply for large grants, sometimes running away with minoritized persons' ideas as they engage in the politics of helping or saving them. According to racial and gender ideologies and racist logic, Black and Aboriginal peoples are "naturally" resource people just as Whites are "naturally" experts. In the process, these sudden experts intensify the marginality and/or exclusion of Black and Aboriginal faculty members, particularly women—those who always did the work—either by excluding them or inferiorizing them as having only experiential knowledge. Thus, Black and Aboriginal people tend to be treated exclusively as resource people, which is another form of exploitation.

Organizing and Struggling for Equity in Academe

African Canadians in Nova Scotia began organizing for anti-racism change in universities in the late 1960s as they became more politically conscious during the civil rights and Black Power movements. Several organizations (such as the Afro-Canadian Liberation Movement [ACLM] and the Black United Front) were formed in Halifax in 1968 to eliminate all forms of anti-Black racism (Calliste 1994, 1996a). Special attention was given to access to universities and the politics of education because of the crucial role of higher education in attaining economic, political and social power. For example, the Transition Year Program (TYP) at Dalhousie University, which provides some African Nova Scotian and Mi'Kmaq students with the academic background and financial assistance necessary to prepare them for university, developed out of the initiative of a group of Black and White students (Dalhousie Graduate Students Association) and the ACLM to increase access to university for Blacks (Calliste 1993, 1996a; Foyn 1998; Moreau 1982).

Before 1990, TYP suffered from chronic lack of funding and human resources because it never received the support of senior university administrators. Although TYP has been successful in preparing some students for admission to university, it has not been effective in redressing systemic racism and educational inequities, given its use as a band-aid policy and, until 1995, an excuse for the province's resistance to educational change (Black Learners Advisory Committee [BLAC] 1994; Calliste 1993, 1994; Task Force on Access for Black and Native People 1989). The forces for the status quo resisted African Canadian demands for institutional transformation at the height of Black protests, and one way they accomplished this was to co-opt some activists and an appeasement policy of multiculturalism (Peter 1981; Stasiulis 1982).

In the 1980s, African Canadians realized that multiculturalism and race relations policies were ineffective in combating racism and that, while a few more African Canadian students were attending university, there were many structural and situational barriers to entry, retention and completion of university education. For example, there was a lack of support services (such as appropriate counselling, culturally relevant curriculum and pedagogical paradigms) for Black and Aboriginal students. Some students decided to organize themselves to seek strategies for change on campuses. In 1987 Aboriginal and Black students at St. Francis Xavier University organized the Ethnic Minorities Association (EMA) to provide support for one another, to promote their history and culture, to combat racism on campus and to exert pressure on the university for systemic anti-racism change. They argued that the university should assume its responsibility to address the issue of racism (Reddick 1992). The association organized guest lectures and symposia on access, anti-racist education and employment equity during its annual "Multicultural Expose" or "Anti-Racism Week" (Williamson and Reddick 1992). The annual symposium also provided an opportunity for students to voice their concerns and to question the university about its commitment (or apparent lack of commitment) to making racial equality on campus a reality (McInnis 1989). However, many students felt that the administration and some faculty members were not listening to their concerns because there was virtually no change. Most discussion audiences consisted of students with a small number of faculty members, administrators and staff.

In 1989, the liaison officer of Black and Native students recommended to the president that he appoint an ad hoc committee to examine the university's awareness of and commitment to racial equality. However, some committee members pathologized African Canadian and Mi'Kmaq communities and blamed them for the severe underrepresentation and low retention rate of students from these communities. Moreover, the committee's mandate was "watered down" to finding ways to assist Black and Aboriginal communities "to take full advantage of educational opportunities and improve their situation" (O'Brien 1990: 8). The committee's sanitized recommendations were limited to providing access to African Canadian and Mi'Kmaq students; including more multicultural content in courses; sensitizing students in the bachelor of education program; and establishing a standing committee on multiculturalism. However, most of the recommendations were not implemented.

EMA was defunct by 1996. Since 1998, Anti-Racism Week has been organized by a coalition of organizations, including the Anti-Racism Caucus,

Brothers and Sisters of the African Diaspora (BSAD), the Students Union and Student Services.

The Anti-Racism Caucus, organized in January 1997 by some faculty members, students and staff, pressured the university administration and the Women's Caucus to include the addressing of race and ethnicity issues (anti-racism) as a key point in their proposal to establish a position of Co-ordinator of Women and Diversity Issues. The meetings reflected the terrain of tensions and conflicts (Henry et al. 1999). The Anti-Racism Caucus argued that the title of the position indicated "othering" ("women and the others"), and they suggested "Equity Co-ordinator." Some members of the Women's Caucus rationalized the exclusion and marginality of anti-racism, sexuality and disability issues by arguing that the job would be unmanageable and that they had asked for the position first. Despite several reminders, they ignored the fact that EMA and the Multiculturalism Committee had been asking for a co-ordinator since 1993. Such a divisive strategy hinders the formation of networks and coalitions among anti-oppressive groups while it benefits those in power. As Anne Bishop (1994: 10–11) points out:

> As long as we try to end our oppression by rising above others, we are reinforcing each other's oppression, and eventually our own.... The idea that one form of oppression, or even one person's oppression, can be solved independently, is of great benefit to the rich and powerful. This belief is enough to keep oppressed people jostling in competition with each other, never reaching a point of unity where we can successfully challenge those with more than their share.

After meeting for eight months, there seemed to have been some progress. The title was changed, the job description included race and ethnicity issues, the Anti-Racism Caucus had representation on the planning sub-committee and on a proposed advisory committee to the Equity Co-ordinator. However, this was a hollow victory given that, with the hiring of an Equity Co-ordinator, racism on the campus has become more subtle and difficult to fight. The university administration and many faculty members refuse to accept the existence of cultural and systemic racism. (See Caplan 1994 and Carniol 1991 on the effects of equity co-ordinators.)

Students of African descent, tired of years of neglect and differential treatment, organized Brothers and Sisters of the African Diaspora (BSAD) in 1999 to pressure the university administration for appropriate support systems such as employing a Black Students' Advisor and allocating space for a Black students' lounge, as well as other anti-racism change. As a result, they have a part-time advisor and a lounge/resource room. Hopefully, these concessions will not serve as an appeasement policy. BSAD continues to demand a policy for dealing with racial discrimination and harassment. However, unlike some nonathletes, Black student athletes do not experience the brunt of racism. They are treated as "exceptional" Blacks; they appear to be popular and have social support from their coach and other team members (personal communications February 2000). It appears that some student athletes become infantalized and dependent on their coach, a mediator who protects his investments and co-opts the voice of students. Thus, some Black student athletes do not develop critical thinking skills, and they do not understand the subtleties of racism (personal communications March 2000).

Another anti-racist strategy was the formation in 1992 of an Anti-Racist Teaching Network (ARTN) by universities in Halifax. This followed a challenge by an African student at St. Mary's University, Ivy Kusinga of Uganda, to a professor who blatantly misused a film depicting "primitive" life in Africa (Millar and Riviere 1993: 3). The ARTN, consisting of students and faculty, organized two successful workshops for faculty on anti-racist teaching. The proceedings of the second workshop, which included forty recommendations, were distributed to all Nova Scotian universities. The two most important recommendations were that the boards of governors of all Nova Scotian universities adopt an anti-racist teaching policy and that "racial harassment ... be accorded equal priority with sexual or other forms of harassment and ... therefore be treated as professional misconduct" (Millar and Reviere 1993: 7–8). However, Nova Scotian universities do not have racial discrimination and harassment policies. Many administrators and faculty members resist anti-racism and equity initiatives because "they are unwilling to question their own belief and value systems, teaching practices, and positions of power and privilege" within the university and the society (Henry et al. 1999: 255). For instance, in the early 1990s, there was strong resistance to Dalhousie University's proposed Discriminatory Harassment Policy on the basis that it constituted "thought policing" and was a threat to academic freedom (Dalhousie University 1992; Watson 1995). Some staff and faculty members who support the policy think that the university is not likely to approve a discriminatory harassment policy, particularly given the current administration's redefinition of racial discrimination and harassment in the workplace as management relations problems (personal communications July 14, 1997, November 1997).

Like those of governments, the response of universities to anti-racism policy demands are shaped by several factors, including the nature of the issue being pursued by the organizers, the group's numerical strength and power, their chosen strategies and the political ideologies of the university administration. They may respond with co-optation of the issue, development of internal divisions, reprisals and repression. For instance, it is alleged that, in the late 1990s, Aboriginal and Black students, staff and faculty members at a university were labelled as "trouble makers" and harassed after they tried to have the issue of racism addressed by faculty in a professional program. As a result, the probationary contract of Janet, an Aboriginal faculty member, was not renewed.

Another faculty member, who resigned from her job, described the "poisoned" working environment as the most hostile one she had ever seen, and a staff member alleged that she was harassed to the point of feeling ill (interviews July 14, 1997). This reflects some of the emotional, psychological and social costs of resistance.

Conclusion

This study of anti-racist organizing and resistance in academia supports my eclectic theoretical perspective (anti-racism, feminism, social closure and Marxism) by illustrating the relational aspects of social difference. The essay also demonstrates some of the emotional, psychological and social costs of resistance.

For universities to be inclusive and equitable educational institutions and workplaces, they need to address the sources of systemic racism. As Carniol (1991: 1) argue,

> [They] will need to acknowledge that these sources stem from the way our system has organized power via (legal, economic, political and cultural) structures which disempower collectivities of people. Conversely, solutions will need to include collective empowerment of those now excluded from institutional decision making.

Students, faculty and staff who are working for anti-racism change must continue to focus on changing structures and policies and participating in decision-making (for example, on student councils). They must also continue to organize at the departmental and university levels and to form meaningful networks and coalitions at the local, national and international levels with other anti-racist groups and other anti-oppression movements.

Notes

1. This research is part of a study on access to universities, which is funded by St. Francis Xavier University Centre for Regional Studies and the Social Sciences and Humanities Research Council grant to universities.
2. Overhead funds pay for the use of university resources (for example, space and equipment).
3. Chun performed extra duties—teaching and supervising graduate students—which were not covered in his research associate's pay.
4. a) Marginality is a process in which a sense of otherness and peripherality is perpetuated and encouraged (Brandt 1986: 104).
   b) The OHRC noted that it could not review some potentially important documents because of incomplete documentation and "shredding of records" (Canadian Association of University Teachers 2000: 4).
5. This information was revealed to me during interviews on July 12, 1997, and in personal communications which took place in February 1998.

6. Grand Bras and Paradise are fictitious names for actual institutions.
7. In 1994, the Status of Women Sub-Committee distributed a survey to examine the characteristics of Canadian sociology and anthropology departments. Fifty-five (70 percent) of the seventy-nine departments contacted returned the survey. Incomplete questionnaires were excluded from the analysis, leaving thirty finished surveys. Although the valid returns represented only 40 percent of the departments, the CSAA findings were consistent with the Canadian Association of University Teachers' (CAUT 1996) statistical profile of university faculty (Canadian Sociology and Anthropology Association 1997: 1).
8. Rules that appear neutral may have a negative impact on minoritized groups.
9. White males do not constitute a homogenous group; nor are they all members of the same cliques or network. Groups have differential economic and political power resources and mobilization resources (such as leadership skills) (Breton 1979).
10. Panis (or Aboriginal) slaves were reported in Montreal in 1670. However, slavery declined in New France (Quebec) because slavery was not profitable given that the fur trade did not require skilled or gang labour (Winks 1971: 2–3).
11. The rationalization that was given for classifying anti-racism, Black and Native Studies courses under criminal justice was that most African American men are in jails and most of the incarcerated people in Western Canada were Native peoples (personal communications January 10, 1997).

Chapter Nine

Resisting Academic Closure:

Rethinking Anti-Racism Education for the New Millennium

George J. Sefa Dei and Agnes Calliste

Over the years we have been moved by the lost sense of entitlement to schooling felt by many disadvantaged youth. This sense of entitlement is not just a question of having a right to be there but of developing a sense of belonging to a collective of shared and conflicting interests and objectives. A new approach to anti-racism could focus on addressing how youths from differing backgrounds can all claim this sense of belonging to our schools and educational institutions. This is a challenging task for educators, practitioners, parents, local community groups and social workers. These are important stakeholders in the education of the future.

As we edge into the new millennium, anti-racist education must confront some key questions about our school systems, and these questions must guide our understanding of education beyond the issues of teaching, learning and administration to access, representation and social equity. How do we (meaning all who read this text and share in the educational politics presented here) ensure that schools respond to the multiple needs and concerns of a diverse student body? How do we ensure that excellence is not simply accessible but also equitable to all social groups? How do we move beyond the bland and seductive politics of inclusion to the pointed questions of transparency and accountability so that administrators can be held responsible for any lack of anti-racism change in schools? Can critical educators move beyond treating everyone the same and begin to work with different models of equity and justice?

In the Introduction we wrote that our society is colour-coded and that a public discourse of a "colour-blind society" is as insidious as the practice of racism itself because it refuses to acknowledge the power differential behind social differences. Here we add that none of us can afford to be blind to the colour of racism or refuse to hear the voices of groups differentially positioned with/by the dominant culture. Those subordinated by societal structures have no option but to hear the voices of pain and suffering and the cry for change. In fact, we should neither want to refuse to hear nor have neutrality as an option. For, as Paulo Freire (1993) writes, there is an inhumanity inherent in the refusal to see and challenge structures and policies that oppress and dehumanize fellow human beings. Moreover, such blindness and deafness inhibit us from critically reading our world, grasping it, reflecting upon it and, through reflection, collectively working to change it.

As argued earlier, taking a position that centres race along with other forms of difference has become even more crucial in light of the quickening pace of global change and the increasing risk of information overload down onto "communities of difference" who do not own the media and, therefore, the means of cultural production and dissemination. In our individual and collective practices (which includes our writing) and with/in our institutions/workplaces, it is ever more important to give priority to groups living with less resources and under conditions of oppression. Failing to do so contributes to a silencing of that reality and impoverishes our communities and the ongoing creation and recreation of cultures. In recognizing the strengths of technological communication we must be ever vigilant to the risk of a dialogue that may be limited to downloaded knowledge imposed onto a flat screen, which can be a powerful tool in homogenizing and silencing the different lived realities.

We bring meanings to texts just as much as texts convey powerful meanings to us. Those of us who work in the academy, who write and read the word on page and screen, have an obligation to ensure that the institutions in which we work are continuously taking up the challenge of equity and social justice in educational access, representation and outcomes. All authors in this collection have continued the dialogue individually (through their articles) and collectively (through this book). We expect that through the engagement of readers the dialogue will reach farther and increase in depth and complexity. Readers will intersect with their own experiences of the textured materials, which are similar and different to varying degrees.

This book contributes to a broad perspective on education from elementary school to university outcomes. Among many things, the book includes issues of teaching practices, student social spaces outside the classroom, programs of access to university, experiences of women of colour in teacher-training institutions and curriculum and texts. Through its broad educational scope, the relations among educational institutions over a student's lifespan is made more visible. This view is informed by a historical perspective on anti-racism and by an outline for a discursive anti-racist theoretical framework. With this we are asking that our responses (readings, writings, actions) take or at times include a centred race position. We articulate this position as the "saliency of race in schooling and education" and the reading of multiple oppressions through the lens of race.

This book has highlighted a particular model of social change through a critical anti-racist practice. This model emphasizes the saliency of race in oppression work while acknowledging the intersections of race and other forms of difference. It is an approach to educational change that acknowledges both the significance of identity to knowledge production and learning process and the importance of acknowledging the situational and contextual variations in intensities of oppressions. As an educational strategy the anti-racist approach must target specific groups, acknowledging severity of issues for certain bodies while at the same time enthusing the interlocking nature of multiple oppressions.

Recognizing that some groups are oppressed or have less power does not diminish the strength and richness of oppositional knowledges and languages. Rather, we have stated that amid dominance and resisting/resistance these knowledges continue to flourish as a testimony to the strength of the struggle and the cultural and political depth of our diverse communities. Throughout history oppressed groups have drawn from within and reached out in alliance for survival. These groups have developed a spirit of continued recreation and revitalization of individual and collective subjectivities. We must be a part of that alliance so that we and our educational institutions can become stronger and richer (culturally and politically speaking) and fulfill the obligations and mandates of educating all of our population as participating citizens actively contributing to the society in which we live.

Anti-racist educational practice in the new millennium must situate equity within the broader definition of education, the varied ways, strategies and options through which subjects come to know their world and act within it for purposeful change. Similarly anti-racist educational practice must work towards a broader definition of equity that recognizes the severity of issues for specific disadvantaged groups. Anti-racist educational practice must lead to an understanding that excellence is equity and equity is excellence.

Anti-racism must acknowledge the limitation of social theory not grounded in practice. Political practice is integral to anti-racism theorizing because writing on anti-racism does not certify anti-racist work. At the same time, anti-racism must herald the importance of understanding the philosophical basis of any educational practice if classroom teaching, instructional and pedagogical practices are to maintain their effects. Anti-racism education is matching the concern over access with a discussion of meaningful outcomes, which is measured beyond the satisfaction of the material and is tangible to the psychological, emotional and spiritual well-being of the learner. Finally all rights have accompanying responsibilities. Therefore as students have a right to education, we and they also have a responsibility to ask critical questions about the absences, omissions and negations in schools. For the teacher, a privilege to teach is also a responsibility to teach about the complete history of ideas and events that have shaped and continue to shape human growth and development.

Bibliography

Abella, R. 1984. *Equality Now: Report of the Special Committee on Visible Minorities in Canadian Society*. Ottawa: Queen's Printer.

Ahamad, Bill. 1987. *Participation of Different Ethnic Groups in Post-secondary Education*. Ottawa: Secretary of State.

Aidoo, Ama Ata. 1992. "African Women Today." *Dissent* Summer: 319–25.

Alexander, J.C. 1992. "Citizen and Enemy as Symbolic Classification: On the Polarizing Discourse of Civil Society." In Michele Lamont and Marcel Fournier (eds.), *Cultivating Differences*. Chicago: University of Chicago Press, 289–308.

Alladin, I., ed. 1995. *Racism in Canadian Schools*. Toronto: Harcourt.

Allen, A. 1997. "On Being a Role Model." In A.K. Wing (ed.), *Critical Race Feminism: A Reader*. New York: New York University Press, 81–87.

Allen, Keith. 1996. "The Transitional Year Program at the University of Toronto: A Life-Line for Blacks Seeking a University Education." In K.S. Brathwaite and C.E. James (eds.), *Educating African Canadians*. Toronto: Lorimer, 234–50.

Amadiume, Ifi. 1987. *Male Daughters, Female Husbands: Gender and Sex in an African Society*. London: Zed.

Amott, T. and J. Matthaei. 1996. *Race, Gender, and Work: A Multicultural Economic History of Women in the United States*. Enlarged ed. Montreal: Black Rose.

Anderson, Benedict. 1991. *Imagined Communities: Reflections on the Origin and Spread of Nationalism*. London: Verso.

Anisef, P., M. Bertrand, U. Hortian and C. James. 1985. *Accessibility to Post-secondary Education in Canada: A Review of Literature*. Ottawa: Secretary of State.

Anisef, Paul and Leslie Andres Bellamy. 1993. "Post-secondary Education and Visible Minorities in Canada: Changes, Expectations and Demands." Paper presented at the 15th Annual EAIR Forum on "Higher Education in a Changing Environment: Regional, National and Trans-national Issues." Turku, Finland.

Anthias, F. and N. Yuval-Davis. 1992. *Racialized Boundaries*. London: Routledge.

Anti-Discriminatory Advisory Group. 1995. *Access Initiative Programme Report*. Toronto: Faculty of Education, York University.

Anti-Racism Forum. 1993. Paradise University. March 31.

_____. 1999. Paradise University. March.

Anzaldua, G. 1987. *Borderlands/La Frontera*. San Francisco: Aunt Lute.

_____. 1990. *Making Faces, Making Soul, Haciento Caras, Creative and Critical Perspectives by Women of Color*. San Francisco: Aunt Lute.

Apple, M. 1982. *Education and Power*. Boston: Routledge and Kegan Paul.

_____. 1990. *Ideology and Curriculum*. New York: Routledge.

Armstrong, P. and H. Armstrong. 1990. *Theorizing Women's Work*. Toronto: Garamond.

Asante, M.K. 1987. *The Afrocentric Idea*. Philadelphia: Temple University Press.

_____. 1988. *Afrocentricity*. Trenton, NJ: Africa World.

_____. 1990a. *Kemet, Afrocentricity and Knowledge*. Trenton, NJ: Africa World.

_____. 1990b. "Afrocentricity and Culture." In Molefi Kete Asante and Karimu Walsh-Asante (eds.), *African Culture: The Rhythms of Unity*. Trenton, NJ: Africa World, 3–12.

Ashcroft, B., G. Griffiths and H. Tiffin, eds. 1989. *The Empire Writes Back: Theory and

Practice in Post-colonial Literatures. New York: Routledge.
Ashrawi, H. 1995. *This Side of Peace: A Personal Account*. New York: Simon and Schuster.
Badets, J. 1994. "Canada's Immigrants: Recent Trends." In Craig McKie (ed.), *Canadian Social Trends: A Canadian Studies Reader*. Vol. 2. Toronto: Thompson.
Bains, H. and P. Cohen, eds. 1988. *Multi-racist Britain*. London: Macmillan.
Bakan, A. and D. Stasiulis. 1995. "Making the Match: Domestic Placement Agencies and the Racialization of Women's Household Work." *Signs* 20, 2: 303–35.
Baker, D. 1983. *Race, Ethnicity and Power: A Comparative Perspective*. London: Routledge and Kegan Paul.
Baker, M., A. Calliste, K. Grant and K. Mirchandi. 1996. *Survey of Canadian Sociology and Anthropology Departments*. Montreal: Status of Women Committee, Canadian Sociology and Anthropology Association.
Bangar, S. and Janet McDermott. 1989. "Black Women Speak." In Hilary De Lyon and Frances Widdowson Migniuolo (eds.), *Women Teachers: Issues and Experiences*. Milton Keynes: Open University Press, 135–53.
Banks, J.A. and C.A. McGee-Banks, eds. 1989. *Multicultural Education: Issues and Perspectives*. Toronto: Allyn and Bacon.
Banks, T. 1993. "The Canon Debate, Knowledge Construction and Multicultural Education." *Educational Researcher* 22, 5: 4-14.
Bannerji, H., L. Carty, K. Dehli, S. Heald and K. McKenna. 1991a. *Unsettling Relations: The University as a Site of Feminist Struggles*. Toronto: Women's.
_____. 1991b. "But Who Speaks for Us? Experience and Agency in Conventional Feminist Paradigms." In H. Bannerji, L. Carty, K. Dehli, S. Heald and K. McKenna, (eds.) *Unsettling Relations: The University as a Site of Feminist Struggles*. Toronto: Women's, 67–108.
Banton, M. 1977. *The Idea of Race*. London: Tavistock.
Barbee, E. 1993. "Racism in U.S. Nursing." *Medical Anthropology Quarterly* 7, 4: 346–62.
Barrett, K. 1996. "Intersections of Race and Gender: Sexual Harassment and International Development." Unpublished paper. Toronto: Department of Sociology in Education, Ontario Institute for Studies in Education/University of Toronto.
Battiste, M. 1986. "Micmac Literacy and Cognitive Assimilation." In J. Barman et al. (eds.), *Indian Education in Canada, Vol. 1: The Legacy*. Vancouver: University of British Columbia Press.
Becker, H. 1963. *Outsiders: Studies in the Sociology of Deviance*. New York: Free.
Beer, V. and D. Marsh. 1988. "A Non-school Curriculum Model Illustrated in a Museum Setting." *Journal of Curriculum and Supervision* 3: 221–39.
Belenky, Mary Field, Blythe McVicker Clinchy, Nancy Rule Goldberger and Jill Mattuck Tarul. 1986. *Women's Ways of Knowing: The Development of Self, Voice and Mind*. New York: Basic.
Belkhir, J. 1996. "Social Inequality and Race, Gender, Class: A Working Class Intellectual Perspective." *Race, Gender and Class* 4, 1: 167–94.
Belkhir, J. and M. Ball. 1993. "Integrating Race, Sex and Class." *Race, Sex and Class* 1, 1: 3–11.
Belkhir, J. and M. Duyme. 1998. "Intelligence and Race, Gender and Class: The Fallacy of Genetic Determinism." *Race, Gender and Class* 5, 3: 136–78.
Bell, S., M. Morrow and E. Tastsoglou. 1996. "Teaching in Environments of Resistance:

Toward a Critical, Feminist and Anti-Racist Pedagogy." Paper presented at the Annual Meeting of the American Sociological Association. August. New York City (forthcoming in Maralee Mayberry and Ellen Cronan Rose (eds.), *Meeting the Challenge: Innovative Feminist Pedagogies in Action.* New York: Routledge).

Bellamy, L. and N. Guppy. 1991. "Women in Canadian Higher Education." In J. Gaskell and A. McLaren (eds.), *Women and Education.* Calgary: Detselig.

Benedict, R. 1999. "Racism: The ism of the Modern World." In R. Harris (ed.), *Racism.* New York: Humanity, 31–49.

Bennet, T. 1990. *Outside Literature.* London: Routledge.

Bernard, J. 1964. *Academic Women.* New York: New American.

Berry, J., M. Joneja, M. Robillard and J. Sinnott, eds. 1993. *Proceedings of the National Symposium for University Presidents on Institutional Strategies for Race and Ethnic Relations at Canadian Universities.* Kingston, ON: Queen's University Press.

Bhabha, H. 1994. *The Location of Culture.* London: Routledge.

Bishop, A. 1994. *Becoming an Ally: Breaking the Cycle of Oppression.* Halifax: Fernwood.

Black Learners Advisory Committee (BLAC). 1994. *BLAC Report on Education: Redressing Inequality—Empowering Black Learners, Vol. 3: Results of a Socio-Demographic Survey of the Nova Scotia Black Community.* Halifax: BLAC.

Boas, F. 1940. *Race, Language, and Culture.* New York: Macmillan.

_____.1969. *Race and Democratic Society.* New York: Biblo and Tannen.

Bolaria, B. and P. Li. 1988. *Racial Oppression in Canada.* 2nd ed. Toronto: Garamond.

Bonnett, A. 1996. "Anti-Racism and the Critique of 'White' Identities." *New Community* 22, 1: 97–110.

Bourdieu, P. 1984. *Distinction: A Social Critique of the Judgement of Taste.* Cambridge, MA: Harvard University Press.

_____. 1989. "Social Space and Symbolic Power." *Sociological Theory* 7, 10: 14–25.

_____. 1990a. *Language and Symbolic Power.* Trans. G. Raymond and M. Adamson. Oxford: Polity.

_____. 1990b. *In Other Words: Essays Towards a Reflexive Sociology.* Trans. Mathew Adamson. Stanford: Stanford University Press.

Bourgeault, R. 1989. "Race, Class and Gender: Colonial Domination of Indian Women." *Socialist Studies* 5: 87–115.

Brand, D. 1987. "Black Women and Work: The Impact of Racially Constructed Gender Roles on the Sexual Division of Labour." *Fireweed* 25, Fall: 28–37.

Brandt, G. 1986. *The Realization of Anti-Racist Teaching.* Lewes: Falmer.

Brant, B. 1994. *Writing as Witness: Essay and Talk.* Toronto: Women's.

Brathwaite, K. and C. James. 1996. *Educating African Canadians.* Toronto: Lorimer.

Breton, R. 1979. "Ethnic Stratification Viewed from Three Theoretical Perspectives." In J. Curtis and W. Scott (eds.), *Social Stratification in Canada.* Scarborough: Prentice-Hall, 270–94.

Brewer, R.M. 1993. "Theorizing, Race, Class and Gender: The New Scholarship of Black Feminist Intellectuals and Black Women's Labour." In Stanlie James and Abena Busia (eds.), *Theorizing Black Feminisms.* New York: Routledge, 13–30.

Briskin, L. 1990. *Feminist Pedagogy: Teaching and Learning Liberation.* Ottawa: Canadian Research Institute for the Advancement of Women.

Britzman, D. 1990. "Could This Be Your Story? Guilty Readings and Other Ethnographic Dramas." Paper presented at the Bergamo Conference. Dayton, OH.

_____. 1993. "Is There a Queer Pedagogy? Or, Stop Being Straight." Paper presented at the Speakers' Series of the Critical Pedagogy and Cultural Studies Forum. Toronto: Ontario Institute for Studies in Education/University of Toronto.

_____. 1996. "'That Lonely Discovery': Anne Frank, Anna Freud and the Question of Pedagogy." Unpublished manuscript.

Brookes, A.L. 1992. *Feminist Pedagogy: An Autobiographical Approach.* Halifax: Fernwood.

Buijs, G., ed. 1993. *Migrant Women: Crossing Boundaries and Changing Identities.* Oxford: Berg.

Burke, M. 1994. "Canada's Immigrant Children." In Craig McKie (ed.), *Canadian Social Trends: A Canadian Studies Reader.* Vol. 2. Toronto: Thompson.

Burton, F. and P. Carlen. 1979. *Official Discourse: On Discourse Analysis, Government Publications, Ideology and the State.* London: Routledge and Kegan Paul.

Butler, J. 1990. *Gender Trouble: Feminism and the Subversion of Identity.* New York: Routledge.

Butler, J. and J. Scott, eds. 1992. *Feminists Theorize the Political.* London: Routledge.

Caldwell, P.M. 1997. "A Hair Piece." In Adrienne Katherine Wing (ed.), *Critical Race Feminism.* New York: New York University Press, 297–305.

Calliste, A. 1991. "Canada's Immigration Policy and Domestics from the Caribbean: The Second Domestic Scheme." *Socialist Studies* 136–68.

_____. 1993."Women of 'Exceptional Merit': Immigration of Caribbean Nurses to Canada." *Canadian Journal of Women and Labour* 6: 85–102.

_____. 1993/94. "Race, Gender and Canadian Immigration Policy: Blacks from the Caribbean, 1900-1932." *Journal of Canadian Studies* 28, 4: 131–48.

_____. 1994. "Blacks Struggle for Education Equity in Nova Scotia. In V. D'Oyley (ed.), *Canadian Innovations in Black Education.* Toronto: Umbrella, 25–40.

_____. 1995. "The Influence of the Civil Rights and Black Power Movement in Canada." *Race, Gender and Class* 2, 3: 123–40.

_____. 1996a. "African Canadians Organizing for Educational Change." In K.S. Brathwaite and C.E. James, *Educating African Canadians.* Toronto: Lorimer, 87–106.

_____. 1996b. "Anti-Racism Organizing and Resistance: Blacks in Urban Canada, 1940s–1970s." In J. Caulfield and L. Peake (eds.), *City Lives and City Forms.* Toronto: University of Toronto Press, 283–302.

_____. 1996c. "Antiracism Organizing and Resistance in Nursing: African Canadian Women." *Canadian Review of Sociology and Anthropology* 33, 3: 361–90.

_____. 2000a. "Resisting Exclusion and Marginality in Nursing: Women of Colour in Ontario." In M. Kalbach and W. Kalbach (eds.), *Race and Ethnicity in Canada.* Toronto: Harcourt.

_____. 2000b. "Nurses and Porters: Racism, Sexism and Resistance in Segmented Labour Markets." In A. Calliste and G. Dei (eds.), *Anti-Racist Feminism: Critical Race and Gender Studies.* Halifax: Fernwood.

Calliste, A. and G.J.S. Dei. 2000. *Anti-Racist Feminism.* Halifax: Fernwood.

Calliste, A., G.J.S. Dei and J. Belkhir. 1995. "Canadian Perspectives on Anti-Racism: Intersection of Race, Gender and Class." *Race, Gender and Class* 2, 3 (Spring): 5–10.

Canadian Association of University Teachers (CAUT). 1996. "Status of Women Supple-

ment." *CAUT Bulletin*, 11.
_____. 2000. *CAUT Bulletin* February: 1, 4.
Canadian Human Rights Reporter. 1983. "Board of Inquiry Decisions under the Nova Scotia Human Rights Act." Vol. 4, Decision 276. *Kamal Baig* v. *Mount Saint Vincent University*. June. D/1365-69.
_____. 1984. "Board of Inquiry Decision under the Nova Scotia Human Rights Act." Vol. 5, Decision 365. *Nirmal Kumar Jain* v. *Acadia University*. May. D/2123-31.
Canadian Sociology and Anthropology Association. 1997. *Report to the Annual General Meeting*. June.
Cannon, Lynn Weber. 1990. "Fostering Positive Race, Class, and Gender Dynamics in the Classroom." *Women's Studies Quarterly* 1 & 2: 126–34.
Caplan, P. 1994. *Lifting a Ton of Feathers*. Toronto: University of Toronto Press.
Carby, H. 1982. "Schooling for Babylon." In Paul Gilroy, Centre for Contemporary Cultural Studies (eds.), *The Empire Strikes Back*. London: Hutchison, 183–211.
Carniol, B. 1991. "The Way We Respond Can Become an Issue." *Remedies for Racism and Sexism in Colleges and Universities: Conference Proceedings*. April 30–May 1. London, ON.
Carroll, C. 1982. "Three's a Crowd: The Dilemma of the Black Woman in Higher Education." In G. Hull, P. Bellscott and B. Smith (eds.), *All the Women Are White, All the Blacks Are Men, But Some of Us Are Brave*. Old Westbury, NY: Feminist, 115–27.
Carty, L. 1991a. "Black Women in Academia: A Statement from the Periphery." In H. Bannerji, L. Carty, K. Dehli, S. Heald and K. McKenna (eds.), *Unsettling Relations: The University as a Site of Feminist Struggles*. Toronto: Women's, 13–44.
_____. 1991b. "Women's Studies in Canada: A Discourse and Praxis of Exclusion." *Resources for Feminist Research* 20, 3 & 4: 12–18.
_____. 1994. "African Canadian Women and the State: Labour Only Please." In Peggy Bristow, Dionne Brand, Linda Carty, Afua Cooper, Sylvia Hamilton and Adrienne Shadd (eds.), *We're Rooted Here and They Can't Pull Us Up*. Toronto: University of Toronto Press.
Castagna, M. 1995. "*Best Practices of Inclusive Schooling in Two Toronto Schools*." Unpublished paper. Toronto: Department of Sociology, Ontario Institute for Studies in Education/University of Toronto.
Chater, N. 1994. "Biting the Hand that Feeds Me: Notes on Privilege from a White Anti-Racist Feminist." *Canadian Woman Studies* 14:100–104.
_____. 1996. "Re-Viewing 'Colour Blindness': Implications for Anti-Racist Educational Praxis." Unpublished paper. Toronto: Department of Curriculum, Ontario Institute for Studies in Education/University of Toronto.
Childers, M. and b. hooks. 1990. "A Conversation about Race and Class." In Marianne Hirsch and Evelyn Fox Keeler (eds.), *Conflicts in Feminism*. New York: Routledge, 61–81.
Chilly Climate Collective, eds. 1995. *Breaking Anonymity: The Chilly Climate for Women Faculty*. Waterloo, ON: Wilfred Laurier University Press.
Christian, B. 1990. "The Race for Theory." In Abdul R. JanMohamed and David Lloyd (eds.), *The Nature and Context of Minority Discourse*. Oxford: Oxford University Press, 37–49.
Churchill, W. 1992. Fantasies of the Master Race: Literature, Cinema and the Colonization of American Indians. Ed. M. Jaimes. Montoe: ME: Common Courage.

Cohen, P. 1985. *The Symbolic Construction of Community*. London and New York: Tavistock.
_____, ed. 1988. *Multi-Racist Britain*. London: Macmillan.
_____. 1989. *Tackling Common Sense Racism: Cultural Studies Project Annual Report*. London.
_____. 1990. *Black Feminist Thought: Knowledge, Consciousness and the Politics of Empowerment*. London: Harper Collins.
_____. 1993. "Toward a New Vision: Race, Class and Gender as Categories of Analysis and Connection." *Race, Sex and Class* 1, 1: 25–46.
_____. 1996. "Learning from the Outsider-Within: The Sociological Significance of Black Feminist Thought." In M. Rogers (ed.), *Multicultural Experiences, Multicultural Theories*. New York: McGraw-Hill, 35–56.
Collins, P. 1990. *Black Feminist Thought: Knowledge, Consciousness and the Politics of Empowerment*. London: Unwin.
_____. 1996. "Learning from the Outsider-Within: The Sociological Significance of Black Feminist Thought." In M. Rogers (ed.), *Multicultural Experiences, Multicultural Theories*. New York: McGraw-Hill, 35–56.
Collins, P.H. 1993. "Toward a New Vision: Race, Class and Gender as Categories of Analysis and Connecting." *Race, Sex and Class* 1, 1: 25–46
Cooper, A. 1991. "Black Teachers in Canada's West, 1850–1870: A History." Unpublished master's thesis. Toronto: Ontario Institute for Studies in Education/University of Toronto.
Cremin, L. 1976. *Public Education*. New York: Basic.
Dalhousie University. 1989. *Breaking Barriers: Report of the Task Force on Access for Black and Native People*. Halifax, NS: Dalhousie University.
Dalhousie University, Committee to Develop a Policy on Racism and Sexism. 1992. "Proposed Statement on Discriminatory Harassment." October. Halifax, NS: Dalhousie University.
Das Gupta, T. 1996. *Racism and Paid Work*. Toronto: Garamond.
Davis, A. 1981. *Women, Race and Class*. New York: Vintage.
Dei, G.J.S. 1993. "The Challenges of Anti-Racist Education in Canada." *Canadian Ethnic Studies* 25, 2: 36–51.
_____. 1994. "Introduction: Anti-racist Education." *Orbit* 25, 2: 1–3.
_____. 1995a. "Examining the Case for African-Centred Schools." *McGill Journal of Education* 30, 2: 179–98.
_____. 1995b. "Integrative Anti-Racism: Intersection of Race, Class, and Gender." *Race, Gender and Class* 2, 3: 11–30.
_____. 1996a. *Anti-Racism Education in Theory and Practice*. Halifax: Fernwood.
_____. 1996b. *Canadian Review of Sociology & Anthropology* 33, 3.
_____. 1997. "Race and the Production of Identity in the Schooling Experiences of African-Canadian Youth." *Discourse* 18, 2: 241–57.
_____. 1998. "The Sociology of Race and Ethnicity." Lecture Notes. Toronto: Ontario Institute for Studies in Education/University of Toronto.
_____. 1999. "The Denial of Difference: Reframing Anti-Racist Praxis." *Race Ethnicity and Education* 2, 1: 17–38.
_____. 2000. "Contesting the Future: Anti-Racism and Canadian Diversity." In S. Nanacoo (ed.), *21st Century Canadian Diversity*. Toronto: Canadian Educators, 295–319.

Dei, G., L. Broomfield, M. Castagna, I. James, J. Mazzuca and E. McIsaac. 1996. *Unpacking What Works: The Examination of 'Best Practices' of Inclusive Schooling in Ontario*. Preliminary report submitted to the Ontario Ministry of Education. August. Toronto, ON.
Dei, G. and A. Calliste, eds. 1996. "Canadian Perspectives on Anti-Racism." Special Issue. *Canadian Review of Sociology and Anthropology* 33, 3.
Dei, G., L. Holmes, J. Mazzuca, E. McIsaac and R. Campbell. 1995. *Drop Out or Push Out: The Dynamics of Black Students' Disengagement from School*. Final report submitted to the Ontario Ministry of Education and Training. November. Toronto, ON.
Dei, G., J. Mazzuca, E. McIsaac and J. Zinc. 1997. *Reconstructing "Drop Out": A Critical Ethnography of Black Students' Disengagement from School*. Toronto: University of Toronto Press.
Deloria, V. 1992. "Comfortable Fictions and the Struggle for Turf: Review of the Invented Indian: Cultural Fictions and Government Policies." In James Clifton (ed.), *American Indian Quarterly* 16: 397–411.
Desai, S. 1996. "Common Issues, Common Understandings." In C.E. James (ed.), *Perspectives on Racism and the Human Services Sector: A Case for Change*. Toronto: University of Toronto Press, 246–51.
Dewey, J. 1916. *Democracy and Education*. New York: Free.
Di Stefano, C. 1990. "Dilemmas of Difference: Feminism, Modernity and Postmodernism." In Linda Nicholson (ed.), *Feminism/Postmodernism*. New York: Routledge, 63–83.
Donald, W. 1993. "Submission to the Multiculturalism Committee, Paradise University." February 22.
Doris Marshall Institute and Arnold Minors and Associates. 1994. *Ethno-Racial Equality: A Distant Goal? An Interim Report to North-Western General Hospital*. Toronto: Doris Marshall Institute and Arnold Minors and Associates.
Du Bois, W.E.B. 1953. *The Souls of Black Folk*. New York: Rue Heron.
Duclos, N. 1992. "Justice and Cultural Difference: The Art of Judging in a Multicultural Society." Paper presented at the seminar on Racial, Ethnic and Cultural Equity. June 6–12. University of Saskatchewan, Saskatoon.
Durkheim, E. 1965. *The Elementary Forms of Religious Life*. New York: Free.
Durkheim, E. and M. Mauss. 1963. *Primitive Classification*. Chicago: University of Chicago Press.
Dyer, R. 1997. *White*. London and New York: Routledge.
Dyson, M. 1993. *Reflecting Black: African-American Cultural Criticism*. Minneapolis: University of Minnesota Press.
Eber, D. 1969. *Canada Meets Black Power*. Montreal: Tundra.
Eisner, E. 1979. *The Educational Imagination on the Design and Evaluation of School Programs*. New York: Macmillan.
Ellsworth, E. 1989. "Why Doesn't This Feel Empowering? Working through the Repressive Myths of Critical Pedagogy." *Harvard Educational Review* 59, 3 (August): 297–324.
Elshtain, J.B. 1992. "The Power and Powerlessness of Women." In Gisela Brock and Susan James (eds.), *Beyond Equality and Difference*. London: Routledge, 111–25.
Essed, P. 1990. *Everyday Racism Reports from Women of Two Cultures*. Alameda, CA: Hunter House.

_____. 1991. *Understanding Everyday Racism: An Interdisciplinary Theory*. Newbury Park, CA: Sage.
Evans, G. 1988. "Those Loud Black Girls." In Dale Spender and Elizabeth Sarah, *Learning to Lose: Sexism and Education*. 2nd ed. London: Women's, 183–90.
Evans, J. and B. Davies. 1993. "Equality, Equity and Physical Education." In J. Evans (ed.), *Equality, Education and Physical Education*. London: Falmer, 11–27.
Feagin, J.R., H. Vera and N. Imani. 1996. *The Agony of Education: Black Students at White Colleges and Universities*. New York and London: Routledge.
Fine, M. 1987. "Silencing in Public Schools." *Language Arts* 64, 2: 157–74.
_____. 1993. "[Ap]parent Involvement: Reflections on Parents, Power, and Urban Public Schools." *Teachers College Record* 94, 4: 682–710.
Fine, M., L. Powell, L. Weis and L.M. Wong. 1997. Preface. In M. Fine, L. Weis, L. Powell and L. Mun Wong (eds.), *Off White: Readings on Race, Power and Society*. New York: Routledge, vii–xii.
Fischer, W. 1996. "Race and Representation in Participatory Research." Unpublished master's thesis. Toronto: Ontario Institute for Studies in Education/University of Toronto.
Fiske, J. 1996. *Media Matters: Race and Gender in US Politics*. Minneapolis: University of Minnesota Press.
Fleras, A. 1996. "Behind the Ivy Walls: Racism/Anti Racism in Academe." In M.I. Alladin (ed.), *Racism in Canadian Schools*. Toronto: Harcourt, 62–89.
Fleras, A. and J.L. Elliot. 1992. *Multiculturalism in Canada*. Toronto: Nelson.
Forsythe, D., ed. 1971. *Let the Niggers Burn!* Montreal: Black Rose.
Foucault, M. 1972. *Power/Knowledge: Selected Interviews and Other Writings*. New York: Pantheon.
_____. 1977. *Language, Counter-memory, Practice*. Trans. D. Bouchard and S. Simon. New York: Cornell University Press.
_____. 1980. "Two Lectures." In C. Gordon (ed.), *Power/knowledge: Selected Interviews and Other Writings*. New York: Pantheon.
Fox-Genovese, E. 1988. *Within the Plantation Household: Black and White Women of the Old South*. Chapel Hill: University of North Carolina Press.
Foyn, S. 1998. "A Troika of Programs: African Nova Scotian Education at Dalhousie University." In V. D'Oyley and C. James (eds.), *Re/visioning Canadian Perspectives on the Education of Africans in the Late 20th Century*. North York: Captus, 178–98.
Frank, D. 2000. "True Identity." Mimeo.
Frankenberg, R. 1993. *White Women, Race Matters: The Social Construction of Whiteness*. Minneapolis: University of Minnesota Press.
Franklin, J.H. 1993. *The Colour Line: Legacy for the Twenty-First Century*. Columbia: University of Missouri Press.
Fredrickson, G. 1971. *The Black Image in the White Mind: The Debate on Afro-American Character and Destiny, 1817–1914*. New York: Harper.
Freire, P. 1972. *Pedagogy of the Oppressed*. New York: Herder.
_____. 1993. *Pedagogy of the Oppressed* Rev. ed. New York: Continuum.
Frideres, J. and W. Reeves. 1989. "The Ability to Implement Human Rights Legislation in Canada." *Canadian Review of Sociology and Anthropology* 26, 2: 311–32.
Fuss, Diana. 1989. *Essentially Speaking: Feminism, Nature and Difference*. New York: Routledge.

Gabriel, J. and G. Ben-Tovim. 1978. "Marxism and the Concept of Racism." *Economy and Society* 7, 2: 118–54.

_____. 1979. "The Conceptualization of Race Relations in Sociological Theory." *Ethnic and Racial Studies.*

Gaskell, J., A. McLaren and M. Novogrodsky. 1989. *Claiming an Education: Feminism and Canadian Schools.* Toronto: Our Schools/Our Selves Education Foundation.

Gillborn, D. 1995. "Racism, Modernity and Schooling: New Directions in Anti-racist Theory and Practice." Paper published at the American Educational Research Association. April 18–22. San Francisco, CA.

Gilroy, P., with the Centre for Contemporary Cultural Studies, eds. 1982. *The Empire Strikes Back.* London: Hutchison.

_____. 1990. "The End of Anti-Racism." *New Community* 17, 1: 49–61.

_____. 1991. *There Ain't No Black in the Union Jack: The Cultural Politics of Race and Nation.* Chicago: University of Chicago Press.

_____. 1993. *The Black Atlantic: Modernity and Double Consciousness.* London and New York: Verso.

Giroux, H. 1983. "Reproduction, Resistance, and Accommodation in the Schooling Process." In H. Giroux, *Theory and Resistance in Education: A Pedagogy for the Opposition.* South Hadley, MA: Bergin and Garvey.

_____. 1991a. "Postmodernism as Border Pedagogy: Redefining the Boundaries of Race and Ethnicity." In H. Giroux (ed.), *Postmodernism, Feminism, and Cultural Politics: Redrawing Educational Boundaries.* Albany: State University of New York Press, 217–56.

_____. 1991b. "Modernism, Postmodernism, and Feminism: Rethinking the Boundaries of Educational Discourse." In Henry Giroux (ed.), *Postmodernism, Feminism and Cultural Politics: Redrawing Educational Boundaries.* Albany: State University of New York Press, 1–60.

_____. 1992a. "Resisting Difference: Cultural Studies and the Discourse of Critical Pedagogy." In Lawrence Grossberg, Cary Nelson and Paula Treichler (eds.), *Cultural Studies.* New York: Routledge, 199–212.

_____. 1992b. *Border Crossing: Cultural Workers and the Politics of Education.* New York: Routledge.

_____. 1993. *Living Dangerously: Multiculturalism and the Politics of Difference.* New York: Peter Lang.

_____. 1994a. "Living Dangerously: Identity Politics and the New Cultural Racism." In H. Giroux and P. McLaren (eds.), *Between Borders: Pedagogy and the Politics of Cultural Studies.* New York: Routledge, 29–55.

_____. 1994b. "Insurgent Multiculturalism and the Promise of Pedagogy." In T. Goldberg (ed.), *Multiculturalism: A Critical Reader.* London: Blackwell, 325–43.

_____. 1997. "Rewriting the Discourse of Racial Identity: Towards a Pedagogy and Politics of Whiteness." *Harvard Educational Review* 67, 2 (Summer): 285–320.

_____. 1998. "Critical Pedagogy as Performative Practice: Memories of Whiteness." In Carlos A. Torres and Theodre R. Mitchell (eds.), *Sociology of Education: Emerging Perspectives.* New York: State University of New York Press, 143–53.

Giroux, H. and P. McLaren. 1986. "Teacher Education and the Politics of Engagement: The Case for Democratic Schooling." *Harvard Educational Review* 5, 3: 213–38.

Giroux, H. and R. Simon. 1989a. "Schooling, Popular Culture, and a Pedagogy of Possibility." In H. Giroux and R. Simon (eds.), *Popular Culture, Schooling, and*

Everyday Life. South Hadley, MA: Bergin and Garvey, 219–35.

_____. 1989b. "Popular Culture as a Pedagogy of Pleasure and Meaning." In H. Giroux and R. Simon (eds.), *Popular Culture, Schooling, and Everyday Life*. South Hadley, MA: Bergin and Garvey, 1–29.

Glazer, N. 1991. "'Between a Rock and a Hard Place': Women's Professional Organizations in Nursing and Class, Racial, and Ethnic Inequalities." *Gender and Society* 5, 3: 351–72.

Goffman, E. 1963. *Stigma: Notes on the Management of Spoiled Identity*. Englewood Cliffs, NJ: Prentice-Hall.

Goldberg, D.T. 1993. *Racist Culture: Philosophy and the Politics of Meaning*. Oxford: Blackwell.

Goldstein, L. 1987. "Standard English: The Only Target for Nonnative Speakers of English?" *TESOL Quarterly* 21, 3: 417–38.

Gramsci, A. 1971. *Selections from the Prison Notebook*. Ed. and trans. Quintin Hoare and Geoffrey Newell Smith. New York: International.

Grand Bras University. 1990. "Multiculturalism Committee Report." April.

Grandy, O.H. Jr. 1998. *Communication and Race: A Structural Perspective*. London: Arnold.

Graveline, F.J. 1994. "Lived Experiences of an Aboriginal Feminist Transforming the Curriculum." *Canadian Woman Studies* 14, 2: 52–55.

_____. 1998. *Circle Works: Transforming Eurocentric Consciousness*. Halifax: Fernwood.

Grayson, J., T. Chi and D. Rhyne. 1994. *The Social Construction of "Visible Minority" for Students of Chinese Origin*. Toronto: North York Institute of Social Research, York University.

Grayson, J. and D. Williams. 1994. *Racialization and Black Student Identity at York University*. Toronto: North York Institute of Social Research, York University.

Gray-White, D. 1985. *Ar'n't I a Woman? Female Slaves in the Plantation South*. New York: Norton.

Grossberg, L. 1994. "Bringin' It All Back Home: Pedagogy and Cultural Studies." In H. Giroux and P. McLaren (eds.), *Between Borders: Pedagogy and the Politics of Cultural Studies*. New York: Routledge, 1–25.

Grossberg, L., C. Nelson and P. Treichler, eds. 1992. *Cultural Studies*. New York: Routledge.

Haggar-Guenette, C. 1994. "Mature Students." In Craig McKie (ed.), *Canadian Social Trends: A Canadian Studies Reader*. Vol. 2. Toronto: Thompson.

Hall, J. 1990. *Proceedings of the Conference on Strategies for Improving Access and Retention of Ethno-Specific and Visible Minority Students in Ontario's Post-Secondary Institutions*. Toronto: Ryerson University.

_____. 1992. "The Capital(s) of Cultures: A Nonholistic Approach to Status Situations, Class, Gender, and Ethnicity." In Michele Lamont and Marcel Fournier (eds.), *Cultivating Differences*. Chicago: University of Chicago Press.

Hall, S. 1980a. "Cultural Studies: Two Paradigms." *Media, Culture and Society* 2: 57–72.

_____. 1980b. "Cultural Studies and the Centre: Some Problematics and the Problems." In Stuart Hall et al. (eds.), *Culture, Media, Language*. London: Hutchinson, 15–48.

_____. 1990. "Cultural Identity and Diaspora." In J. Rutherford (ed.), *Identity, Community, Culture, Difference*. London: Lawrence and Wishart, 222–37.

_____. 1991. "Ethnicity: Identity and Difference." *Radical America* 13, 4: 9–20.

_____. 1992a. "New Ethnicities." In J. Donald and A. Rattansi (eds.), *Race, Culture and Difference*. Newbury Park, CA; Sage, 252–59.
_____. 1992b. "What Is this "Black" in Black Popular Culture?" In M. Wallace (ed.), *Black Popular Culture*. Seattle: Bay, 21–33.
_____. 1998. "Identity and Representation in the Media." North Hampton, MA: Media Educational Foundation.
Hall, S., C. Critcher, T. Jefferson, J. Clarke and B. Roberts. 1981. *Policing the Crisis: Mugging, the State and Law and Order.* London: Macmillan.
Hall, S. and T. Jefferson, eds. 1976. *Resistance Through Rituals: Youth Sub-cultures in Post-war Britain*. London: Hutchinson and the Centre for Contemporary Cultural Studies, University of Birmingham.
Hammonds, E. 1993. "Clarence Thomas, Affirmative Action, and the Academy." In B.W. Thompson and S. Tyagi (eds.), *Beyond a Dream Deferred: Multicultural Education and the Politics of Excellence*. Minneapolis: University of Minnesota Press, 66–79.
Haraway, D. 1991. *Simians, Cyborgs, and Women: The Reinvention of Nature*. New York: Routledge.
Harkavy, I. and J. Puckett. 1994. "Lessons from Hull House for the Contemporary Urban University." *Social Service Review* September: 300–21.
Harlow, Barbara. 1987. *Resistance Literature*. New York: Methuen.
Harris, B. 1996. "Reading Whiteness and Anti-Racism Education." Unpublished paper. Toronto: Department of Sociology in Education, Ontario Institute for Studies in Education/University of Toronto.
Harris, C. 1993. "Whiteness as Property." *Harvard Law Review* 106: 1714.
Harrison, Faye. 1995. "The Persistent Power of 'Race' in the Cultural and Political Economy of Racism." *Annual Review of Anthropology*. Palo Alto, CA: Annual Reviews.
Hatcher, R. and B. Troyna. 1993. In C. McCarthy and Warren Crichlow (eds.), *Race, Identity and Representation in Education*. New York: Routledge, 109–25.
Head, W. 1975. *The Black Presence in the Canadian Mosaic: A Study of Perception and the Practice of Discrimination Against Blacks in Metropolitan Toronto*. Toronto: Ontario Human Rights Commission.
Heller, M. 1993. *Gender and Language Choice in Minority Education*. Paper presented at the American Anthropological Association Conference. November.
Henry, F. 1978. *The Dynamics of Racism in Toronto: Research Report*. Toronto: York University Press.
Henry, F. and C. Tator. 1994. "Racism and the University." *Canadian Ethnic Studies* 26, 3: 74–90.
Henry, F., C. Tator, W. Mattis and T. Rees. 1995. *The Colour of Democracy: Racism in Canadian Society*. Toronto: Harcourt.
_____. 1999. *The Colour of Democracy: Racism in Canadian Society.* 2nd ed. Toronto: Harcourt.
Herrnstein, R. and C. Murray. 1994. *The Bell Curve: Intelligence and Structure in American Life*. New York: Free.
Hesch, R. 1996. "Antiracist Educators Sui Generis? The Dialectics of Aboriginal Teacher Education." *Canadian Review of Sociology and Anthropology* 33, 3: 269–90.
Hick, S. and R. Santos. 1993. "Anti-Racism Student Organizing in Canadian Universi-

ties." Paper presented at the Canadian Ethnic Studies Association Biennial Meeting. November. Vancouver, BC.

Hicks, D.E. 1988. "Deterritorialization and Border Writing." In Robert Merrill (ed.), *Ethics/Aesthetics: Post-Modern Positions*. Washington, DC: Maisonneuve, 47–58.

Higginbotham, E. 1990. "Designing an Inclusive Curriculum: Bringing All Women into the Core." *Women's Studies Quarterly* 1 & 2: 7–23.

Hoodfar, H. 1992. "Feminist Anthropology and Critical Pedagogy: The Anthropology of Classrooms' Excluded Voices." *Canadian Journal of Education* 17, 3: 303–20.

hooks, bell. 1981. *Ain't I a Woman? Black Women and Feminism*. Boston: South End.

_____. 1984. *Feminist Theory: From Margin to Centre*. Boston: South End.

_____. 1988. *Talking Back: Thinking Feminist, Thinking Black*. Toronto: Between the Lines.

_____. 1990. *Yearning Race, Gender, and Cultural Politics*. Toronto: Between the Lines.

_____. 1992a. *Black Looks: Race and Representation*. Toronto: Between the Lines.

_____. 1992b. "Representing Whiteness in the Black Imagination." In L. Grossberg et al. (eds.), *Cultural Studies*. New York: Routledge, 338–46.

_____. 1993. *Sisters of the Yam*. Boston: South End.

_____. 1994a. *Outlaw Culture: Resisting Representations*. New York: Routledge.

_____. 1994b. *Teaching to Transgress: Education as the Practice of Freedom*. New York: Routledge.

_____. 1995. "Black Women: Shaping Feminist Theory." In B. Guy-Sheftall (ed.), *Words of Fire*. New York: New, 270–82.

_____. 1997. "Sisterhood: Political Solidarity Between Women." In A. McClintock, A. Mufti and E. Shohat (eds.), *'Dangerous Liaisons': Gender, Nation and Postcolonial Perspectives*. Minneapolis: University of Minnesota Press, 396–411.

hooks, b. and C. West. 1991. *Breaking Bread*. Toronto: Between the Lines.

Howard, B. 1997. Letter to C. Baptiste, February 3.

Hull, Gloria T., Patricia Bellscott and Barbara Smith, eds. 1982. *All the Women Are White, All the Blacks Are Men, But Some of Us Are Brave*. New York: Feminist.

Ibrahim, A. 1997. "Ethnography of Performance: Race, Language, Culture, and the Politics of Identity." In *Qualitative '97: Interdisciplinary Perspectives: Using Qualitative Methods to Study Social Life*. Toronto: Ontario Institute for Studies in Education/University of Toronto.

_____. 1998. *"'Hey, Whassup Homeboy?' Becoming Black: Race, Language, Culture, and the Politics of Identity. African Students in a Franco-Ontarian High School."* Unpublished doctoral thesis. Toronto: Curriculum Department, Ontario Institute for Studies in Education/University of Toronto.

Inglis, S., J. Mannette and S. Sulewski. 1991. *Paqtatek: Volume I, Policy and Consciousness in Mi'kmaq Life*. Halifax: Garamond.

Jackson, J. 1998. "The Resurgence of Genetic Determinism: Is It a Distraction?" *Race, Gender and Class* 5, 3: 76–89.

James, A. 1981. "'Black': An Inquiry into the Pejorative Associations of an English Word." *New Community* 9, 1: 19–30.

James, C. 1963. *Beyond a Boundary*. London: Hutchinson.

_____. 1990. *Making It: Black Youth, Racism and Career Aspirations in a Big City*. Oakville, ON: Mosaic.

_____. 1994a. "Access Students: Experiences of Racial Minority Students in a Canadian University." Paper presented at the Society for Research in Higher Education Annual Conference, "The Student Experience." University of York, York, England.
_____. 1994b. "I've Never Had a Black Teacher Before." In Carl James and Adrienne Shadd (ed.), *Talking about Difference*. Toronto: Between the Lines, 125–40.
_____. 1994c. "The Paradox of Power and Privilege: Race, Gender and Occupational Position." *Canadian Woman Studies* 14, 2: 47–51.
_____. 1995a. "Reverse Racism: Students' Response to Equity Programs." *Journal of Professional Studies* 3, 1: 48–54.
_____. 1995b. "Multicultural and Anti-Racism Education in Canada." *Race, Gender and Class* 2, 3: 31–48.
_____. 1996. "Proposing an Anti-Racism Framework for Change." In C.E. James (ed.), *Perspectives on Racism and the Human Services Sector: A Case for Change*. Toronto: University of Toronto Press, 3–12.
_____. 1997. "The Distorted Images of African Canadians: Impact, Implications, and Responses." In C. Green (ed.), *Globalization and Survival in the Black Diaspora: The New Urban Challenge*. Albany: State University of New York Press, 307–27.
James, C. and J. Mannette. 1996. "'So Close to the Fire': Problematizing Diversity in the University." Paper presented at the Canadian Sociology and Anthropology Association Annual Meetings, Learned Societies Conference. June. Brock University, St. Catharines, ON.
James, I.M. 1996. "Paradigms of Resistance: Towards Anti-Racist Feminist Criminology, and Repairing Inequality for Black Women in the Criminal Justice System." Unpublished paper. Toronto: Department of Sociology, Ontario Institute for Studies in Education/University of Toronto.
James, J. 1993. "African Philosophy, Theory and 'Living Thinkers.'" In Joyce James and Ruth Farmer (ed.), *Spirit, Space and Survival: African American Women in (White) Academe*. New York: Routledge, 31–46.
James, J. and R. Farmer. 1993. Introduction. In Joy James and Ruth Farmer (eds.), *Spirit, Space and Survival: African American Women in (White) Academe*. New York: Routledge, 1–10.
Jeffcoate, R. 1984. "Ideologies and Multicultural Education." In M. Craft (ed.), *Education and Cultural Pluralism*. Lewes: Falmer, 161–87.
John, M. 1989. "Postcolonial Feminists in the Western Intellectual Field: Anthropologists and Native Informants?" *Inscriptions* 5: 49–73.
_____. 1999. "Racialized Bodies: The Social Construction of Black Identities in Popular Cinema." Unpublished master's thesis. Toronto: Department of Sociology and Equity Studies, Ontario Institute for Studies in Education/University of Toronto.
Jordan, G. and C. Weedon. 1995. *Cultural Politics: Class, Gender, and the Post-Modern World*. Oxford: Blackwell.
Joyce, M. 1995. "Class Communication, 1947S: 'Principles of Anti-Racism Education.'" Toronto: Department of Sociology in Education, Ontario Institute for Studies in Education/University of Toronto.
Kailin, J. 1994. "Anti-Racist Staff Development for Teachers: Considerations of Race, Class, and Gender." *Teaching and Teacher Education* 10, 2: 169–84.
Kalbach, W., R. Verma, S.Y. George and S.Y. Dai. 1993. *Population Projections of Visible Minority Groups, Canada, Provinces and Regions, 1991–2016*. Ottawa: Employment Equity Data Programme, Statistics Canada.

Kamboureli, S. 1993. "Of Black Angels and Melancholy Lovers: Ethnicity and Writing in Canada." In Sneja Gunew and Anna Yeatman (eds.), *Feminism and the Politics of Difference*. Halifax: Fernwood, 143–56.

Keene, J. 1992. *Human Rights in Ontario*. 2nd ed. Toronto: Carswell.

Keeshig-Tobias, L. 1990. "Stop Stealing Native Stories." *Globe and Mail*, February.

Kehoe, J.W. n.d. "The Limitations of Multicultural Education and Anti-Racist Education." Unpublished paper.

Kennelly, I., J. Misra and M. Karides. 1999. "The Historical Context of Gender, Race and Class in the Academic Labor Market." *Race, Gender and Class* 6, 3: 125–55.

Keung, N. 2000. "Cronyism Cited in U of T Hiring." *Toronto Star*, February 7, A1.

King, T., C. Calver and H. Hoy. 1987. *The Native in Literature*. Toronto: ECW.

Kirby, S.N. and L. Hudson. 1993. "Black Teachers in Indiana." *Educational Evaluation and Policy Analysis* 15, 2: 181–94.

Kivel, P. 1996. *Uprooting Racism: How White People Can Work for Racial Justice*. Gabriola Island: New Society.

Ku, J. 1995. "The Invisibility of Race in the Experience of Visible Minorities." Unpublished paper. Toronto: Department of Sociology, Ontario Institute for Studies in Education/University of Toronto.

_____. 1996. "Legitimation of Minority Discourses: Challenges and Choices." Unpublished paper. Toronto: Department of Sociology in Education, Ontario Institute for Studies in Education/University of Toronto.

Labov, W. 1972. *Language in the Inner City: Studies in the Black English Vernacular*. Philadelphia: University of Pennsylvania Press.

Laclau, E. and C. Mouffé. 1985. *'Hegemony and Radical Democracy.' Hegemony and Socialist Strategy: Towards a Radical Democratic Politics*. London: Verso.

Lamont, M. and M. Fournier, eds. 1992. *Cultivating Differences*. Chicago and London: University of Chicago Press.

Lamy, P. 1994. "Offenders, Victims and Academic Freedom." *Society/Société* 18, 2: 9–11.

Lather, P. 1988. "Feminist Perspectives on Empowering Research Methodologies." *Women's Studies International Forum* 11, 6: 569–81.

_____. 1991. *Getting Smart: Feminist Research and Pedagogy with/in the Postmodern*. New York: Routledge.

Lattas, A. 1993. "Essentialism, Memory and Resistance: Aboriginality and the Politics of Authenticity." *Oceania* 63: 240–67.

Lavery, J. 1996. "Racism in the Canadian Education System: The Experiences of Aboriginal and Black University Students." Unpublished honours thesis. Antigonish, NS: St. Francis Xavier University.

Lawrence, S.M. and B.D. Tatum. 1997. "Teachers in Transition: The Impact of Antiracist Professional Development on Classroom Practice." *Teachers College Record* 99, 1: 162–78.

Leah, R. 1995. "The Emergence of Anti-Racism Studies: An Integrative, Holistic and Transformative Paradigm." *Race, Gender and Class* 2, 3: 105–22.

Lee, E. 1985. *Letters to Marcia*. Toronto: Cross Cultural Communication Centre.

_____. 1989. *Letters to Marcia: A Teacher's Guide to Anti-racist Education*. Toronto: Cross Cultural Communication Centre.

_____. 1991. "An Interview with Educator Enid Lee: 'Taking Multicultural, Anti-Racist Education Seriously.'" *Rethinking Schools* V6, 1.

_____. 1994. "Anti-Racist Education: Panacea or Palliative?" *Orbit* 25, 2: 22–25.
Lee, S. and R. Wiley. 1992. *By Any Means Necessary: The Trials and Tribulations of the Making of Malcolm X ... Including the Screenplay*. New York: Hyperion.
Lewis, M. 1990. "Interpreting Patriarchy: Politics, Resistance, and Transformation in the Feminist Classroom." *Harvard Educational Review* 60, 4 (November): 467–88.
Li, P. 1990. "Race and Ethnicity." In P. Li (ed.), *Race and Ethnic Relations in Canada*. Toronto: Oxford University Press, 3-17.
Loney, M. 1977. "A Political Economy of Citizenship Participation." In L. Panitch (ed.), *The Canadian State*. Toronto: University of Toronto Press, 446–72.
Lorde, A. 1984. *Sister Outsider*. Freedom, CA: Crossing.
_____. 1995. "Age, Race, Class, and Sex: Women Redefining Difference." In B. Guy-Sheftall (ed.), *Words of Fire*. New York: New, 284–91.
Lumsden, D. 2000. "True Identity." Mimeo.
Lutz, C.A. and J.L. Collins. 1993. *Reading National Geographic*. Chicago: University of Chicago Press.
Lynch, J. 1992. *Education for Citizenship in a Multicultural Society*. London, UK: Cassell.
Lyons, C. 1994. "Teaching Tolerance: Multicultural Education and Anti-Racist Education." *McGill Journal of Education* 29, 1: 5–14.
Macchiusi, J. 1993. "The Origins of Racism and the Rise of Biological Determinism." *Paradox of Racism, Prize Winning Essays*. Vol. 6. Toronto: York University Press, 53–63.
MacPherson, J. 2000. "OHRC Report Follow-Up." Letter to CAUT Equity Listserv, March 2.
Manicom, Ann. 1992. "Feminist Pedagogy: Transformations, Standpoints, and Politics." *Canadian Journal of Education* 17, 3: 365–89.
Mannette, J. 1988. "'A Trial Which No One Goes to Jail': The Donald Marshall Inquiry as Hegemonic Renegotiation." *Canadian Ethnic Studies: Special Issue on Atlantic Canada* 20, 3.
_____. 1990. "Cross Cultural Education and the University." *Rapport de la conférence, Congrés de l'Association des ombudsmans des universités et collèges du Canada* (AOUCC). June. Laval University, Quebec City, PQ.
_____. Forthcoming. "'Revelation, Revolution or Both': Black Art as Cultural Politics." *Callaloo*.
Matthews, S. 1996. "Excavating the Invisible: Deconstructing White Hegemony within a Discourse of Anti-Racism." Unpublished paper. Toronto: Department of Sociology in Education, Ontario Institute for Studies in Education/University of Toronto.
Mazurek, K. 1987. "Multiculturalism, Education and the Ideology of the Meritocracy." In T. Wotherspoon (ed.), *The Political Economy of Canadian Schooling*. Toronto: Methuen, 141–63.
McCarthy, C. 1995. "Multicultural Policy Discourses on Racial Inequality in American Education." In Roxana Ng, Pat Staton and Joyce Scane (eds.), *Anti-racism, Feminism, and Critical Approaches to Education*. Toronto: Ontario Institute for Studies in Education/University of Toronto, 21–44.
McCarthy, C. and W. Crichlow, eds. 1993. *Race, Identity and Representation in Education*. New York: Routledge.
McClintock, A. 1995. *Imperial Leather: Race, Gender, and Sexuality in the Colonial Contest*. New York: Routledge.

McCombs, H.G. 1989. "The Dynamics and Impact of Affirmative Processes on Higher Education, the Curriculum and Black Women." *Sex Roles* 21, 1/2: 127–43.
McInnis, P. 1989. "St. F.X. Holds Cultural Expose." *The Casket*, March 15.
McIntosh, P. 1990. "White Privilege: Unpacking the Invisible Knapsack." *Independent School* Winter, 31–36.
McIntyre, S. 1987/88. "Gender Bias within the Law School: 'The Memo' and Its Impact." *Canadian Journal of Women and the Law* 2, 2: 362–407.
McLaren, A. 1990. *Our Own Master Race: Eugenics in Canada, 1885–1945*. Toronto: McClelland and Stewart.
McLaren, P. 1994. "Multiculturalism and Postmodern Critique: Toward a Pedagogy of Resistance and Transformation." In H. Giroux and P. McLaren (eds.), *Between Borders: Pedagogy and the Politics of Cultural Studies*. New York: Routledge, 192–222.
_____. 1997. "Unthinking Whiteness, Rethinking Democracy: Or Farewell to the Blonde Beast: Towards a Revolutionary Multiculturalism." *Educational Foundations* 11, 2: 5–39.
Messner, M. 1991. "Masculinities and Athlete Careers." In L. Kramer (ed.), *The Sociology of Gender: A Text Reader*. New York: St. Martin's, 105–19.
Middleton, S. 1993. *Educating Feminists: Life Histories and Pedagogy*. New York and London: Teachers College.
Miles, A. 1996. *Integrative Feminisms: Building Global Visions 1960s-1990s*. New York: Routledge.
Miles, K. 1997. "Body Badges: Race and Sex." In N. Zack (ed.), *Race/Sex: Their Sameness, Difference and Interplay*. New York: Routledge, 1–18.
Miles, R. and R. Torres. 1996. "Does Race Matter? Transatlantic Perspectives on Racism after Race Relations." In V. Amit-Talai and C. Knowles (eds.), *Re-Situating Identities: The Politics of Race, Ethnicity and Culture*. Peterborough, ON: Broadview, 24-46.
Miles, Robert. 1980. "Class, Race and Ethnicity: A Critique of Cox's Theory." *Ethnic and Racial Studies* 3, 2: 169–81.
_____. 1989. *Racism*. London: Tavistock.
Millar, H. and R. Riviere. 1993. *Towards Anti-Racist Teaching in Nova Scotia's Universities: Proceedings from the Second Workshop on Anti-Racist Teaching*. April 27. Halifax: Saint Mary's University Press.
Mitchell, A. 1998. "Face of Big Cities Changing." *Globe and Mail*, February 18: A1 & A3.
Mohanty, C.T. 1990. "On Race and Voice: Challenges for Liberal Education in the 1990s." *Cultural Critique* Winter: 179–208.
_____. 1991. "Cartographies of Struggle: Third World Women and the Politics of Feminism." In Chandra Talpade Mohanty, Ann Russo and Lourdes Torres (eds.), *Third World Women and the Politics of Feminism*. Bloomington and Indianapolis: Indiana University Press, 1–47.
_____.1993. "On Race and Voice: Challenges for Liberal Education in the 1990s." In B.W. Thompson and S. Tyagi (eds.), *Beyond a Dream Deferred: Multicultural Education and the Politics of Excellence*. Minneapolis: University of Minnesota Press, 41-65.
Monture-Angus, P. 1995a. *Thunder in My Soul: A Mohawk Woman Speaks*. Halifax: Fernwood.

_____. 1995b. "Flint Woman: Surviving the Contradictions in Academia." In P. Monture-Angus, *Thunder in My Soul: A Mohawk Woman Speaks*. Halifax: Fernwood, 53–73.

Monture-Okanee, P. 1995. Introduction. "Surviving the Contradictions: Personal Notes on Academia." In the Chilly Climate Collective (eds.), *Breaking Anonymity: The Chilly Climate for Women Faculty*. Waterloo, ON: Wilfrid Laurier University Press, 11–28.

Moore, D. 1980. "Multiculturalism: Ideology or Social Reality." Unpublished doctoral thesis. Boston: Department of Sociology, Boston University.

Moore, D.S. 1997. "Remapping Resistance: 'Ground for Struggle' and the Politics of Place." In S. Pile and M. Keith (eds.), *Geographies of Resistance*. London: Routledge, 87–106.

Moreau, B. 1982. "Programme Innovation: The Transition Year Programme at Dalhousie University." Unpublished master's thesis. Halifax: Dalhousie University.

Morrison, T. 1992a. *Playing in the Dark: Whiteness and the Literary Imagination*. Boston: Harvard University Press.

_____, ed. 1992b. *Racing Justice, Gendering Power: Essays on Anita Hill, Clarence Thomas, and the Construction of Social Reality*. New York: Pantheon.

Mouffé, C. 1988. "Radical Democracy: Modern or Postmodern?" Trans. Paul Holdengraeber. In Andrew Ross (ed.), *Universal Abandon? The Politics of Postmodernism*. Minneapolis: University of Minnesota Press, 31–45.

Mukherjee, A. 1994. "The Race 'Consciousness' of a South Asian (Canadian of course) Female Academic." In Carl James and Adrienne Shadd (eds.), *Talking About Difference*. Toronto: Between the Lines, 201–07.

Mullard, C. 1980. *Racism in Society and Schools: History and Policy*. London: Centre for Multicultural Education.

_____. 1985. *Race, Power and Resistance*. London: Centre for Multicultural Education.

Mullings, L. 1997. *On Our Own Terms: Race, Class and Gender in the Lives of African American Women*. New York: Routledge.

Multiculturalism Committee Forum. 1992. Paradise University. October.

Multiculturalism Policy of Canada. 1988. "Excerpts from the Canadian Multiculturalism Act." July.

Murphy, R. 1988. *Social Closure: The Theory of Monopolization and Exclusion*. New York: Oxford University Press.

Nanacoo, S., ed. 2000. *21st Century Canadian Diversity*. Toronto: Canadian Educators.

Nazim, Z. 1996. "Managing Diversity." Doctoral thesis proposal. Toronto: Department of Sociology, Ontario Institute for Studies in Education/University of Toronto.

Nelson, C., P. Treichler and L. Grossberg. 1992. "Cultural Studies: An Introduction." In Lawrence Grossberg, Cary Nelson and Paula Treichler (eds.), *Cultural Studies*. New York: Routledge, 1–22.

Newson, J. and H. Buchbinder. 1988. *The University Means Business: Universities, Corporations and Academic Work*. Toronto: Garamond.

Ng, R. 1991. "Sexism, Racism and Canadian Nationalism." In Jesse Vorst et al. (eds.), *Race, Class, Gender: Bonds and Barriers*. Toronto: Garamond.

_____. 1994. "Sexism and Racism in the University: Analyzing a Personal Experience." *Canadian Woman Studies* 4, 2: 41–46.

_____. 1995. "Multiculturalism as Ideology: A Textual Analysis." In M. Campbell and A. Manicom (eds.), *Knowledge, Experience, and Ruling Relations: Studies in the*

Social Organization of Knowledge. Toronto: University of Toronto Press.
Ng, W. 1995. "On the Margin: Challenging Racism in the Labour Movement." Unpublished master's thesis. Toronto: Department of Education, University of Toronto.
Nixon, J. 1984. "Multicultural Education as a Curriculum Category." *New Community* 12: 22–30.
Nova Scotia Interuniversity Committee on Access to Under-represented Populations. 1992. *Report to Council of Nova Scotia University Presidents*. Halifax.
O'Brien, K. 1990. *Multiculturalism Committee Report*. April 6. Antigonish, NS: St. Francis Xavier University.
Ogbu, J. 1990. "Minority Education in Comparative Perspective." *Journal of Negro Education* 59, 1: 45–57.
Okpewho, I. 1992. *African Oral Literature: Backgrounds, Character, Continuity*. Bloomington: Indiana University Press.
Omi, M. and H. Winant. 1983. "By the Rivers of Babylon: Part One." *Socialist Review* 13, 5: 31–65.
_____. 1993. "On the Theoretical Concept of Race." In C. McCarthy and W. Crichlow (eds.), *Race, Identity, and Representation in Education*. New York: Routledge, 3–10.
_____. 1994. *Racial Formation in the United States from the 1960s to the 1990s*. New York: Routledge.
O'Neil, M. 1993. "Teaching Literature as Cultural Criticism." *English Quarterly* 25, 1: 19–25.
Ontario Human Rights Commission (OHRC). 1976. *Ramesh* v. *Cameron and Algoma University College*. Toronto: OHRC.
_____. 2000. *Chun* v. *University of Toronto: Case Analysis*. February 1. http://www.utoronto.ca/acc/chun/ohrc/ohrc01.htm.
Oommen, T.K. 1995. "Contested Boundaries and Emerging Pluralism." *International Sociology* 10, 3 (September): 251–68.
Orris, M. 1990. *Proceedings of the Conference on Strategies for Improving Access and Retention of Ethno-Specific and Visible Minority Students in Ontario's Post-Secondary Institutions*. Toronto: Ryerson Polytechnic University.
Palmer, Eustace. 1972. *An Introduction to the African Novel*. Ibadan: Heinemann.
Parkin, F. 1979. *Marxism and Class Theory: A Bourgeois Critique*. New York: Columbia University Press.
Peter, K. 1981. "The Myth of Multiculturalism and Other Political Fables." In J. Dahlie and T. Fernando (eds.), *Ethnicity, Power and Politics in Canada*. Toronto: Methuen, 56–67.
Philip, M.N. 1995. "How White Is Your White? Ethnicity, Race and the Bernardo/Homolka Trial." *Border/Lines* December: 38–39.
Pierson, R. 1991. "Experience, Difference, Dominance and Voice in the Writing of Canadian Women's History." In Karen Offen, Ruth Pierson and Jane Randall (eds.), *Writing Women's History: International Perspectives*. Bloomington: Indiana University Press, 79–106.
Post, R. and M. Rogin, eds. 1998. *Race and Representation: Affirmative Action*. New York: Zone.
Pratt, M.L. 1992. *Imperial Eyes: Travel Writing and Transculturation*. London: Routledge.
Price, E. 1993. "Multiculturalism: A Critique." Unpublished paper. Toronto: Department of Sociology and Equity Studies, Ontario Institute for Studies in Education/

University of Toronto.
Proctor, S. 1996. "Natives Appeal to PM to end Harassment in School." *Chronicle Herald*, November 29: 1.
Raines, H. 1977. *My Soul Is Rested: The Story of the Civil Rights Movement in the Deep South*. New York: Penguin.
Razack, Sherene. 1991. "Issues of Difference in Women's Studies: A Personal Reflection." *Resources for Feminist Research* 20, 3 & 4: 45–47.
_____. 1998. *Looking White People in the Eye: Gender, Race, and Culture in Courtrooms and Classrooms*. Toronto: University of Toronto Press.
_____. 2000. "Your Place or Mine? Transnational Feminist Collaboration." In A. Calliste and G. Dei (eds.), *Anti-Racist Feminism: Critical Race and Gender Studies*. Halifax: Fernwood, 39–53.
Reddick, T. 1992. "Does St. F.X. Have the Will to Stop Racism?" *The Xaverian Weekly*, April 1, 7.
Reed, C.A. 1994. "The Omission of Anti-Semitism in Anti-Racism." *Canadian Woman Studies: Racism and Gender* 14, 2: 68–71.
Rex, J. 1999. "Racism, Institutionalized and Otherwise." In R. Harris (ed.), *Racism*. New York: Humanity, 141–60.
Reyes, Maria de la Luz and J. Halcon. 1988. "Racism in Academia: The Old Wolf Revisited." *Harvard Educational Review* 58, 3 (August): 299–314.
_____. 1990. "Racism in Academia: The Old Wolf Revisited." In N. Hidalgo, C. McDowell and E. Siddle (eds.), *Facing Racism in Education*. Reprint Series No. 21. Harvard Educational Review, 69–83.
Rezai-Rashti, G. 1995. "Multicultural Education, Anti-Racist Education, and Critical Pedagogy: Reflections on Everyday Practice." In Roxana Ng, Pat Staton and Joyce Scane (eds.), *Anti-Racism, Feminism, and Critical Approaches to Education*. Toronto: Ontario Institute for Studies in Education/University of Toronto, 3–19.
Rich, Adrienne. 1979. *On Lies, Secrets and Silence*. New York: Norton.
Richardson, R.C. Jr. and E.F. Skinner. 1991. *Achieving Quality and Diversity: Universities in a Multicultural Society*. Toronto: Maxwell Macmillan.
Roediger, D. 1991. *The Wages of Whiteness*. London: Verso.
_____. 1994. *Towards the Abolition of Whiteness: Essays on Race, Politics and Working Class History*. London: Verso.
Roger, K. 1996. "Empathy, Fetish and Whiteness." Paper presented at the Learned Societies Conference. Brock University, St. Catharines, ON, June 4.
Roman, L. 1997. "Denying [White] Racial Privilege: Redemption Discourses and the Uses of Fantasy." In M. Fine, L. Weis, L. Powell and L. Mun Wong (eds.), *Off White: Readings on Race, Power, and Society*. New York: Routledge, 270–82.
Roper, L. 1990. "Face up to Racism on Campus." *Democrat and Chronicle*, December 19, 13A.
Rose, T. 1991. "Fear of a Black Planet: Rap Music and Black Cultural Politics in the 1990s." *Journal of Negro Education* 60, 3: 276–90.
_____. 1994. *Black Noise: Rap Music and Black Culture in Contemporary America*. Hanover, NH: University Press of New England.
Ruemper, W. 1996. "Antiracist Education for Universities and Colleges." *Canadian Review of Sociology and Anthropology* 33, 3: 317–35.
Said, E.W. 1985. "Orientalism Reconsidered." *Cultural Critique* 1, Fall: 89–107.
_____. 1993. *Culture and Imperialism*. New York: Vintage.

Samuel, J.T. 1992. *Visible Minorities in Canada: A Projection.* Ottawa: Carleton University Press.
Sarup, M. 1989. *An Introductory Guide to Poststructuralism and Postmodernism.* Athens: University of Georgia Press.
Saunders, C. 1989. "Barriers to Achievement Must be Broken." *Daily News*, October 1, 16.
Schenke, A. 1993. *Being 'Access'/Doing Change: Confronting Difference in Teacher Education: A Reading of Teacher Candidates' Experiences of the Faculty of Education Access Initiative and Consecutive Program, York University, 1992/93.* Toronto: York University Press.
Schmidt, S. 2000. "Rights Panel Sees Racism in Hirings at U of T." *Globe and Mail*, February 7, A1.
Schuster, M.R. and S.R. Van Dyne. 1985. "The Changing Classroom." In M. Schuster and S. Van Dyne (eds.), *Women's Place in the Academy.* Totowa, NJ: Rowman and Allanheld, 161–71.
Scott, J.W. 1991. "The Evidence of Experience." *Critical Inquiry* 17, 3: 773–97.
Segal, E. and K. Kilty. 1998. "The Resurgence of Biological Determinism." *Race, Gender and Class* 5, 3: 61–75.
Shields, R. 1991. "The True North Strong and Free." In Rob Shields (ed.), *Places on the Margin: Alternative Geographies of Modernity.* New York: Routledge, 162–99.
Silver, H. 1990. *Education, Change and the Policy Process.* London: Falmer.
Silvera, M. 1983. *Silenced.* Toronto: Williams-Wallace.
_____. 1993. "Speaking of Women's Lives and Imperialist Economics: Two Introductions from Silenced." In Himani Bannerji (ed.), *Returning the Gaze: Essays on Racism, Feminism and Politics.* Toronto: Sister Vision.
Simmel, G. 1950. "The Stranger." In Kurt Wolff (trans. and ed.), *The Sociology of Georg Simmel.* New York: Free, 402–08.
Simmons, A. and D. Plaza. 1998. "Breaking Through the Glass Ceiling: The Pursuit of University Training Among African-Caribbean Migrants and their Children in Toronto." *Canadian Ethnic Studies* 30, 3: 99–120.
Simon, M. 1998. Letter to R. Edwards, November 9.
Simon, R.I. 1992. *Teaching Against the Grain: Texts for a Pedagogy of Possibility.* New York: Bergin and Garvey.
Singleton, S. n.d. "Faculty, Personal Comfort and the Teaching of Content on Racial Oppression." *Journal of Multicultural Social Work* 3, 1: 5–16.
Skilliter, D. 1995. Epilogue. "Studying Science, Playing Politics." In the Chilly Climate Collective (eds.), *Breaking Anonymity: The Chilly Climate for Women Faculty.* Waterloo, ON: Wilfred Laurier University Press, 387–90.
Skinner, L. 1997. "Black Masculinity in Relation to Work, Sex and Sports." Mimeo, April 2.
Sleeter, C. 1991. "Introduction: Multicultural Education and Empowerment." In Christine Sleeter (ed.), *Empowerment through Multicultural Education.* Albany: State University of New York Press, 1–23.
_____. 1993. "How White Teachers Construct Race." In Cameron McCarthy and Warren Crichlow (eds.), *Race Identity and Representation in Education.* New York: Routledge, 157–71.
_____. 1994a. "White Racism." *Multicultural Education* Spring: 5–8, 39.
_____. 1994b. *Multicultural Education, Social Positionality and Whiteness.* Paper

presented at the Annual Meeting of the American Educational Research Association. April 12–18. New Orleans, LA.

Small, S. 1994. "Racialized Barriers." *The Black Experience in the United States and England in the 1980s*. London: Routledge, 1–40.

Smith, D. 1974. "The Social Construction of Documentary Reality." *Social Inquiry* 44, 4: 237–68.

_____. 1977. *Feminism and Marxism*. Vancouver: New Star.

_____. 1984. "Textually Mediated Social Organization." *International Social Science Journal* 36, 1: 59–75.

_____. 1987a. "An Analysis of Ideological Structures and How Women are Excluded: Considerations for Academic Women." In Jane S. Gaskell (ed.), *Women and Education: A Canadian Perspective*. Calgary: Detselig, 241–64.

_____. 1987b. *The Everyday World as Problematic: A Feminist Sociology*. Toronto: University of Toronto Press.

Smith, David. 1991. "Colonialism, Science, and Secularism, and the Question of Narrative in the Experience of Postmodernity." Paper delivered at the Speakers' Series of the Critical Pedagogy and Cultural Studies Forum. Ontario Institute for Studies in Education/University of Toronto, Toronto, ON.

Smitherman, G. 1994. *Black Talk: Words and Phrases from the Hood to the Amen Corner*. Boston: Houghton.

Snapp, Mary Beth. 1992. "Occupational Stress, Social Support, and Depression among Black and White Managerial Women." *Women and Health* 18, 1: 41–79.

Solomon, R.P. 1992. *Black Resistance in High Schools: Forging a Separatist Culture*. Albany: State University of New York Press.

_____. 1995. "Why to Teach from a Multicultural and Anti-Racist Perspective in Canada?" *Race, Gender and Class* 2, 3 (Spring): 49–66.

Solomos, J. 1986. "Varieties of Marxist Conceptions of 'Race,' Class and the State: A Critical Analysis." In J. Rex and D. Mason (eds.), *Theories of Race and Ethnic Relations*. Cambridge: Cambridge University Press, 84–109.

Solomos, J. and L. Back. 1995. "Marxism, Racism and Ethnicity." *American Behavioural Scientist* 38, 3: 407–20.

Special Committee on Visible Minorities in Canadian Society. 1984. *Equality Now: Participation of Visible Minorities in Canadian Society*. Ottawa: Supply and Services.

Spence, C. 1999. *The Skin I'm In: Racism, Sports and Education*. Halifax: Fernwood.

Spivak, Gayatri Chakravorty. 1990a. *The Post-colonial Critic: Interviews, Strategies, Dialogues*. New York: Routledge.

_____. 1990b. "Gayatri Spivak on the Politics of the Subaltern. Interview with Howard Winant." *Socialist Review* 20, 3: 81–97.

St. Lewis, J. 1996. "Identity and Black Conscious in North America." In J. Littleton (ed.), *Clash of Identities: Essays on Media, Manipulation and Politics of Self*. Englewood Cliffs, NJ: Prentice Hall, 21–30.

Stalker, J. and S. Prentice, eds. 1998. *The Illusion of Inclusion: Women in Post-Secondary Education*. Halifax: Fernwood.

Stasiulis, D. 1982. "Race, Ethnicity and the State." Unpublished doctoral thesis. Toronto: University of Toronto.

_____. 1990. "Theorizing Connections: Gender, Race, Ethnicity and Class." In P. Li (ed.), *Race and Ethnic Relations in Canada*. Don Mills, ON: Oxford, 269–305.

Steckley, J. 1999. *Beyond Their Years: Five Native Women's Stories*. Toronto: Canadian Scholars.

Stewart, P. 1994. "Finding Their Way: The Experiences of Undergraduate Women in University." In L. Erwin and D. MacLennan (eds.), *Sociology of Education in Canada: Critical Perspectives on Theory, Research and Practice*. Toronto: Copp Clark Longman.

Stoler, A.L. 1995. *Race and the Education of Desire: Foucault's History of Sexuality and the Colonial Order of Things*. London: Duke University Press.

Takaki, R. 1993. *A Different Mirror: A History of Multicultural America*. Toronto: Back Bay/Little, Brown.

Takata, Susan. 1991. "Who Is Empowering Whom? The Social Construction of Empowerment." In Christine Sleeter (ed.), *Empowerment through Multicultural Education*. Albany: State University of New York Press, 251–71.

Task Force on Access for Black and Native People. 1989. *Breaking Barriers: Report on the Task Force on Access for Black and Native People*. Halifax, NS: Dalhousie University.

Tator, C. and F. Henry. 1991. *Multicultural Education: Translating Policy into Practice*. Ottawa: Multiculturalism and Citizenship Canada.

Tatum, Beverly Daniel. 1992. "Talking about Race, Learning about Racism: The Application of Racial Identity Development Theory in the Classroom." *Harvard Educational Review* 62, 1: 1–24.

Taylor, S. 1994. "Black Academics Face Racism." *Share* March 3, 9.

Thatcher, R. 1986. "The Functions of Minority Group Disrepute: The Case of Native Peoples in Canada." In B. Maclean (ed.), *The Political Economy of Crime*. Scarborough: Prentice-Hall, 272–94.

Thomas, B. 1984. "Principles of Anti-Racist Education." In Tim Rees (ed.), *Currents* 2, 3. Toronto: Urban Alliance on Race Relations.

_____. 1987. "Anti-Racism Education: A Response to Manicom." In J. Young (ed.), *Breaking the Mosaic: Ethnic Identities in Canadian Schooling*. Toronto: Garamond, 104–07.

Thompson, B. and S. Tyagi. 1993. "A Wider Landscape … Without the Mandate for Conquest." In B.W. Thompson and S. Tyagi (eds.), *Beyond a Dream Deferred: Multicultural Education and the Politics of Excellence*. Minneapolis: University of Minnesota Press, xiii-xxxiii.

Tomaskovic-Devey, D. 1993. *Gender and Racial Inequality at Work: The Sources and Consequences of Job Segregation*. Ithaca, NY: ILR.

Traweek, Sharon. 1992. "Border Crossings: Narrative Strategies in Science Studies and among Physicists in Tsukuba Science City, Japan." In Andrew Pickering (ed.), *Science as Practice and Culture*. Chicago: University of Chicago Press, 429–65.

Troyna, B. 1984. "Multicultural Education: Emancipation of Containment." In L. Barton and S. Walker (eds.), *Social Crisis and Educational Research*. London: Croom Helm, 75–77.

_____. 1987. "Beyond Multiculturalism: Toward the Enactment of Anti-racist Education in Policy, Provision and Pedagogy." *Oxford Review of Education* 62, 1: 1–24.

Troyna, B. and J. Williams. 1986. *Racism, Education and the State*. London: Croom Helm.

Tynes, M. 1992. *Borrowed Beauty*. Porters Lake, NS: Pottersfield.

Usher, R. and R. Edwards. 1994. *Postmodernism and Education*. New York: Routledge.

van Dijk, T. 1993. *Elite Discourse and Racism*. Newbury Park: Sage.

Varma, M. 1996. "Anti-Racist Education: A Guide for White Schools." Unpublished paper. Toronto: Department of Sociology in Education, Ontario Institute for Studies in Education/University of Toronto.

Verdecchia, Guillermo. 1993. *Fronteras Americanas/American Borders*. Toronto: Coach House.

wa Thiong'o, N. 1993. *Moving the Centre: The Struggle for Cultural Freedoms*. London: James Currey.

Walcott, Rinaldo. 1990. "Theorizing Anti-Racist Education." *Western Canadian Anthropologist* 7, 2: 109–20.

_____. 1994. "The Need for a Politics of Difference." *Orbit* 25, 2: 13–15.

_____. 1996. "Reading the Queer Narrative of Clement Virgo Rude: The Politics of Third Cinema in Canada." In M. Pomerance and J. Sakeris (eds.), *Pictures of a Generation on Hold: Selected Papers*. Toronto: Media Studies Working Group.

Wallace, M. 1990a. *Invisibility Blues: From Pop to Theory*. London: Verso.

_____. 1990b. *Black Macho and the Myth of the Superwoman*. London: Verso.

_____. 1990c. *A Feminist Ethic of Risk*. Minneapolis: Fortress.

_____. 1992. "Boyz N the Hood and Jungle Fever." In M. Wallace (ed.), *Black Popular Culture*. Seattle: Bay, 123–31.

Watson, S. 1995. "Discriminatory Policy Handed Back and Forth … and Back Again." *Dalhousie News*, March 8, 3.

Weaver, John A. 1995. "Popular Culture and the Shaping of Race, Class and Gender: Exploring Issues and Imploding Academic Boundaries." *Race, Gender and Class* 2, 3 (Spring): 167–75.

Weiler, K. 1991. "Freire and a Feminist Pedagogy of Difference." *Harvard Educational Review* 6, 4: 449–74.

West, C. 1990. "The New Cultural Politics of Difference." In Russell Fergusson, Martha Gever, Trinh T. Minh-ha and C. West (eds.), *Out There: Marginalization and Contemporary Cultures*. New York: Museum of Contemporary Art.

_____. 1991. "The Dilemma of the Black Intellectual." In bell hooks and Cornel West (eds.), *Breaking Bread: Insurgent Black Intellectual Life*. Toronto: Between the Lines, 131–46.

_____. 1993a. "The New Cultural Politics of Difference." In B.W. Thompson and S. Tyagi (eds.), *Beyond a Dream Deferred: Multicultural Education and the Politics of Excellence*. Minneapolis: University of Minnesota Press, 18–40.

_____. 1993b. *Race Matters*. Boston: Beacon.

Williams, R. 1981. *Culture*. London: Fontana.

_____. 1990. *Culture and Society*. London: Hogarth.

Williamson, P. and T. Reddick. 1992. "Ethnic Minorities Society." *The Xaverian Weekly*, September 30.

Winant, H. 1994a. "Racial Formation and Hegemony: Global and Local Implications." In A. Rattansi and S. Westwood (ed.), *Racism, Modernity and Identity*. London: Polity, 266–89.

_____. 1994b. *Racial Conditions*. Minneapolis: University of Minnesota Press.

_____. 1997. "Behind Blue Eyes: Whiteness and Contemporary U.S. Radical Politics." In M. Fine, L. Weis, L. Powell and L. Mun Wong (eds.), *Off White: Readings on Race, Power and Society*. New York: Routledge, 40–53.

Winkler, Karen. 1998. "Robin Kelley's Work on Race and Class Explores Culture,

Politics, and Oppression." *Chronicle of Higher Education* February 6: A13–14.
Winks, R. 1971. *The Blacks in Canada: A History*. Montreal: McGill-Queen's University Press.
Wolfe, Alan. 1992. "Democracy Versus Sociology." In Michele Lamont and Marcel Fournier (eds.), *Cultivating Differences*. Chicago: University of Chicago Press, 309–25.
Wray, M. and R. Newitz, eds. 1997. *White Trash: Race and Class in America*. New York: Routledge.
Wright, Handel Kashope and Rinaldo Walcott. 1992. "How Esu's Children Signify at the Zoo: The Praxis of Being Black in the Academy." Paper presented at the African Studies Association Conference. Seattle, Washington.
York University, Faculty of Education. 1995. "Access Initiative Programme." Toronto: York University.
Young, D. 1992. *The Donna Young Report*. Toronto: Ontario Human Rights Commission.
Young, D. and K. Liao. 1992. "The Treatment of Race at Arbitration." *Labour Arbitration Yearbook* 5: 57–79.
Yudice, George. 1988. "Marginality and the Ethics of Survival." In Andrew Ross (ed.), *Universal Abandon? The Politics of Postmodernism*. Minneapolis: University of Minnesota Press, 214–36.
Yuval-Davis, N. 1994. "Identity Politics and Women's Ethnicity." In V.M. Moghadam (ed.), *Identity Politics and Women: Cultural Reassertions and Feminisms in International Perspective*. Boulder, CO: Westview.